arlena de Blasi has worked as a chef and a food and wine consultant. She lives in Italy, where she assembles and conducts gastronomic tours of the various regions. She is the author of two previous memoirs as well as three books on the foods of Italy.

The Lady in the Palazzo

AT HOME IN UMBRIA

Marlena de Blasi

virago

VIRAGO

Published in Great Britain in 2007 by Virago Press
First published in the United States in 2007 by
Algonquin Books of Chapel Hill, a
division of Workman Publishing

Copyright © Marlena de Blasi 2007

ISBN 978-1-84408-273-5

Typeset in Perpetua by M Rules
Printed and bound in Great Britain
by Clays Ltd, St Ives plc

Virago Press
An imprint of
Little, Brown Book Group
100 Victoria Embankment
London EC4Y 0DY

An Hachette Livre UK Company

www.virago.co.uk

Per l'amore mio, Fernando Filiberto Maria
Il gran bel gentiluomo di Venezia

Per Alberto Romizi
Il gran bel gentiluomo di Perugia

Per Chuck Adams
Il gran bel gentiluomo di Chapel Hill

Per Alberto Bettini
Il gran bel gentiluomo di Savigno

Per Rosalie Siegel
La gran bella donna di Pennington

Per Edna Tromans

Dolcezza con occhi blu

Contents

ix

PART THREE: IN VIA DEL DUOMO

The Feast

The
Lady in the
Palazzo

*I*t was Don Paolo's birthday and all the people of the village were gathered in the piazza to celebrate him. The band played, the wine flowed, the children danced, and, as he stood for a moment alone under the pergola, a little girl approached the beloved priest.

'But Don Paolo, are you not happy?' she asked him.

'Of course I am happy,' he assured the little girl.

'Why, then, aren't you crying?'

PART ONE

The Next House

A Life Lived Well Moves Backward

*T*he sausages had been roasted in the baker's oven earlier in the day. Now, plumped and crisp and still in their shallow metal pans, they warm over the embers of a charcoal burner, the scent of them rousing hunger and perfuming the piazza. Nearby, on another table, there sits a large kettle over a gas burner filled with what must be gallons and gallons of local red wine. Whole oranges pricked with cloves float about in the purply depths of it, and a woman in a fur hat with a cardigan over her pinafore stands on a stepladder and stirs the wine with a long wooden spoon. Nearly everyone who passes by tells her the same thing: 'Don't let it boil, Mariuccia. *Per carità, non farla bollire*. For pity's sake, don't let it boil.'

Mariuccia goes jealously about the business of her infusion, all the while talking easily across the piazza to the polenta man, whose copper cauldron, black and battered, hangs, by virtue of a wrought iron stand, over a pile of red-and-white ashes smoldering in a small circle of stones. A long white apron wraps his jeans, and only a U2 T-shirt keeps him against the late-January afternoon, the thin cotton of it straining across his chest as he whips his savory pap with a broomstick, moving it always in the same direction. Stirring polenta counter-clockwise is to flirt with calamity. Any Umbrian will assure you of that.

'Polenta incatenata stasera,' he tells Mariuccia. Polenta in chains tonight. He points to a great bowl of white beans, which he'll fold into the cornmeal when it's thickened and smooth. Some fanciful eye in one past century or another must have thought that white beans running through the thick yellow pudding looked like a chain. How a thing happened matters less to an Umbrian than that the thing is preserved, and so 'polenta in chains' the dish will always be.

One side of the piazza is enclosed by a stone wall in which there is a low wooden door. Through the door and down half a flight of steep steps is a grotto, a large cave that has been trans-formed into a village kitchen, complete with generator and lights. A slab of marble resting on trestles serves as a worktable, covered now in a storm of flour. Oil bubbles in two deep pans set over a wood-fired stove. Tonight the kitchen is the scene of the mixing and rolling and frying of bread dough, all of it per-formed by women upholstered in the local uniform of flowered pinafore and shawl or sweater, accessorized for winter with stocking cap or woolen kerchief. These women live a few meters from the piazza, some of them inside apartments in the palazzi that sit directly on the square. But rather than cook alone – each one in her own place – they prefer to gather in the cave to prepare for village feasts or to save a windfall of fruit, a bounty of tomatoes, to set their cheeses to age and the wine-washed haunches of their pigs to dry. And one senses that the kitchen serves some other, more sympathetic purpose, as a club or a bar or a card room does for their men. Two of the women enter the kitchen now, sharing the weight of a sack of flour; two others exit, each one holding her half of a wooden wine case filled with just-fried flats of bread. *Tortucce,* they are called. A moment later, another woman exits the cave kitchen, her bread-piled wooden case balanced quaintly on her head. Swinging her prosperous hips through the crowd, an old blue sweater falling open, uncloaking Junoesque bosoms, soft and brown and bursting over the confines of her dress, she raises cries of joy. One man bites the side of his finger, a gesture of desire, of admiration.

'*Ciao, bellezza. Ciao, Miranda bella mia.* Ciao beauty, ciao Miranda my lovely,' shout the men.

Miranda sets her load of bread down near the sausages, and then, to spur their collective amusement, she lifts one of the smaller men off his feet, promising him a death by grilling if he doesn't behave. Miranda is nearly seventy, and the man she taunts is past eighty. Both will tell you that they are younger now that they are older, that a life lived well moves backward.

Like the only way to stir polenta, this is another Umbrian truth. Truth number two.

And so Sant'Antonio's birthday supper is ready. The saint is the patron of this Umbrian village, and his presence and image are as familiar to these people as an endearing uncle. They live as at ease with the hallowed as they do with one another, both relationships being mysteries which need no solution. And I begin to think that this must be Umbrian truth number three.

All the cooks come out from the cave kitchen now, wiping hands on aprons, buttoning sweaters and wrapping shawls more tightly, joining in among the hundred or so people milling about the place in greeting and expectation. The few, like us, who've come from neighboring villages in both Umbria and Tuscany are welcomed as guests, taken here and there about the piazza to meet the others. The air is charged. It's nearly time. There is suspense even in the light. As though old red satin had been stretched too tightly across the sky, the leaving sun pokes through the frays in it, causing a great hot splendor over the pageant, freezing it for a moment and surely forever, like the squeeze of some antiquated camera or the strokes of a gold-dipped brush. The crowd seems made of children waiting for the doors to open upon a party. A church full of people looking for the bride. They wait for their saint and the fire that will honor him. But it's colder now without the sun, and the waiting begins to feel too long.

Rescue comes from the back of the square. Three men stride forward with fagots of twigs in their fists, holding them high like unsheathed swords. They are three generations of a family – a man flanked by his son and his father. Each of them is named Antonio. From the other direction, a small, bareheaded and purple-robed man appears and, brandishing a burning torch, walks, smiling, toward the trio of Antonios. He is the bishop. Like altar boys, the men kneel on the cobbles of the pavement before him. The bishop kisses the tops of their bent heads, lights each of their fagots with the flame of his, and in a move swift, balletic like discus throwers in a sandy field, all four men heave their flames onto a great pyramid of wood. Trenchers of oak, split and drenched in benzine, piled one atop another; it is a totem, primitive and dreadful, that they set alight. Sixty feet high it is, but higher still it seems, the flames licking now, gasping in a rampage up and over the oily black skin of the wood. The crowd sways in a primal thrall and, save a sacrificial lamb or a pale-skinned virgin, the ritual flames are barely removed from those of the ancients. In a single brazen voice, they are a pagan tribe saying psalms in the red smoke of Saint Anthony's fire. They are reminding themselves and one another how small we all are in the scheme of the world. And this is Umbrian truth number four.

'*Ti piacciono, heh?* You like them?' asks the baker of a man who is shamelessly ravishing of a lush, dripping package made of sausage and fried bread. '*Le ho arrostite io,*' says the baker. I roasted them.

'*Ma, io le ho preparate.* But they were made by me,' says the butcher.

'*Ma, guardate, ragazzi, sono io che ho ammazzato il maiale.* But, look, my fellows, it was I who killed the pig,' said the farmer, whose boast causes a volley of backslaps and a reckless clinking of glasses.

Like a reliquary in a shrine, there is a wheel of cheese set on a white-draped table and flanked by candles. *Pecorino ignorante,* someone calls it. Ignorant pecorino. It is ewe's-milk cheese made the old way, which means it was made by 'ignoring' the State's new-fangled sanitary laws. Bootleg pecorino it is, made by a shepherd the way cheese was meant to be made, says the shepherd who made it, tapping at the form with his knuckles, looking for a natural crack. Like a sculptor seeking acquaintance with a stone.

Why does one always expect a shepherd to be of a certain age, toothless and swathed in skins, a peaked hat pulled low on his brow? This one is perhaps thirty, with eyes green and liquid as just-pressed oil set wide in his heart-shaped face. With his creamy turtleneck sweater and a fine pair of boots, he is a sixth-generation sheep farmer and cheese maker who lives with his family in an eighteenth-century stone house surrounded by the moors and meadows where his herds graze. He rides a Harley but leaves it in a shed on the edges of his land so as not to disturb his sheep. His cheese — this one a tobacco-leaf-wrapped three-kilo form that has been aged for two years in an heirloom terra-cotta urn — falls into bronze crumbles as he breaks its crust with a pallet knife and a small hammer. People wait in line for the cheese, each one holding a paper cup of black honey. One claims his piece and, before biting into it, drags the cheese through the honey, eats it then as though it were the only food in the world. Ignorant cheese, indeed.

Another table is set with nine or ten versions of an olive oil and orange-blossom-scented cake. Each one looks and tastes just a little bit different from the others, according to the hand and the soul of the baker. Most people, surrendering to politeness and greed, taste all of them. Meanwhile, Mariuccia still hovers over her kettle, dosing it with cold wine at the first sign of a gurgle, and Miranda-of-the-Bosoms tells of the miracles of Saint Anthony to a group of children who sob and choke in battle over the rights to a silver balloon.

WE'D LEARNED ABOUT this festival of Saint Anthony from signs – handwrought in bold, bleeding script – fastened to every lamppost and under every bridge along the lakeside road: FESTA DI SANT'ANTONIO ABATE, 17 GENNAIO.

'Did you see that sign? It's tonight. Tonight is Sant'Antonio. Would you like to go?' I'd risked the question despite the down-turned pitch of my husband's mouth, the bilious tint of his cheeks, the rhythmic slapping of his palms on the steering wheel. We were returning to San Casciano after another day dedicated and lost to the hunt for a house. *The next house,* as Barlozzo calls it.

Over time, one becomes hardened to the dupe, the dazzle, the genteel hiss of scorn which can be symptoms of the business of buying and selling – or even of the renting – of something as subjective as walls and the space within them. But today was made of mockery. And so when he didn't answer my question about Saint Anthony, I stayed quiet. I understood that he was bent on putting immediate distance between his murderous thoughts and a certain red-bearded agent.

Said agent had taken us to see what he'd called a 'country house' in one of the communes that surround the gorgeous hill town of Todi. All the while we were in the auto with Redbeard, he'd rhapsodized about light, about the amazing softness of the light and how it illuminated the house he was taking us to see, no matter the time of day.

'*Luminosissima,* the lightest of lights,' he'd said as we approached the place. And so it was. Unfettered as it was by much of a roof.

'Ah, yes, the roof. It has been arranged for – we are waiting only for the *permessi,* the permits, from the *Comune,* the city hall. You know very well that these things are not in our control, but we have been assured that the work can begin within another week. It will be finished in a matter of months.'

How many times had we heard the song of the *permessi,* how many times had our questions and perplexities been crushed by an agent's automatic absolution with his single mention of *il Comune?*

'But in the meantime, look: there are an additional two rooms in the wine cellar,' he'd said, pushing open the rotted door to a fetid cave piled with tools and pots, the dross of better days.

I'd felt suddenly spent, wanting nothing more to do with

Redbeard or *permessi*. And as for the grand concept of *il Comune,* well . . .

'You will admit, *signori,* that it does provide the dream of all strangers, does it not?' Redbeard had continued. 'To live under the Italian sun.' He'd said this while plucking at the dried petals of a hortensia bush, even he, now, too tired for the play. Thwarted and silent, he'd driven us back to the center of the town, unwinding a handsome green scarf from his neck as we went. An actor stepping out of costume. But Redbeard had provided only the day's finale. The scenes had begun at eight that morning.

The first stop was to keep an appointment to see *un apparta-mento in affitto, centro storico di Todi; terzo piano di un palazzo prestigioso del settecento, restaurato in modo pittoresco:* an apartment for rent in the historic center of Todi; the third floor of a prestigious seventeenth-century palace, restored picturesquely. Apart from the advertisement itself, we'd been besotted just stepping through the *portone,* the great door, into the courtyard at this address. A long dim hall, a fallow of broken marble — wine and russet columns – strewn everywhere, half supine and lustrous in the powdery light.

Hearts racing, grinning to each other over our luck, we mount shallow steps. Barely touching the velvet cord banister, barely touching the steps themselves, which curve and careen three stories up to an abrupt end in front of a pair of great wooden doors – carved, beveled, corniced, the sheen of them the color of ripe black grapes – I stop to catch my breath. Two brass moors' heads are the doors' knockers. I strike one sharply, three times. I stand back to await entrance to my new home, smoothing my jacket, pulling my hat so it sits just above my eyebrows. Where's Fernando? Huffing, he rounds the final curve as the door is opened by Signor Luca from the estate agency. The bowing and hand shaking take place in front of the door.

Only the threshold rests between the sublime and the 'picturesque.' Lowered ceilings, perfect plasterboard walls, pimpled milk-glass shades over high-wattage bulbs, and rubber baseboards are the stuff of the *salone,* all of it clinically strangled, vandalized of every Renaissance architectural and cultural trapping, motif, and sentiment. But surely it will get better, I tell myself. I know that the agent and my husband banter behind me, but I hear nothing save my own peevish growl. I open and then shut one hollow wooden door after another, at first quite slowly, then faster and faster until I've touched them all, until I've seen the butchering, complete. The six bedrooms are postmodern cubes, each an eight-foot square. There are two baths with metal shower cabinets pressed against the Lilliputian facilities of a nursery school loo. The cherry on the cake is a factory-assembled kitchen plumped down in a dark corner behind a half wall of embossed plastic. Dark yellow embossed plastic. Fernando, more polite than I in the face of most horrors, listens to a sheep-eyed Signore Luca reciting the apartment's potentials.

We can rent rooms to foreign students who come to Todi to study the Italian language, he says, or to those who will attend music courses, or to paint and sculpt. Better yet, we can establish some sort of *rapporto* – euphemism for 'kickback' – with the local theater management, who will send us actors and rock stars. Technicians. Do we know how many lighting and sound engineers it takes to put on the humblest of shows? All we'd have to do is to keep our tariffs a thousand lire or two under those of the cheapest hotel and *pffft,* it's done, he says, brandishing his arms and throwing back his head as though lowering the baton on the Appassionata. That we are searching for an apartment for our personal use, that we have never breathed the tiniest word to him or anyone else about a desire to run a home for traveling cellists has not been considered by Signor Luca.

Out from a yet unnoticed cubicle that opens from a door set flush into one of the bedrooms steps this performance's second banana. He is Adolfo, and together these two are convinced to rent this place. *This* morning. To us or to any one of the twelve – I've counted them, twelve – other appointments printed in twenty-two point Book Antiqua on a page clipped to Luca's leather agenda. Fernando continues his obliging, feigned interest, his head cocked fetchingly in thought, unresponsive to my fierce pinching of his forearm. The cat and the fox want signatures, deposits, the repeated thumping of their notary's stamp on the at least three hundred pages of state-composed and printed and collated forms, which await only the addition of the renter's personal data. They want all this before lunch.

I take Fernando's lead. I stop the pinching and my not quite sotto voce repetitions of English, French, and Spanish oaths. I cock my head, too. If head cocking will get us out of here faster than whispered oaths, I'll do it. All I want is to escape down those majestic stairs, through that splendid courtyard, and out into the crackling cold of the Umbrian winter. And then I'd like an espresso.

WE ARE SEATED in a *caffè*, our emptied cups pushed aside. I know that my husband is preparing himself for a quietly spoken tirade on cultural posture.

'Here, let me read the advertisement to you once again.'

In his vulpine voice, he does so. And in the same tone, he explains that each and every word is true. Is the apartment not in the historic center of Todi? Is it not housed on the third floor of a prestigious seventeenth-century palace? And, since style is subjective, it could very possibly be accepted that the restoration of this space has been done in a picturesque fashion. 'Picturesque,' as a term, does not promise that it will be picturesque to anyone but the restorer.

'That you are sickened by what they've done with the space does not mean that a ruse was thrust upon you. It's your expectations that have foiled you. Someone, someday, will come along and find that place absolutely satisfactory. Exterior architectural judgments are the domain of city planners, of the keepers of the patrimony. What an owner does *inside* his real property is of no concern to the town fathers. *Abusivi,* abusive restorations, apply only to the exterior of a palazzo. Not a single window frame, not the slope of a roof, not the height of a chimney;

nothing exterior can be "adjusted" in the least evident or intrusive way. But the interior is a blank page, architecturally. If you will acccept that as an absolute, house hunting in this part of the world will become easier for you.' He finishes his discourse with a horizontal movement of his hands. As though he's pulling taffy. A sign that means there's nothing left to be said. Least of all by me.

I sit there, processing what I can of the speech, adding the bits and pieces of Italian real estate truths with which I'd made my peace long before this morning. Indeed, there is a far greater national coherence regarding real estate than any other sector of the Italian culture. It's the same everywhere in the country. One buys a ruin and restores it himself, or one rents a former ruin that someone lovingly, faithfully restored for *himself* and now can't quite afford to live in but is loath to let go of for good. But the properties that fall into the latter realm are almost always available only to the seasonal renter. It is rare and becoming more so to find an honorably restored place to rent long-term. The highest categories of apartments or town houses or country houses or villas are rented in the summer season for a ransom, the ransom sliding only slightly south at other times of the year. Our experience this morning is a variation on the theme of what's available to rent long-term, not only in an Umbrian or Tuscan hill town but all over Italy.

But even Fernando's steady reason wears thin over the hours, dissolving, finally, with the January light. Redbeard had pocketed the last of the Venetian's indulgences. And so now he seethes, takes the curves faster than he might, reviling the peninsula, whole. Its population, entire. I don't attempt comfort. He is Italian, and the day has gifted him all these wonderfully legitimate motives for agony. He will rage and curse in the privacy of his car, with me his only audience. There is joy in *sfogo,* in unburdening, and he will have his, uninterrupted. Fernando had sauntered through the day's events, or so he wished all witnesses to believe, his *bella figura* – good image – showing not a wrinkle. I, however, had responded as I'd felt, inviting – *figuraccia* – bad image – at every step. Fernando cares about how he is perceived. I care about how I *feel.* I know there will be at least one more palm slam on the steering wheel. And maybe there'll be time for another beseeching for vendetta. And then I wonder if he might not be ready for a bonfire and a roasted sausage. A cup of hot spiced wine. And so he was. And so did the fire and the food, Mariuccia's hot wine, the kindness of strangers – so did all of these work to soothe him. Once again, Fernando is in love with his country. His countrymen.

THE BISHOP, DIVESTED of his official purple in favor of corduroy pants and down-filled vest, is calling for attention. The drawing of the winning ticket for the evening's prize is near. A wheelbarrow – a glossy black number, on loan for the evening from the *ferramenta,* the hardware store – is lined with a tablecloth, faded yellow and nicely ironed. It is precariously stacked with *salame* and prosciutto and cheese, necklaces of dried figs and bay leaves threaded on kitchen string, pomegranates, persimmons still on their leafless branches. Nests of homemade pasta wrapped in kitchen towels are leaned up against the dried kind in paper boxes. Breads, cakes, jam tarts, biscotti shed sugar over all of it. And there are jugs and jugs of housemade wine. Each item is a donation from a villager, his 'tariff' for the evening. Additionally, the villagers each buy a raffle ticket, the price of which is 5,000 lire, about two dollars and fifty cents. The proceeds from the sale of the tickets are handed over to the village women, who use it, as needed, to fund the festival and, with what might remain from their thrift, to stage some other impromptu supper. I like that nothing in the wheelbarrow is separate from the other things, how the fruit lies on the unwrapped cheese, how the cakes totter as they will, the whole of it an artless study in abundance. *182.709*

Another study in abundance is the winner. He is a small, round boy with great chestnut eyes and red blooms over his olive cheeks. He seems shy at first, pulling at his mother's hand, wanting her company as he goes to claim his prize. Noting his hesitation, the bishop steers the barrow to the boy, and the crowd screams its approval. The boy's brown-mittened hands take over the cart and, after some small consulting with his mother, he pushes it about the piazza. Having decided to distribute his riches to the crowd, he asks people to choose what they'd like. Sometimes, the boy stops to tell someone how to cook a thing, how to slice it, what to serve with it. Often he rolls his eyes in delirium over his own descriptions and suggestions.

Of his preening mother, I ask his age. He will soon be ten. She is flustered and teary, pulling at her sweater, running a hand through the curls of her thick black hair. No one, least of all she, will talk about the circle of grace just closed by her son here in a small town in Umbria by the light of Saint Anthony's fire.

INSIDE THE CHURCH hall there is dancing. An accordianist and a keyboardist – their stage a precariously shifting table skirted in red paper for the occasion – play with eyes tightly shut, the two of them singing different words. There is no room at the top for the trombonist, who slides and puffs below them. They play a kind of West Indian polka, and I want to dance. Fernando says all he needs to seal the day is to suffer my dancing. I tell him not to look.

Mostly children and older women twirl and lope about soberly, risking some fillip now and then. The result a shuffling sort of beguine. I stay at the edge of the dancers, waiting to be invited, but when no one beckons I reach for the hand of a woman, who, missing not a beat, pulls me into the troupe. I follow what they do for a while, then slowly begin to break off on my own. Then they follow what I'm doing, until we fall into laughing, pull ourselves together for a final twirl.

I look for Fernando and see him outside the hall, leaning his elbows back against the side of a palazzo. His face arranged in a crooked smile, he is shaking his head in that *I can't believe you'd do that but I'm so happy you did* sort of way. Then, through a

Bogart crunch on his cigarette, he purses his lips in a kiss. I go out to stand next to him. He pulls me close and we stand and watch. I think how these people are as invigorated by the fragility as by the eternity of things. I think back to Umbrian truth number four: *to remind oneself and each other how small we all are in the scheme of the world.* Humble masters of perspective, they stage these homemade spectacles not to forget but to remember.

The kitchen ladies are strolling now en masse, a sort of victory walk about the crowd. Miranda-of-the-Bosoms breaks stride when they pass by us, stops to ask if we're enjoying the *festa.* As though it had been a plan, we begin walking with her, a rear guard to the pinafored heroines. Miranda tells us she is from the hill town of Orvieto, the widow of a man from this village, where she'd lived for twenty years. When he passed away, she returned to Orvieto to care for her aging parents.

'They've been gone for almost ten years now,' she says, 'but I've just stayed on in Orvieto. I'm not ready to part with my childhood home, which was also my mother's childhood home, and her mother's as well. I can't seem to let go of all that history. I come up here to visit my friends nearly every Sunday, *ma io sono nata Orvietana e morirò Orvietana.* But I was born Orvietana and I'll die an Orvietana.'

She says she's a *tuttofare,* a maid-of-all-work, for the family for whom her mother was the cook for fifty years, her father the gardener for many more than that. She shakes hands with us, looks at us as though she wants to say something else, perhaps to ask a question; but she only smiles, wanders off to find her friends.

'I like her. If I were ever going to open my little one-table, twelve-seat *taverna,* I'd invite her to come work with me,' I say to Fernando as I watch Miranda sashaying through the crowds.

'There's not going to be any *taverna* in our lives. At least not anytime soon. First we have to find a place to *live.*'

'And why can't our place to *live* also be our place to *work*?'

'Because there are such things as permits and zoning and regulations. You know, all those tiresome things that hold no interest for you. Yet the smallest infraction would bring the *finanza* racing to the door.'

'I'd open the door. Invite them to supper. Even men wearing pistols and high boots have appetites. Everyone else pays them off; I'd pay them off in warm cornmeal bread with walnuts and some dark, winey stew.'

'What really frightens me about your ideas is that they are almost as clever as they are brash. Most of them would probably work.'

I say not another word, tuck away his remarks for some other time. He, too, is quiet – chagrined, I think, by his small concession. The clouds and the wasting fire have locked arms now, and when the wind blows, leaves shiver and stars show like flung crystal cracking across the night. But there is some new perfume coming up from the kitchen. Something is being fried and sugared down there. Just my imagination. We're ready for the winding road back home, hardly remembering Redbeard or the roofless house. We are saying our till-we-meet-agains, our thank-yous when one of the kitchen ladies holds out a sack — warm, decorated with delicate patches of oil.

'*Ciambelle di Sant'Antonio,*' she says.

It seems that Saint Anthony also had a fondness for dough-nuts.

Truth, Hard and Hot,
Has Its Pleasures

Nearly a year has passed since Floriana's death, time we've spent peacefully if very much alone in our rambling old place on the hill. As if saving a chair at table for Elijah, we are always at home when the bells ring four, just in case Barlozzo should come by. When he does — only rarely and with the spaces growing always longer in between — he smiles and pats us on our shoulders, tells us we're looking fine. He remains aloof. Nearly all his time is spent working on his finally acquired ruin, porting debris from one place to another, replacing broken roof tiles, mending the electrical system. He is replanting a vineyard. At first we'd follow him there, ready to be useful, ready to continue with the plans as he'd presented them to us. But Florí was at the center of those plans, and now — like so much else without her — they seem fragments, irredeemable. He works for the sheer motion of it, restlessness being the shape of his grief. Rather than making a home, he neatens pieces of despair.

Neither of us having a telephone, we leave messages for each other at the Centrale. *June 6, Will you come to supper tonight? Braised beef with puree of white beans. No dessert. 8:30. Love, Chou.* The system is feeble against his unpredictable comings and goings. He stays days up at the ruin, sleeping in his truck or beside the hearth in the summer kitchen, where he is rebuilding a wood-fired oven. A woeful beast gone back to his lair. He works until he is too tired to drive back to San Casciano, too tired even to eat or undress. Too tired to miss her. Bathing is not an issue with the old duke. On more than one morning after not hearing from him, we'd rounded, pell-mell, the curves tilting over the lake of Corbara, past the morning skin of the Tiber gleaming gold – cappuccino going cold in a paper cup, bread and ham in a sack – to find him, curled fetally and still sleeping, on and under the fusty stinks of coverlets and cushions, assets bequeathed from the former owner and only once removed from errant sheep and goats. As though her leaving is erasing him, he is made mostly of bone, a veneer of pallid skin stretched over him, thin as moonlight. All that's left are his eyes. Long black eyes where silver swims. And even when he laughs, the pain still roars there in the place where the undimmed sight of her lives. Florí is gone but not wholly.

'She won't go away, Chou. I try to tear at her face, but the next time I dare to look, she's back again like a spider web. And then, sometimes in the night, I wake and I can't find her, can't put all the pieces of her face together, and I think I've lost her once and for all, and that's worse. Listen, I'm not the best company for you now. And I don't know if I will be anytime soon or ever again, but what I do know is that it's the right moment for you to get off this bridge you've been living on.'

His metaphors always take me unawares, and for a moment I try to think where this bridge could be. Meanwhile, I notice that his voice is different these days, too; the gargoyle in him gone away. He speaks in singsong: up and down, up and down, soft and then powerful, guttural, desperate, before fading into a whisper as his breath grows short. And when he begins again, his voice is younger, timid almost. And the whole cant repeats.

'That's really all life in San Casciano was meant to be. A bridge from Venice to, I don't know, *to the next place*. But I'm worried that you'll stay for me. Or that I'll begin to want you to. I love you, Chou; I love you and that husband of yours. Blood being the least necessary part of love, you are my children. And because that's true, I want you to go. You've outgrown this place. And I think that means you've outgrown me, too. At least the physical, day-by-day part of who we are to one another. If you stay too long, you won't be able to go. You're on your way to becoming that quaint couple who live up on the Celle curve. You've successfully escaped the bank and the lagoons, you've got a collection of memories fat and sweet as September plums. Take them and run. San Casciano is changing, and not in the direction you'd have it. The reconstruction of the old spa will hardly be attracting ladies in hoop skirts arriving in liveried carriages with gaslights flickering. There'll be big black autos full of sun-spoiled women and men who wear seven-hundred-dollar shoes but no socks. You know who I mean; those men who seem to have spent all their money on shoes and have nothing left for socks. That's who'll be peopling this place. Taking it over like Hannibal. A posh invasion by warriors believing that hot mud and cold Champagne will do the trick, whatever trick might be desired, but an invasion nevertheless. If you stay, you'll have to change your ways, Chou. You'll have to fall in with the times or they'll take you for a Byzantine.'

'I am a Byzantine.'

His eyes begin to laugh, but his recovery is quick as a serpent's tongue. 'Every merchant stands to get rich, every house will quadruple in value, and even the rags of that past we've been passing back and forth to each other and calling them tradition, even those, in case you haven't noticed, are falling apart in your hands. You know what I think? I think you've been here for the best of it. For the last of the best of it. It's time to go. Besides, you're paying rent that's who knows how many times more than your place is worth. I think the Lucci still sit by their noble fire over the dregs of their noble wine and snigger at you.'

'Have I ever told you that you are the longest-winded creature of my life?' I ask him, getting up from the back steps, where we'd been sitting in the sun. I want to stand before him, to look at him. 'Aren't you going a little too quickly? San Casciano isn't going to evanesce overnight just because the spa will reopen. Some of the changes might be good ones. Why do you make it sound as though we'll need to decamp, take refuge in the woods? I am hardly fearful of big black cars and men with no socks.'

'But are you not afraid of staying beyond your welcome?'

'What does that mean? Whose welcome? Yours?'

'No. Not mine. I mean that welcome you felt when you first arrived, the one that came from inside of you. What happened to your elegant sense of timing? Your knowing when to arrive, when to depart? You've missed an ending, Chou, a natural ending which might have been this morning or a year ago. I don't know exactly when it was, but I do know that you've stayed too long. Even without the damn spa, I just can't believe that this is the *last place* for the two of you. There is no purpose to your staying.'

He rakes me like a fire, trying to raise the sparks. Trying to make me dance.

'I don't understand that,' I say. 'Let's begin with your telling me what purpose there is to anything. And who ever said it was a *last place*? Neither Fernando nor I have ever thought we'd spend the rest of our lives at Palazzo Barlozzo. But it still feels right to be here, neither like hiding nor like pretending. We're not staying here because of you. We're here because of us. And you.' I say the last more quietly, looking at him hard.

'It's been so long since we've had a good fight, Chou. Truth, hard and hot, has it pleasures. I've missed you. But I am not suggesting that you set sail for Tasmania. I'm talking about an apartment, a house, somewhere in an even minimally larger town, a Tuscan town if you will, where there would be more.'

'More what?'

'More people, more stimulation, more possibility, I guess. And after a couple of winters without it, I'm thinking you might like to have some heat. And a kitchen.'

'I like my kitchen.'

'You've gotten *used* to your kitchen. And that's what you've both done about everything else that's wrong with that house. And with this life. You've gotten *used* to it all.'

Perhaps he's right. What if he's right? What's wrong with *adjusting*? *Compensating*? Living here feels good.

'Are you writing?' he wants to know.

He never asks about work or small progresses, whether I've finished a book or am starting another one. What sort of program we're preparing for guests or even if there are guests booked at all. And so he catches me off guard when he asks this. My answer is in shorthand.

'Second book almost ready to submit. My editors are talking about wanting a memoir next. The story about my meeting Fernando. About how it felt to leave a culture, a life. What it was like to jump ship, sell the house, leave behind the familiar, set up with a stranger on the edges of the Adriatic Sea. That sort of thing.'

'From what I can tell, these cookbooks you've been writing aren't cookbooks as much as memoirs anyway. Not much transition necessary for the next one, do you think?'

As usual, he surprises me with his precise knowledge of things undiscussed. Unrevealed.

'And what about money? Are you eating regularly? And Fernando, how is he?'

I just keep nodding my head in the affirmative. He's quiet for a moment, and I think he's waiting for breath until I understand it's the words he can't catch.

'When you're ready, please tell me the rest of it,' I say.

'What do you think the rest of it might be?'

'I think it might be something about you. Just you.'

Another silence.

'I wish I'd done what you did.' He whispers this. 'I wish I'd loved someone more than myself. Myself from whom, over time, I couldn't distinguish from my sadness. As though I were *made* of sadness and there was nothing to do about it and so I got *used* to it. Came to cherish it. Obedient as to a king, I followed where it led me. I thought it was I who was obliged to shelter the past. To keep it burning at all costs. A fire in the rain. Except for Florí and the beautiful respite of her, my life has been made of other people's lives. I wish I'd done what you did and claimed one for myself. That's why I'm telling you to protect yours, to shape it and steer it with the same courage you did when you left Venice. Don't get comfortable, Chou. You do remember about the danger that comes with comfort?'

I THINK THAT'S WHEN it began – the earnest talk between Fernando and me about leaving San Casciano. Surely one or the other of us had already raised the subject before Barlozzo did. Our brand-new and homemade business in which we tour with English-speaking guests – those exuberantly inclined toward dining and sipping their way through the hill towns – thrives in small, steady fashion. But San Casciano itself, at least until the spa reopens, seems to hold little sway in the traveler's Tuscan dream, which is made of more than the ancient stones of a medieval hamlet trod upon by farmers going about their rural life. And so we have based our journeys in one or another of the more seductive hill towns, lodging our guests in handsome palazzi inside their walls or in villas that sit in the environs of them. Our guests want to be in Montepulciano, Montalcino, Pienza, Siena, San Gimignano, Volterra, the wine villages of the Chianti region, among other places, and all these are somewhat distant from San Casciano. We know it would be better to live and work in the same place, that if our lives were so arranged we could offer a greater intimacy to our guests, nearly as though we were inviting them to stay in our home. As it is now, we, too, are travelers, even if only from fifty kilometers or so down the road, across the mountain.

But if our work is a reason to go, the duke is a reason to stay. Or so we'd thought until now, until this morning's trenchant talk of bridges and natural endings and sun-spoiled women and the quaint couple on the hill. *Last house. Next house.* Maybe it *is* time to go.

*

IF WE ASKED the duke to help us look about for this next house, the search itself might provide a way for us to spend more time together, to take him with us, emotionally. And so our Saturdays we compose of half ruse, half mission.

Like old times, we breakfast together at the Centrale, collect a sackful of white pizza from the *forno, due etti di prosciutto,* a cut of fresh pecorino, and we're off. One Saturday to Montalcino, the next to Montepulciano. Wherever we go, the pattern is the same. A knock at the estate agent's office, a heart-to-heart with a barista or two, each of whom who has a sister-in-law or a cousin who is thinking about renting a place. A fruit seller who knows a farmer who has a wonderful house just outside of town that is available. That is, if his son decides not to get married. We go three weeks in a row to Pienza, believing the agent who tells us each time that it is once again inconvenient for *la padrona* of the advertised apartment to receive us. *Dispiaciuta,* she was, *terribilmente dispiaciuta,* he assures us. And one Saturday we were sure we'd found the perfect place in Siena.

It sat in a dark, crooked street, on the second floor of a great, tragic-faced palazzo, the sort that would be wonderfully forlorn in the rain or the moonlight. A warren of interior alleyways and small courtyards led to the apartment door. We entered directly into a *salone* – its walls upholstered in pale green taffeta – and I was ready to sign contracts, stifling screams of disbelief at the black marble floors sprawling under my racing feet, the vaulted, frescoed ceilings overhead. Each room was magnificently conceived, and I thought that surely the owner must be decorator to the Aga Khan. Or he, himself, a Magyar prince. There was a red marble fireplace *in the kitchen*. I looked again at the printed list of properties that we were scheduled to see that morning, assuring myself of the price of this one. It cost 200,000 lire less per month than we were paying for Palazzo Barlozzo. This is our house, I said. Barlozzo and Fernando were quiet – their own sort of cat and wolf kind of quiet.

I was about to break into song, to throw myself upon the cashmere-covered chest of the agent to beg a pen, when the duke said, 'And the dearth of windows? That wouldn't be disturbing, Chou? I know that taffeta goes a long way with you, and I know, too, that you've managed well enough without heat and electricity, but could you really live in a house with no windows?'

'What do you mean, no windows? Of course there're . . .'

There wasn't a window in the place. Cunningly, the apartment had been carved from an inside space, from one large room or two, perhaps. There was no outside wall. Like dwindling Russian dolls, it was an apartment contained within another, an Egyptian architectural recourse, intentional or fouled. I began to ask questions of the agent, but Fernando steered me away, thanking him. Barlozzo was already back on the street.

After more than three months of the Saturday journeys, the duke began to excuse himself from the chase, preferring to resume, full-time, his ruined empire among vines and the sheep.

'Keep me posted,' he told us. 'You're sure to find something soon. The only place left to look in Tuscany is Elba. Maybe Napoleon left something nice. A place full of cherubs and faded silk. Stay on the trail. You'll know when you've found it. Besides, you can always move in here with me . . .'

3

Once in a While, Let Life Shape Itself

*M*ore months pass until even we are convinced it's only Elba that remains untried. We enlarge the Tuscan field to embrace Umbria, the region next door. After Todi and Redbeard and the roofless house, there was Perugia and Spoleto. There was Gubbio, Foligno, Bevagna, Spello, and Assisi. By now the rhythm of the search seems nearly liturgical, each event in our Saturday mornings prescribed. Drive up to the *centro storico*, locate the *agenzia immobiliare*, tell the agent our story, to which he hardly pretends to listen, nod our heads in perfect unison at his lament, offer and accept cigarettes, blow smoke through our noses in collective depression, suffer his attempts to sell us a deconsecrated church or to rent us a few rooms in a castle under reconstruction by a group of recovering addicts – a State penal project in need of funds. We decline and turn to go. He will then recite, faithfully as evensong, his sudden recall of *some glorious place or other, newly and splendidly reconstructed, sixteenth or is it seventeenth century? No matter, it's one of those treasures that befall the market only once in a poor agent's lifetime and I'll surely call you as soon as . . . d'accordo?*

D'accordo, we agree, drifting periously toward defeat.

Destiny rides up to the Centrale one morning in the form of a Hollander. A painter who lives in Rome. His companion is an Englishwoman, also a painter, and they've stopped in San Casciano this morning on their way to the Umbrian village of Castelviscardo, where they've just bought a farmhouse. Jan spontaneously introduces himself to us in the way that expatriates often will, one to another, in their common adopted country. His companion is hardly so voluble and sits thumbing a *London Sunday Times*. It's Wednesday.

When we mention to Jan that we, too, are looking for a place, he puffs his meaty breast, quaffs the last of his eight A.M. beer, and, from his wallet, pulls an oversized business card.

'*Samuele Ugolino.* My agent in Orvieto. He's the man to see. Knows everything. A Monaldeschi count, by the way. Honorable as they come,' says Jan, hoisting his bulk up from the little *caffé* chair, holding out his hand in farewell.

Only now it's his companion who wants to talk.

'But whatever you do, don't consider living up on the rock,' she commands, chin pointed nearly to her chest, glasses straddling the tip of her nose. 'I'm Katherine, by the way.'

'Marlena. Pleasure,' I say, mildly intrigued by her ferocity.

'If you're going to talk about Orvieto, I'm going to drink another beer,' announces Jan as he invites Fernando to retire with him to a terrace table. Fernando looks back at me with rolling eyes.

'We'll just be a moment,' I say.

'Have you ever been to Orvieto?' Katherine wants to know.

'Yes, of course. It's beautiful, isn't it?'

'Probably the *most* beautiful of all the hill towns. In either Tuscany *or* Umbria. Floating up there on that great flat rock, it seems bewitched. And demographically as well as spatially, it's of perfect dimensions. Large enough but small enough. Architecturally, it's quite rare in that there are Roman remnants among the medieval and the Renaissance palaces. Did you know that it was the second seat of the Etruscan nation? Oh, yes. Its pre-Roman evidence is unsurpassed in central Italy.'

I can't tell if it's the artist in her who speaks or if she aspires to a mayoral appointment. On the heels of her grisly warning, I'd not expected hosannas.

'We've crossed out Orvieto on our list,' I tell her, 'put it back and crossed it out again. Besides its beauty, it's also famous for being expensive.'

'That's true, but that is not all that's wrong with it. It's closed, pretentious, *un isola infelice,* an unhappy island. We rented a place in one of the rural communes of Orvieto a few summers ago, then took the same farmhouse again last winter when we were looking to buy a property. We went up into town nearly every day to shop and walk, and, as lovely as it is, I was never at ease there. I felt spurned, like Hester. Only the merchants smile. And only at those with open purses. Old money oils the place. Too much old money, which too many people are trying to make older yet by hoarding it under their fifteenth-century beds. I tell you, even in the markets, these fur-wrapped women haggle like Arabs. Imagine a woman in lynx to her ankles asking for *qualcosa in omaggio,* something for free, of a woman trying to stay warm in her husband's cardigan? And they live in tight little family tribes behind closed doors, social-ize only in the bars or on the street. A strange race are the Orvietani. I've lived in several parts of Italy, and I can tell you they're like no other Italians. Neither southerners nor north-erners. They don't even like each other. Just as soon step over your dying body than hold out a hand. Essentially Orvieto is nothing but a medieval countinghouse.'

With that and a firm slap of her three-day-old newspaper on the table, Katherine leaves me.

Save the medieval part, Orvieto-according-to-Katherine sounds a lot like Santa Barbara. I am no longer stunned by the force of the expat indictment of Italy. Yet each time I hear a slur, I wonder why he stays, why she does. Go back to the Cotswolds, to Berlin. Go back to New York. And how can it be that a person who sets up life in another country either bur-lesques or scorns its culture? Katherine's tale of the extortions of the Orvietana in fur reminds me of a Venetian woman I knew. She, too, wore her riches.

She, too, would taunt the farmers, walk away from each of

them with some gifted fistful of herbs, one perfect brown-skinned pear for her lunch, two more long, slender leeks to flavor her soup than those she'd paid for. She was most brutal of all with the fishmongers. And, too, it was she – with delicacy – who paid for more than one of their children to study the violin with a professor in Padua, or directed the tortuous route of another one's application for a post in the Benedetto Marcello Conservatory. She was, in truth, immensely fond of the market fraternities just as they were of her, each side demonstrating its affection in a culturally accepted way. La Veneziana behaved as it was expected she should, both her taking and her giving carried out according to the refinements of Venetian civility. When an outsider is scandalized by the comportment of another society, it is because he measures it against his own set of cultural expectations – often idealized – as though his own were universal. The new society must adjust to him rather than he to it. A colonial approach, the swagger of which keeps us all separate. The Katherines see to that.

'We have an appointment with Signor Ugolino this evening at six. Jan set it all up. It certainly can't hurt to talk to him. Can it?'

'What do you know about Santa Barbara?'

'Only that she is the protectress of seafarers. Are you preparing to set sail?'

'Touché.'

'Is that somewhere in France?'

*

ANOTHER FLIGHT OF marble stairs to another agent's office. It's six o'clock in Orvieto and we climb. Eyes wrapped in smoked aviator glasses, hands pulling at sleep-tousled, bottle-black hair, blue Converse high-tops unlaced, Samuele Ugolini opens his door. He has the perfect place for us. There is no question about it. He tells us this before we've spoken a word. Before the exchange of cigarettes, before the lament. Before all of it. Samuele says he's got our house.

If he does nothing else, he's already refreshed our spirits. Made us laugh. *But tell us about it, show us a photo, a floor plan. Where is it, how large, how old? How much does it cost? Is it for rent or for sale?* To each question he responds with a half toss of his raven head. We are clearly behaving impertinently. We must only stay calm and all things will be unfurled. Impatience is the work of the devil. He says all of this in a hoarse, whiskeyed voice, as though he'd just awakened. *Because* he'd just awakened. Summoning the requisite young man from the requisite adjoining room, Samuele hands him two keys strung on a black cord — one of them long and rusted as a castle keep's — tells him to escort us the few meters from the office up Via del Duomo to number 34. Our escort is called Nicola. Lashes thick as a pony's frame his pale caramel eyes, and in the darkling light of a looming storm he walks between us, offering each one the crook of an arm. Thunder murmurs like a seer.

A *tabac,* a small grocery, an artisinal jeweler, a take-away pizza shop, and a trattoria comprise the street floor of the palazzo that sits at number 34.

'It's called Palazzo Ubaldini,' Nicola tells us. 'Originally the summer home of a family of medieval Roman nobles.'

Fernando and I are quiet. We stand to watch the homely afternoon scene on Via del Duomo. People come and go from a small chapel that sits two meters across from the Palazzo Ubaldini. Its doors are wide open and the smell of frankincense spills onto the street, mingling with the scents of espresso and wine from the tiny bar next door. Sacks of vegetables hung from their wrists, boxes of pastry held by paper ribbons, the Orvietani are out gathering the pieces of supper. Some rest on a bench to recount and receive the day's news or stand in the bar, tilting back a tall flute of Prosecco. After our slumbering refuge on the hill, how would it be to live midst all of this bustle? Not to be in the same town with it or to visit it, but to be *at home* in it?

In rapid recitation of the palazzo's history, Nicola opens the great derelict doors and we step inside a courtyard. Dark, dank. I look up four stories to the roof, to a Roman vault open to the sky. Like beaten silver, rain falls, splashes onto the broken stones. It's lovely. A shabby, crumbling beauty. A beauty nevertheless. Nicola is telling Fernando about electrical boxes and *magazzini* and I attempt the thigh-burning stairs. Once in front of the apartment door on the *piano nobile,* I screech over the balustrade, begging them to hurry.

Nicola pulls out the long iron key, holds it to the light to determine the correct position, slips it into the lock.

'Please stay back for a moment, signora,' he says.

His lower torso steady, he tilts the rest of him frugally inside. Is there someone there, I wonder? What ghost does he think to disturb? He pushes one half of the double door to the right, all the way to the interior wall.

'*Ecco. Guarda, signora, guarda il tuo salone.* Behold. Look, look at your living room.'

In gallant body language, he now invites me to do what he did. To lean into the debris. Save a few skeletal boards, there is no floor. I flash to the house with no roof, the apartment with no windows, but this is altogether something else. The room is soaringly vast. Seventy, perhaps eighty square meters. The walls are bared to medieval bricks. Where a chandelier once hung, a handwrought iron chain swings from a twenty-foot, frescoed cupola. Like a hangman's rope. With a tempestuous calculation of its potential, I turn to Nicola.

'I'll take it,' I say.

Fernando still putters in the courtyard. Finally he takes the stairs. Breathless, bluish, cigarette with two inches of unbroken ash clenched between his lips, he cantilevers his upper body into the apartment. He stays that way for a long time. He straightens up and looks back at me. Bends back inside.

'Welcome home' is what he says.

Still standing in front of the apartment door, Nicola pulls out a floor plan, spreads it out upon the crackled brown paint of the door. Besides the *salone,* there are three bedrooms, two baths, a kitchen, a pantry, a *studiolo,* two small terraces. The place is large. He assures us that in two months, perhaps three, the work on the apartment can be accomplished. The permits have already been granted, the crew contracted.

'*È tutta una fesseria.* It's all simple work,' he tells us.

Fernando knows that this is a lie, and I do, too. But I've lived long enough among the Latin cavaliers to understand that Nicola says this because he wants us to be happy. He wants us to be happy now, in this very moment. Why should he diminish our joy by putting forth the longer-range possibilities, the unavoidable twists and turns along the path to the completion of the work? The caramel-colored eyes say, *Perché no?* Why not? The eyes also say that only fools would hesitate over such a glorious place. I know that his desire for our happiness is more compelling than his need to scribble estimates and projections. Too, I know that he is not lying as much as he is telling the truth in pieces. After all, the work *could* take only three months, but should it take more, he knows that in the meantime we will have adjusted to the situation, however it may have unfolded. Besides, what joy is there in prudence? Or in certainty? Even if certainty really did exist. Once in a while, let life shape itself.

We run back down Via del Duomo to tell Samuele that he was right. Strangely enough, he still looks as though he's just awakened. He breaks into a timid grin and invites us to sit. He has things to tell us, he says. *Piccoli problemi* regarding Palazzo Ubaldini. Now comes the ritual offering and lighting of cigarettes, the blowing of smoke through our noses. This time we blow not in despair but expectation. But Samuele stays quiet inside the thick exhalations from his nonfiltered Gitane. Tantalus with hurly-burly hair.

Of course, it's I who treads upon the silence. 'What does the place cost? I still don't understand if it's for sale or for rent.'

'I believe that both are the case. It is for sale. Partly. And it is for rent. Partly.'

Perhaps this is an Umbrian game. I puff furiously on my cigarette, aiming my smoke at Samuele's, then at Fernando's. Yes, that must be it. Before Samuele will begin to speak, we must be obliterated, one from the other, inside our entwining smoke. I puff and I wait, reminding myself that *all things will be unfurled*. The silence seems mercilessly long, and as Samuele lights another Gitane I think he must still be inventing the next piece of the business. Toward the end of the second Gitane, he begins to speak of *una bega familiare,* an ancestral blood battle between two factions of the owning family. The apartment has been abandoned for thirteen years. The matriarch who lived in the apartment, until her death at 107 years old, bequeathed the palazzo to both factions. A Neapolitan clan and a Roman one. The Roman clan is willing to sell, while the Neapolitans are willing to rent. And for thirteen years, neither one has budged.

'So what part of it do we buy and what part do we rent? And the work that has to be done, who will pay for what?'

He removes his glasses for the first time, all the better to show me his disdain. Again, I am going too fast. I am punished with another silence. More smoke.

When he speaks, the solution he recommends seems rigorously medieval. He will draft a very particular contract, the archaic language of which will say that, though we are not the owners of the property, said property belongs rightfully to us and to our heirs. He thinks again. No, no. It will be better to write that we are, indeed, the owners, but that the deed must remain in the names of the warring family for the next one hundred years. He assures us that all of this conundrum is only posturing, that once funds have passed hands, we'll never hear another word from either of the clans. He says the truth is that they both want to sell and they both want to rent, but any sort of overt agreement between the clans would speak of surrender. And surrender is as unthinkable as impatience.

Hands clasped beseechingly on my breast, I channel Teresa the Little Flower who dares: 'How much does the apartment cost?'

'We can make it cost what we'd like it to cost.'

I want desperately to gnaw at my palms, but rather I try, 'Do you intend that the family will hold the mortgage?'

'What mortgage? There will be no mortgage. *Per se*. You will, let's say, write a check for *tot,* which will initiate the long, happy relationship between you and the family. Families. Monthly, thereafter and until your passing, you will write a check for *tot*. Call it what you like – rent, mortgage. A monthly check.'

But what are we buying? And how much does it cost? And why won't Fernando say a word? And what in hell is *tot*? All this

47

I ask only of myself, fearing that two silences for impertinence can only lead to a third. I feel muffled and strangled as a smiling Fernando rises, shakes hands with Samuele, makes plans to meet again tomorrow. I get up too, offer my hand to be brushed by the count's Gitane-flavored lips. His eyes are softened now, telling me not to worry. *Stai tranquilla*. Be tranquil. I'm sure *he'll* be tranquil. Probably going right back to bed. But Samuele is not Redbeard. No, he's not a knave. Rather, this past hour has been made of his Italian finesse. What is life without suspense and mystery? Our leaving with no more illumination than that which he'd so solemnly meted out can only fire our desire to know the rest. Like a matinée serial. Samuele understands that we want the house and, too, that we'll want it more tomorrow. If today we were butter, tomorrow we shall be cream. His is another kind of device, the shape of which is not crooked but serpentine.

'So will you tell me what happened in there?'

We are walking down Corso Cavour, running nearly, as though toward or away from something, and I can't tell which. What I do know is that Fernando is processing the events in the insider's way that I cannot.

He pulls me down onto a stone bench in Piazza della Repubblica.

'I think the situation is this. Yesterday when Jan called Samuele, I heard him say that you are a chef and a writer, that I'm a retired banker, that we have lived in Venice and, for the past two years, in San Casciano, that we host small groups of Americans, from time to time, who are particularly interested in food and wine.'

'He told him all that?'

'Yes, of course he did. Jan wants his commission, too. He wanted Samuele to be sold on us. And Jan knew exactly which parts of our curriculum vitae would persuade him.'

'So he left out the part about our being poor, right?'

'I don't think I mentioned the state of our poverty to Jan.'

'So, of what was Jan trying to persuade him?'

'That we were, let's say, "interesting" enough for him to take us on, to arrange something for us. Every time someone buys or rents a property in Italy, he or she becomes a scout of sorts. Jan performed as Samuele's scout. And so, after Jan had convinced Samuele, Samuele set out to convince whoever represents the Ubaldini, and together, they set some flexible parameters. I think what both clans are after is the cash to put the place in order. Once that's done, even a relatively small monthly check would probably suffice. Remember, they haven't had any income on that space for thirteen years. It's clear they can't, or won't, let the property be sold outright. We'd never be able to buy it anyway. So this is good. In fact, if all goes the way I think it will, we've just had a kiss from Fortune.'

'How, exactly, can you think that without knowing about those "flexible parameters"? What is the amount needed to "put the place in order"? Whatever it is, it's either more than we have or all that we have. What's to stop them from taking money from us to fix up the place and then asking us to leave six months later?' Somebody has to take the devil's part here.

'Nothing at all. Except the understanding that we struck with Samuele.'

'What understanding? Every time I opened my mouth I was castigated like a milkmaid with a white mustache.'

'Understandings, agreements, contracts even are not only spoken or written. Samuele shook my hand and I shook his, and I believe he will conspire to do whatever it takes for us to live in that house until *we* don't want to live there anymore. What the owners will receive is some money up front to cover the work, and what we'll get is a wonderful apartment with either a very low monthly payment or no payment at all until our — let's call it a deposit — is amortized. And even then, we'll never pay what the place would be worth on the rental market. That was implicit in what Samuele said as well as what he didn't say. Samuele liked us. Couldn't you feel that? He liked us *a pelle*. From the skin. A form of instinct. And I liked him, too.'

'But how could you get all of that out of smoke and silence and a few phrases about warring clans and a hundred years' wait before the passing of deeds?'

'Listen, Italy is the most corrupt nation in Europe. Being Italian, I can acknowledge that. But when these sorts of *arrangements* are struck between individuals, they become far more than legal contracts. More like vows. The parties are joined in conspiracy. Everyone moves to the same side of the table. In fact, this may be the single form of collaboration that thrives in this land of individualists. Does any of this make sense to you?'

'Not yet. Not exactly. What seems most curious is that a Hollandish painter telephones an Umbrian count with news of an American cook and a Venetian ex-banker who might want to live in Orvieto, and suddenly the count brings forth some vertiginous plan for the cook and the ex-banker to take possession of an apartment that's been abandoned for thirteen years. Other than trying to sort that out, I'm doing fine. Do you think Samuele has tried this plan with others?'

'Maybe. But maybe not. He's got dozens or more of these places tucked away in his wily head. Apartments, whole palazzi, villas, even a castle or two, surely a monastery and a windmill; all of them needing restoration, all of them owned by people who can't afford to fix them and can't justify selling them. And so they go to a man like Samuele to tell him their stories. Samuele files away the stories until a ripe someone comes before him and then he makes the deal. No one is in a hurry. That a property would stay another fifty or hundred years in passive ruin won't much alter the life of its owner. He'll pass on the patrimony to the next generation. It's the continuing possession of things that matters more to Italians than what those possessions could buy or produce. A bid for immortality. More than he is an agent, Samuele is a kind of matchmaker. Much of the "passing of the keys" in Italy is done by people like him. Let's just let the business play out. Then we'll decide.'

'But tell me this. Why did Nicola say that permits have been granted and workers contracted? Why was that all arranged before we climbed those stairs this afternoon?'

'That was an illustration of Nicola's clumsiness. He didn't want to lose us. Besides, he knows that Samuele can arrange for the permits and the crew in a moment. There are no long lines for the count. What you might be forgetting is that I did as much of the bank's business in bars and drawing rooms as I did in my office. Right now, Samuele understands that better than you do.'

EACH DAY THEREAFTER we meet with Samuele, and each time, like heels of bread for the birds, he pulls forth another morsel of the plan. One day an architect is present, flourishing blueprints and floor plans and explaining the wants and desires of the Ubaldini. The *salone* is the only room that needs total restoration, the remainder of them only patching. The bathrooms and kitchen need fixtures and appliances. Some rewiring. All in all, it's not a formidable task, he tells us. The Ubaldini will consult us at every juncture of the work, invite us to follow it as closely as we'd like. The work can begin almost immediately. The projected date for completion is set at six months hence. No one has yet to mention money.

By now I am steeled against clarity. The thing is a blind horse. And I ride it, neither craven-hearted nor stout. I just ride. I want to talk to Barlozzo, ask his counsel, his affirmation, but I fear he would only wallop the horse, tell me to hang on. After all, even the word Umbria must derive from *ombra*. Shade.

Besides, what was it I'd said about one adjusting to his new society rather than it adjusting to him?

A black velvet jacket buttoned above his jeans, Converse high-tops traded for Ferragamo, Samuele greets us one afternoon with a full smile. The first one I've seen from him. We're off to meet the Ubaldini, he tells us. *Aperitivi* in the bar of the Palazzo Piccolomini hotel. But why didn't you call us? I wonder. I would have worn another dress. More truthfully, I would have chosen the pieces of other drapes or curtains sewn together into a dress rather than this brown taffeta leftover from a Venetian bedcover. Why are we meeting them anyway? In the style to which I have become accustomed, I ask these questions only of myself. We are hurried down the stairs and out onto the *corso,* Samuele and Fernando chattering about soccer. Two paces behind them, I rattle my sword. I think I would prefer an open swindle over this genteel opacity. I thought I'd long ago learned my Italian lessons from the sugared, gilded cunning of the Venetians; perhaps in the opaline pause of San Casciano, I'd forgotten the essential postures. But Fernando knows them all. I am Candide *in lapsus* being led through the ancient world. I fling my long black braid over my shoulder. I fling it over the other shoulder. Already I'm weary of this Umbria.

I stow my sword in time to have my hand kissed by the Neapolitan and the Roman. Somewhere beyond seventy, they could be twins. Their pomaded hair smells of limes, the skin of them has been roasted to the color of almonds, and despite my will not to, I purr under their courtliness. Blond and dainty, two women who'd been talking with a group in the entry hall come toward us, hands extended as to old friends.

'*Ah, la Chou-Chou. Finalmente ci incontriamo*. Finally we meet.'

An Amazon in a tea dress and work boots, I feel huge and graceless against their diminutive chic. Cashmere sweaters over spare little Armani dresses, they totter on high, slender heels, and I don't know whether to dip into a curtsy or pull them to my breast. I decide to bask. So much for being spurned like Hester, I think. I am mildy perplexed, though, when they, too, present themselves as Ubaldini, since Italian women keep their maiden names for life. These women must be the gentlemen's sisters rather than their wives. The Roman, who is called Tommaso, addresses my half moment of hesitation.

'Ah, yes, signora, we are all Ubaldini. Lidia, my wife,' he says, standing behind her, his hands caressing her shoulders.

'And I am Concetta, married to Ciro,' says the other woman, holding out her hand to the beaming Neapolitan.

'We are first cousins, each of us sired by an Ubaldini brother. From Rome and Naples, all of us gathered in Orvieto to summer with Zia Beatrice. Ah, such memories we all have of number thirty-four.' A salacious crinkle in his cornflower eyes, Ciro steps closer to me, whispers, 'We were all, shall we say, *begotten* in that palazzo? Yes, and I think most of our children were as well.'

Charged with holding fast to the ancestral riches, with opening the conjugal doors only to those who might ornament the coffers, the Ubaldini first cousins married each other, a common enough practice among the nobles. And so all of them are Ubaldini. All of them charm us. Console me. As Fernando and I walk back to the car, he burns to tell me what I'd missed while listening to the women's tales of *la zia* Beatrice – the aunt who lived *in the apartment that will now be yours,* they'd kept repeating.

Concetta had said, 'Bah, Beatrice was a singular woman. The last matriarch, she was as benevolent as she was severe. There used to be a *macellaio,* a butcher downstairs from the apartment. Where the jeweler is now. He both slaughtered and sold his animals. Yes, right there. And Beatrice had a pulley basket – I think it's still somewhere in the apartment – that she would send down from her terrace when she'd hear the thwack of the butcher's cleaver. She'd yell, "Don't bother sending up anything but the best part of that animal or I'll heave the mess down on your ugly head." Some version of that. Apart from those savage moments, she'd wander about in her silk dresses, demure as a Belgian queen. By then she was already nearing ninety, and the life to which she was raised had ended long before. After the Second World War, most of the liquid money was gone. People began living on memories and promises. An account with the grocer, one with the tailor. No one could sell much because no one else had money with which to buy. Most of the jewels were disposed of, though. There's always a market for vanity.' Concetta had fingered a sapphire bangle. Lidia had picked up the story.

'And when *i nonni,* our grandparents, passed on, it was

Beatrice to whom they bequeathed the palazzo and whatever else that was left, she having been the one to renounce her life and stay at home with them. And it was she who, for survival, cut up the palazzo into apartments. Sometime in the fifties, I believe. We were all still young. But I remember how it changed her. Ashamed, enraged, overnight she crumpled like a smothered rose. After all, the palazzo had been the Ubaldini family home since the early 1500s. She felt reduced to a landlady. *La locandiera,* she would call herself, adjusting her perfect hair, touching her only string of pearls. She took the best floor for herself, though. Your apartment. Did you know that it was once the ballroom? All two hundred eighty square meters of it was an open room. Think of the history waiting for you there.'

Romanced by the stories, the first flush I'd felt for Via del Duomo 34 was piqued again. It *would* be a wonderful place to live in.

'So what do you think?' Fernando asks me.

'That they're kind people. And that I suppose I really would love to live in their home. Our home. Or would it be a collective "our"? Would Lidia and Concetta and all of them still want to spend their summers there? Why don't we just change our name to Ubaldini? But they seem neither people with thin pockets nor those at war with one another.'

'Things aren't always as they seem, are they? It could be that they'd simply *prefer* not to pay for the restoration. Or this evening we might have witnessed a case of pure *bella figura*.

56

They may have dressed up like that in their one and only set of expensive clothes. Anyway, we talked about the estimates for the work. We can afford to do this.'

I am silent.

'And the monthly payments wouldn't begin for seven years after we take possession of the apartment. The amount of those payments will be set now to avoid the moods of inflation. Do you remember when the duke said we were paying far too much to the Lucci? He was right.'

'You know, not one of them is very young. What about their children, their heirs?'

'That was addressed. During our lifetime, the house belongs to us. Their heirs become our heirs as far as the apartment is concerned.'

'But why wouldn't one of their children want to fix up the place and move in now?'

'Maybe none of them wants to live in Orvieto. Remember, they're Romans and Neapolitans. Or maybe these people haven't offerred it to their children. You impose yourself too much. Let it be.'

'But if we do this, we're obliged to stay. To live there for a long time, maybe always. How can we be sure that's what we'll want? I mean, what if we want to live in Barcelona someday?'

'*Amore mio,* can we leave Barcelona for another moment?' Fatigue boils up, spills over into exasperation. He sits with his face in his hands. So blithe he'd seemed through all of this that I'd worried about my toll and not his.

I take his hands away and hold them. 'Barcelona was only a "what if."'

'I know. Being the gypsy princess, you might just as well have said Budapest. And I agree that we can't be sure that Via del Duomo is where we'll want to live until we die. All we're ever going to be sure of is that we'll be together.'

'I know, I know. *Let life shape itself.* Still, it's all so strange.'

'Oh, and Samuele has found another house for us. An *intervallo.* An interim house, furnished, right down the hill from the Duomo. Owned by his physician. He says it has a beautiful garden with apricot trees. And the doctor will rent it to us by the month. We can spend the summer there, keep an eye on the work in progress. Much better than commuting back and forth from San Casciano. Samuele offered us a *magazzino* where we can store all our things meanwhile. It's a very good plan. We can give notice to the Lucci tomorrow. Darling, do you want that apartment? All I've done is what I said I'd do: see the business through. Now there's finally something to decide. Let's think about it.'

'Okay. Did you know that the apartment used to be a ball-room? We'd be going from a stable to a ballroom.'

'Shall we dance?'

4

Life Is Lived in Epochs

Yes, *let's dance,* we say, and so we do. We give Samuele approval to proceed on all counts. We write a check; he prepares contracts. We pack supper in a basket and drive to the ruin to tell Barlozzo that we will soon have a ruin of our own. We don't tell him that the *salone* has no floor or that I've been wooed by hand-kissing, lime-scented nobles. We don't tell him even one of the particulars of the agreement with the Ubaldini. I sense it's enough for him to know that the deed is done, that we'll be leaving the old house, his old house, leaving the past to itself. And leaving the Lucci to await the next pair of doves. Having inspired this disencumbrance, knowing now that we will be 'safe away,' as he calls it, I sense, too, that this will be his license to crouch deeper into aloneness. His work as a father is finished.

'We're going to need your help,' I say. 'Not so much with the moving but once we get there. This interim house has a garden that wants tending and—'

'Stop worrying, Chou. Stop inventing jobs for me. I've got all I can do here. I'm not going to starve or let mice sleep in my beard. And I'm not going to die. You're not leaving me any more than I'm leaving you. We're all just going about our lives. You've already saved me, Chou. Florí and Fernando and you have already done that. You see, when I do die, I won't die never having been loved. So I'm safe. Stop fretting and sparring with me. All it does is make me nervous. I'm fine Chou, I'm better. I really am.'

WE PACK WHAT FITS into boxes and cartons and call upon Gondrand, once again, to load them up, to ease the furniture into the big blue truck. We half expect to see the clandestine Albanians who brought us from Venice two years earlier, but this crew is Tunisian. Also clandestine. In the leaving light, we stand on the front steps, watch the driver heave shut the truck doors and climb up into his perch. He'll take it all directly to the *magazzino* which Samuele has indicated. The boxes marked for the interim house fit nicely in the BMW. I go inside, run through the rooms, pretending to search for something forgotten. Nothing is forgotten. Not Florí's voice. Not her great topaz eyes looking up at me from her chair by the window. Not the boy who became the duke. Not his father. And not his mother. Conjuring the devil, I hear Barlozzo's truck grinding up the stones out back.

'I just wanted to send you off to Etruria with some decent wine,' he says, lifting the lid of our boot, stuffing a bottle here, a bottle there among the boxes.

'So you'll come to supper next Saturday, right?' I ask. 'That's a week from tomorrow. I'll call the bar and leave a reminder message for you, but we might even see you at the ruin first – it's only an hour away . . .' He smothers me in his bony arms, the only way to quiet me.

'Stop writing an ending.'

I begin to climb back upstairs, saying I'll turn off the lights that glow in every room. But the duke says no, says to leave them be, and I don't know whether it's a small disrespect for the Lucci or because he doesn't want me turning around, looking back at the darkness.

'Just go, you two. Just go, and I'll close up.'

He stands there looking at the house, a shattered ancient gazing through the windows at the boy he used to be. I know he can see himself, see her and the others, scenes tumbling fast: light, cold, dark, whispers, screams. And I know that this is, indeed, an ending. The last wander through the old house for the duke. I begin to understand why he'd been so pontifical about our going away from this place. It was the only way that he could go away, too.

OVER THE BACK ROADS from San Casciano to the *autostrada*, at Fabro, the exit for Orvieto is thirty-six kilometers away. We're not going so far, and yet it's another world, this Orvieto. From a sleepy Tuscan hamlet cradled in sheepfolds to a great stone island raised up from some convulsion before history. A slow-moving palanquin plowing the amber mists, the place seems. For all the times we've climbed this hill during these past weeks, I should be accustomed to the improbable beauty of it. I'm not. Tonight we're going to stay. Tonight we've come to live here.

For some last-moment and, of course, unrevealed reason, we can't take the keys to the interim house until tomorrow. Samuele had called the Centrale to leave this message and also to tell us that he had a surprise for us. Would we meet him at his office at seven? Dear old Vera of the oyster-colored eyes had written this on a paper napkin in her big, slanted scrawl, handed it to us like the path to a treasure. Then she'd recited it aloud, asked us to repeat it after her, as though we were children on our way to buy bread. We'd not said good-bye to her or to anyone in the village, convinced as we were to position the thirty-six kilometers of separation as a bagatelle. We'll see you all the time, we'd said. And you'll come to visit, we'd also said, even though we'd not been back to Venice for two years. Life is lived in epochs.

As we leave the car in the park behind the *biblioteca comunale* in Orvieto, I feel suddenly-not-so-suddenly exhausted and sad, and I don't care a whit about Samuele's surprise.

He is waiting for us in the *vicolo* downstairs from his office. As I'd expected, he doesn't explain the change in the arrangements for the interim house. Rather, he tells us that he's booked a lovely room at the Piccolomini for us, and a quiet supper in the trattoria that sits on Vicolo Signorelli – the little alleyway off the Via del Duomo – on the street level of Palazzo Ubaldini.

He walks with us to La Grottina, introduces us to Franco, a small, frenetic man wrapped in a starched white apron from high on his pale-blue-shirted chest to the tips of his patent leather loafers. He smells deeply of musk and long-simmered tomatoes and I like him instantly. He's been in the kitchen – he explains that his cook has an earache – and he's serving, too, since his waiter has yet to arrive. Diners sit at only two of the ten or so tables, but Franco is a knife-wielding dervish whirling from breadboard to haunch of pig; he parts the curtains to the kitchen – a silent-movie hero entering center stage – banging pots, singing *Don Giovanni* in falsetto, erupting back out through the curtains, a plate of pasta raised up like a chalice, delivering it with a flourish. He is never silent or still.

The room is small, the white walls of it splashed in violent amaranthine murals – payment from a hungry Japanese artist who wandered through Orvieto a few years before, Franco tells us. Against the soberness of these, all else is abundance. Racks and shelves of wine are everywhere; a wheel of Parmigiano, aged to crumbling and the color of old gold, is stuck with a small silver palette knife and set on a marble column. One steps gingerly about the room, among baskets of peaches and plums still clinging to their branches, and artichokes nodding on foot-long leafy stems, all of which strew the stone floor. A demijohn of olive oil holds court by the door. On a great oak dresser sits a long, narrow, thin-crusted tart lavished in blackberries; a small crystal ice bucket is piled with thick cream, and a tall stick of cinnamon bark stands up in its middle. Wild violets are carelessly fluttered about each table. I look up at the vaulted ceiling of the room and think, *There, right up there above those red tiles is our* salone *with no floor which was once a ballroom which I hope will soon have a floor where we'll light fires and candles and sit over long winey suppers and go on with our lives.* Everything about this evening is both exquisite and bewildering and I can't decide if I want to go on with this dream or run back down the yellow-lit rock to the stable. But the stable door is closed.

We dine on Franco's beautiful and simple food, drink a Primitivo from the Campanian hills, stand still for his crushing hugs, walk outside into the alleyway and start for the hotel. Fernando looks up at the ironwork and the weeds of what will be our little terrace. Blows a kiss. Save the slinking of a cat and the chinking of plates, all is quiet in Vicolo Signorelli.

PART TWO

Waiting for a

Ballroom

5

That's Umbria Out There

The next morning, we meet Samuele at the interim house. Though we'd made a brief passage through some of its rooms with him a week or so earlier – during the apogee of my disenchantment with the whole deal – I'd paid scant attention. I recall little about the space except for an overall sense of order and a pronounced scent of furniture polish. Now he passes the keys to us, says he must run, that we should call him whenever we need him, and, blowing kisses, leaves us standing in the middle of Via Postierla. I tell Fernando that Samuele is just in a hurry to get back to bed.

But it's lovely, this interim house. A seventeenth-century *'casa povera'* – an unadorned, or 'poor,' house that was once a Dominican cloister – stuccoed in pale yellow with black shutters and a wrought iron gate. A narrow walk separates it from the street. The rooms are all quite small, with very low ceilings. The living room, dining room, and study sit half a story underground, while up a long flight of stone stairs there are bedrooms and baths. Throughout there are dark-rubbed, wide-board floors and rough white walls, scant space of which is visible what with a gallery's worth of artwork hanging nearly everywhere, especially in the lower rooms. White canvas fabric stretches over fat sofas and chairs arranged about a low marble table in front of a small wooden fireplace. Two walnut armoires hold mismatched piles of antique Deruta pottery; angled cupboards display an antiquarian's collection of silver serving pieces and crystal decanters. An immense candelabra sits on the floor near the hearthstone, and a gilt-framed mirror leans against the opposite wall, covering every centimeter of it. A fine red kilim carpets the dining room, and on it rests a long mahogany trestle table flanked by six armchairs, all cloaked and skirted in charcoal velvet. Upstairs, the larger of the two bedrooms is dressed in more of the white canvas – drapes, upholstered chairs, bedskirt. The duvet is yellow satin. There is a rectangular marble bathtub – the stone of it wonderfully cracked and worn – raised up on a platform a few feet in front of the bed. I turn the green brass faucets and scream with joy when the water bursts forth and the coil of cable attached to the telephone-style showerhead shoots up like a fountain. An Umbrian baptism. A small terrace off the bedroom is arranged like a breakfast room, with table and wrought iron chairs cushioned in more of the canvas. The bathrooms are as spare as they are stunning.

'Why can't we just live here forever?' I ask Fernando as we open and close doors.

'Because it's not being marketed for long-term rent. Samuele said the restoration has just been completed, that we're the first tenants. The owner wants, eventually, to rent it weekly or monthly to tourists. It will be advertised at five million lire weekly in high season, maid service included. I think Samuele must have called in a marker from the owner. Whoever he is, he must be indebted to Samuele for "a courtsey," as they say. And Samuele passed it on to us. Or, more accurately, to the Ubaldini. Anyway, for a summer and part of an autumn, this is home.'

'And the kitchen?' I ask. 'Where is the kitchen?'

The only room in all this glory we have yet to see is a kitchen. We go downstairs and start reopening doors. Wine cellar. Laundry room. A guest bath, which we'd somehow missed. Fernando opens a louvered door behind which we'd thought would be a *ripostiglio,* a storage room, but rather it is the lost kitchen. Only it's not a kitchen at all. It's an *angolo cottura,* a cooking corner, as Italian estate agents are wont to call the closet spaces furnished with armoires into which sinks and stoves and fridges are folded like Murphy beds. All the rage in Milano, we'd been assured more than once.

After Venice, after San Casciano, I must be pliant before the Fates, who refuse me a proper kitchen. I calm the viper in me, stare at the shiny black lacquered cabinet, turn the key in the latch. The doors fall open to a sink built like an office water fountain, a single-burner stove, a dishwasher that might support as many as four plates, a refrigerator crafted in the same PlaySkool design as was mine in San Casciano. Two shelves. A freezer the size of a glove box. Two blue trays for ice cubes. There are three microwave ovens. Closing the doors, setting them right with only the softest of poisonous kicks, I promise myself a summer of *composed* meals rather than cooked ones. I'll bring things home from the markets or take bits of this and that already prepared in the shops. It's a luxurious camping arrangement, I tell myself. No, wait, we'll be proper gypsies and roast our suppers in the fireplace, wash the kettles and pots outside in the garden, with a hose. But the kettles and pots are packed. Safe with all our other possessions in the *magazzino*. All we've brought here with us are suitcases full of summer clothes, a box of books, the computer, bed and bath linens, bolts of fabric from which I'll begin cutting drapes for Via del Duomo.

It doesn't matter. We'll be fine, I tell Fernando, and he tells me in return. We tell each other, nodding and shrugging and saying it again and again, as though testing which delivery is most credible. Brief, very brief. A summer. A month or so in autumn. This is fine.

Then I notice that Fernando is standing with his back up against the wall in the dining room. He's hiding something. He distracts me from it with yet more assurances that the house is perfect for our needs. He's still gurgling about the beauty of it all as I pull him toward me, away from the wall. He harbors a patch of mold. Acid-green dust from which black hairs grow.

'We'll just scrub and paint.'

'I am Venetian, remember? I know about mold. These walls were painted less than a month ago. Repainting them or, *Dio buono,* washing them will only feed the mold, help it to grow faster.'

I patrol the rooms, look behind some of the artwork, one painting, another painting; I tilt the wall-size mirror and sniff behind it. The hydra is everywhere.

'We can't live in this house.'

'Yes, we can. If you leave everything as it's been arranged, we'll never even see it. I am not going to look about to rent another house for this period just because of a little mold. A lot of mold.'

'This is a stage set, Fernando; it's not a place where people really *live,*' I shout, but he's fled for the garden and a cigarette.

I peek behind the mirror a few more times, size up the enemy, find a long-handled dish sponge, parry with the beast. I am pitiful against it. Who cares: it's a house done in early-antibiotic friezes and, anyway, the mirror is spectacular, the paintings quite wonderful. In anticipation of further encroachment, I tack up sheets and lengths of the drapery stuff on the only two bare walls in the house. The effect is tentlike, adding nicely to the baroque camping motif. But nothing on the inside matters much at all when I step onto the terrace. That's Umbria out there.

Beveled territories of wheat and tobacco shudder in the wind, and yellow corn struts down fields piped in the ruffled silk of cabbages. Lush as a Turkey rug, poppies blow, tangling in the lavender and, here and there, spangling the disheveled grasses of the sheepfolds. Trees of fig and mulberry hold out great leafy arms to each other across narrow avenues of grapes and olives. A shade against the sun. A remnant of Etruscan farming – romantic, sensical, as was their society. Rambling roses festoon red-roofed houses; woodpiles, lettuce patches, and pink pigs decorate each garden. The bawdy squawking of geese and ganders is a duet of old men laughing, old women scolding. And here, just outside the back door, we've our own walled garden with two lush apricot trees, a magnolia. A venerable lime. A disowned flower bed is blowsy against the steps, and Italy's most splendid Gothic cathedral sits fifty meters up the hill. 'It's only mold,' I say out loud.

IT'S NOON AND we eye the bread and cheese that Franco pressed upon us last evening as we left him.

'Will you go to fetch the wine?' Fernando asks, his arms full of clothes ready to hang. In Orvieto, that's the same as saying *Walk twenty paces either left or right or up or down*. Orvieto is a town built as much by wine as it was with tawny stones.

I head up Via Postierla. It's true, I swear it: nineteen paces I take before arriving at the first *enoteca,* a minuscule shop filled with cases and cartons. Two dogs sleep, and a leather-aproned man is bent over a box of *amabile.*

'*Buongiorno, signora,*' he says, his head still down.

'*Buongiorno, signore. Volevo un classico, bello fresco.*'

'*Ah, siete già sistemati? Una bella casa, quella. Benvenuti.*'

He knows where we've moved, though we've been there for only two hours, and he's welcomed us. Now he is pulling a misted green bottle from his cold case, wrapping it, then, in thick white paper.

'*Ci vediamo, signora. Ci vediamo, senz'altro.* We'll see you. Without a doubt, we'll be seeing you.'

I reach for the lire in the pocket of my skirt. He puts two fingers to his lips.

'*Ancora, benvenuti a Orvieto.*'

What was it that the Englishwoman had said about Hester?

We sit on the terrace with our bread and cheese and wine, anticipating this next period. We make lists of what we must do, what we'd like to do. We decide upon a month of delicious indolence. I won't even set up the computer until August, when I'm due to receive a manuscript back from my editor. Our next groups of clients will arrive in September for the grape harvest in Montalcino. All of those arrangements are fixed. We'll spend our days learning about Orvieto, visiting the workers in Palazzo Ubaldini, walking the markets every Thursday and Saturday, taking *gitarelle,* little journeys to explore the towns and villages nearby. We'll draw our own sentimental map of our new town, mark our routes, make it our home. We will give ourselves time.

All that deciding, all that wine; we close our eyes, lift our faces to the sun, and we sleep that way, awakened by the six o'clock breezes. We head for the marble tub, dress for the *passeggiata* and supper at Franco's.

6

Everywhere in Orvieto There Is the Suspicion of Glory

*I*n a lilac sky, red clouds, thin as tulle, shake down light like sugar. Water-splashed faces, each other's perfume in our hair, yesterday's clothes. It's just before seven.

'*Sei pronta, amore?*'

'Ready,' I say, and we race out the door to find coffee, to make our way through this first full day as Orvietani.

On the route to or from Rome, tourist buses are already parked in Piazza Cahen, just outside our door, spewing forth bicycle-panted, baseball-hatted pilgrims bent on acquisition, on the thrill of accumulating brown-paper-wrapped evidence, be it wine or shoes or a pottery jug with a rooster's-head spout. Often it's the proofs of their journeys for which they are eager more than the journeys themselves. This we learned well in Venice, and we think it must be much the same here.

Everywhere. We cluck and shake our heads, wend our way among them up the hill to the Piazza del Duomo, walk down past Palazzo Ubaldini. I look up at the *piano nobile* yearning to see scaffolding and hear the shouts of an army of workers. But all is dark and silent in the ballroom above.

'They really are going to begin work on our apartment right away, don't you think? Any day now, they'll get started, I'm sure.'

I'm not so sure, but I say this so that Fernando will tell me it's true. He only flashes his trout smile, thin-lipped and vague, as we round the corner onto the *corso*.

'Let's try this bar,' he says.

Latin music throbs. The barista – tall, sallow-skinned, black mustachioed – sways modestly at the hips, presents a menu of five beans and their particular characteristics, from which he can brew our morning coffee. '*Buongiorno*,' he says, with the slightest crunch of his shoulders as the music peaks. This is a South American Starbucks, and I'm about to run away when Fernando orders two Ethiopians as though they were what he'd come for. There is a pastry case beset with cream-swirled cakes and a poster that promises the good black rum hoisted most often in the worst bars of Caracas and I'm moving my sandaled feet like hoofs in dirt. Where are the farmers in muddy Wellies knocking back grappa? Who are these seersucker suits with briefcases asking for *latte scremato*, skim milk? I ask for my Ethiopia *corretto*, and Fernando throws his head back in laughter, knowing that I do so in memory of my beloved *Centrale*. If there were a raw egg

75

in sight, I'd crack it right into my mouth like the duke does, chase it with red. I'd like to show them how a San Cascianese takes breakfast.

'There must be twenty bars in this town; we just chose the wrong one,' Fernando tells me as we walk. 'Four thousand people live here, not two hundred. The town is big enough to support workingmen's bars, slick ones, and, I suspect, ones that attract only tourists. We'll find our way.'

We take cuts of white pizza wrapped in rough gray paper from a shop on the *corso* and go to sit on the sun-soaked steps of Sant'Andrea. Across from us a lovely scene unfolds. To a convention of ancients sitting in the Piazza della Repubblica, a woman is speaking perfect Italian with an even more perfect Australian accent. Charming enough in itself. She wheels a carriage back and forth in front of the sitters, from which a baby's rosy limbs are seen flailing. A very small baby's rosy limbs, the feet of it shod in gold kidskin.

The woman is saying, 'I just want to buy some wine. And some shoes. My husband is sketching up at the Duomo and I don't know a better place to leave my baby than with you. She's seven months old and her name is Sabine. She loves to be held. She'll sing if you sing first. I'll be back in half an hour. *Va bene?*'

'*Va benissimo,*' clucks the convention as one. They all begin to sing. As though the baby girl were a sainted relic, they pass the sweet, precious plump of her one to another, each woman kissing an ankle or an elbow or a furrow in her thigh. And amid the

76

sympathy of the lullabying ancients and Sabine's own lusty refrain, we look at each other, say *Welcome home.* We say, too, that these steps are just the place from which to begin a first day. A next life.

This is the church where Innocent III blessed the Fourth Crusade, sent the cavaliers off to murder and rape in the name of the Holy Roman Church. A recent event, this, in the Orvieto time line, for under these same stone steps sit the husks of an Etruscan temple that the conquering Romans later claimed as a house for their own troupe of pagan gods. And over the heads of Jupiter and Apollo and Diana and Minerva, the medieval Christians raised up a Romanesque house, and it is their work – save some Renaissance embellishment – that composes the present face of this church of Sant'Andrea. The passages of civilizations are clearly imprinted on Orvieto, though it is the medieval that remains most conspicuous.

Illuminating the town are the legacies of the artisans' guilds and the golden coffers of the nobility – both historically nourished by agricultural wealth from the thousand-year-old and still thriving winemaking culture. Stout medieval towers guard Renaissance palaces, triumphal arches invite strolls over crooked stones down darkened alleys, which open upon the dazzle of some grand piazza, some small square, titillating with a whiff from the open doors of an *osteria* with no name. In European art and music and gastronomic circles, the town is known as *La Divina,* the Divine. Everywhere in Orvieto there is the suspicion of glory.

We learn that on Monday and Thursday and Saturday, a wood-fired roaster is stoked in the cellars of a place called Gli Svizzeri, and each time we go there we ask the red-smocked lady to grind only fifty grams of the gorgeously fragrant black beans, sufficient to fill the old Bialetti for two days. Until the next roasting session. Gli Svizzeri is a *drogheria* as well as a coffee roaster – a spice shop. We queue with ladies who call for twenty grams of dried fennel flowers or *un pizzico di cannella,* a pinch of cinnamon. They take only what they will need in their cooking for that day, not because they fear a more abundant stash would grow stale – the contents of the great glass spice jars are all pre-Flood – but so they can come back again tomorrow. Standing in line together to talk and lament is social intercourse.

Eyes rolling like saints in ecstasy, we make the rounds of every *pasticceria,* crunching, chewing, sugaring our fronts, glossing our lips as we walk, practicing only enough restraint so we can finish the morning with the modest gluttony of truffled *salame* and shavings of pecorino laid on thick cuts of new bread, built and wrapped and handed to us by a man called Giovanni.

What's lovelier than the caress of the sun or the hissing of the Faema as one's *barista* of choice pulls the levers to release one's thrice-daily jolt of espresso, dark and thick as hot molasses? Or the sanctity of ten o'clock pizza when the whole town craves its paper-wrapped dose of it, warm, perfumed with rosemary and crunchy with sea salt? Babies in strollers clap their hands for it, school-children race, screaming, from classrooms into the shops for theirs, women rest their shopping bags on benches and sit down to theirs, old men playing *briscola* on the terraces of the *caffès* call for theirs, and even the seersucker suits stroll forth from the law offices and the city hall, bending forward as they devour theirs, protecting Gucci ties from drips of the good green oil.

And the greatest risk of a morning for an Orvietano might be to linger twenty minutes longer in the sun before stopping by to pick up the bread for lunch, trusting that the baker will have saved his usual *pagnotta, ben cotta,* a round loaf with a crispy crust. Yes, an old man will tell you, risk sharpens the appetites. The danger of the wait is wonderful, when it comes to bread or the other components of lunch.

Will there be *due palline di burrata,* two balls of a mozzarella-like cheese, soft as butter and wrapped in asphodel leaves to protect its delicacy, delivered this morning by a *casaro,* a cheesemaker, who drove – through five dark hours across the confines of four regions – from Puglia, his lush cargo consigned in a twig basket to Piero, the grocer in the Piazza della Repubblica? But all the little *gastronomie,* groceries, present some specialty or other along with the traditional Umbrian stuffs, and each one boasts the loyalty of its own society of shoppers. Each day they congregate, three or four deep in horizontal queues, seemingly immersed in the corroboration of small scandals but all the while scrutinizing one another's purchases. They note that extra *etto* of Parmigiano (perhaps her 'friend' is stopping by once again today; that's three times this week, isn't it?), only one dollop of the black olive and truffle paste rather than the usual two (the daughter-in-law must still be down with *la grippe*). As the bells strike noon, a restlessness overcomes the crowd. It's getting late. Must finish the shopping. It's nearly *aperitivi* time.

The primordial alarm rings at precisely half noon and the streets are instantly thick with citizens off to the bars. The rigors of the office or the shops or of chats with neighbors in yet other bars must be relieved with something cool, perhaps alcoholic or not, either oversweet or penitently bitter. And it must be shaken by the *barista* with the mildly lewd, two-hands-over-one-shoulder-and-then-over-the-other-shoulder sort of gymnastic, the potion then set down in a frosted, sugar-rimmed glass, preferably with some extravagant fruit accessory. The bar itself is already set with plates and bowls of roasted nuts and fat green olives and shards of crumbling cheese, tiny salted pastries, prosciutto-wrapped breadsticks. Excitement for the palate since lunch is, after all, a half hour away. And besides, nothing matters as much as living does, they'll tell you. Life will proceed with a million lire less or more, a hundred million less or more, but lunch is lunch. And after it, there is the sacred nap, a stroll back to the office, a little more work, sparkled by another espresso, some tiny marzipan-stuffed confection, or the smallest cup of gelato – pistacchio or hazelnut or one made of white peaches and black rum. A good stretch, a yawn, and back again for an encore in the bars. The evening *aperitivi*. Then *la passeggiata,* the walk down the *corso* to take the air. A quick stop for more bread and home, then, to the table. And early to bed, since all of it begins again tomorrow. We take on the same motions of this ebulliant life. We do what the Orvietani do, but clearly we are mimes rather than players in the star troupe.

There is a harsh ring of exclusion in this Camelot to which we have come, unbidden, and, early on, we begin to move through it warily. Unlike our beginning in San Casciano, here there is no Barlozzo to shepherd us. Life up here on the pale stone palisade is bequeathed, endowed, a continuum of blood for which there is no entry save heredity. The unblemished peace of the place belongs to the Orvietani, and, at best, I – or anyone else not born to it – must content myself to flit about its edges. Life here is a birthright, a slot earned long ago, lifetimes ago, in a battle, in a challenge, in a coupling and saved for the continuing dynasty – humble or grand – that would bear their names. And the slant of their eyes. But the battles have all been fought. The spoils secured. The Orvietani need only to trace the template. Live within the lines. Here, up on the rock among the nobles and the *alta borghesia,* one begins a life not from the beginning but from the accumulation of the beginnings of all those who came before them. And, either bequeathed or bestowed, there is also land and a palazzo, a part of a palazzo, a mountain house, some little place by the sea, a craft, an art, a métier. A perfect yellow diamond. The tracks are laid, and the journey upon those tracks is too seductive to ignore. The young here don't aspire to another place. Or, should they, a lark somewhere else is just that. A tolerable interruption in the order of things. To walk to the edge for an Orvietano means to stroll along the cliffs at sunset on his way to dinner.

It is said that in Orvieto, life is lived *a misura d'uomo,* to the measure of man. In other words, the proportions of life in Orvieto, the very rhythms of it, are *human.* And this seems true, especially and perhaps only, if the human, himself, is Orvietano. The life into which he is born has been plotted to suit him at every juncture. It is a life that comforts him, supports and bows to him. And to whomever he may be or might become, almost without condition. And should he reach toward some additional purpose apart from what's already been arranged for him, well, that, too, shall pass. Mother, father, grandmother, grandfather, and all the aunties and uncles and cousins who claim him will gather together to remind him of his riches. He can work and sleep and dine and drink and make love and grow up and grow old and he can even die, all within the legacies and the preconceived notions of his place in the family. In the town.

And though the concept of life *a misura d'uomo* might hold true for men of stations besides those cradled in the upper berths, the measuring stick itself is made of other, rougher stuff. Country people have their own sets of legacies and preconceived notions. At first glance there seems little distinction among the classes, what with the nobles, the merchants, the farmers, the emerging *borghese,* the very young, the very old all thronging together in the markets and the bars, the shops and the churches. Yet an unblushing distinction there is, veiled by a pose upheld only for the duration of a particular range of encounters. Apart from these encounters – for-instance, should a farmer and an attorney who are apt to joke together in the bars happen to come upon one another in the waiting room of a medical office – one will hardly acknowledge the other's presence. An unsmiling glance suffices. But I find the very same behavior, let's say, between two men of the *same* upper class who meet outside the prescribed route. Even they seem inconvenienced by having come upon one another, contorting their faces as though a rotting flounder has swung by on a string. Yet I have never seen this rudeness pass between two villagers or farmers, no matter where or when. And so the snuffy sort of loftiness that the nobility give, unstintingly, to their perceived lessers, they give also one to another. And so who am I to imagine they might give anything *but* that loftiness to me? What was it that Katherine had said? *And they live in tight little family tribes behind closed doors, socialize only in the bars or on the street. They don't even like each other.*

FROM THE FIRST DAYS, people look at us askance. All discourse assumes the form of rhythmic chant thrown back and forth, the litany of a mass.

'*Buongiorno.*'

'*Buongiorno, signori.*'

'*Un caffè, per piacere.*'

'*Eccolo.*'

'*Buona sera.*'

'*Buona sera, signori.*'

'*Due prosecchi, per piacere.*'

'*Ecco, due prosecchi.*'

Who are they, that perfectly 'normal' man with that woman with all the hair, the one with le gonnone, *the big skirts.* Some already know who we are, from whence we came, the plans we've made, the agreements we've struck. They tell each other in whispers as we leave a bar, enter a restaurant. Those who don't yet know, wonder, stare beadily, ogle us as at waxen images. I could tame my hair and heave my lipstick over the cliffs, wrap myself in a tube skirt and a blazer, trade my work boots for a pair of navy Louis heels, but all of that would change nothing. According to Samuele, I am the first American to live in the *centro storico,* the very first one, and so that I would be taken as one of the Celtic fringe seems just. Not since the invasion of the Lombards in the fifteenth century have strangers scaled the rock, *come to stay*. Tourists and holidaymakers and pilgrims are of another ilk, a soothing part of which is their temporariness. They descend in herds, fling their currencies about the shops, run for their trains, their buses. Their chauffeurs. Certainly American and English and Dutch and German, among others, have lived from time to time, and many of them still, in the sur-rounding valleys, the hamlets that compose the *comune* of Orvieto. Tucked safely apart. Coming up into town to shop or dine or stroll, retreating then. Away and separate from the high fastness of the town. And, remembering the Australian mother who left her baby in the care of the ancients in Piazza della

Repubblica that day, I think how wise she was to choose a bench full of ladies who'd come up onto the rock to shop from the villages below. I wonder with what sort of greeting she'd have been met had she chosen a bench full of Louis heels.

We will learn that the Ubaldini have been criticized for their brash accord with us. Better, say the Orvietani, that the Ubaldini, like all the rest who have inherited palazzi that they don't need or can't afford, leave them to the bats and the ghosts. Yes, better any day to bats and ghosts than to strangers.

When I'd come to marry Fernando, been set adrift in Venice, kithless and without language, the sense of not belonging was keen. But being the stranger was, even then, not unknown to me. I'd lived among an avoiding society as a child and, hence, was long past the pain of it. When I was young, instinct provided me two roads. I could be sweet and yielding and, thus, occasionally invited inside, the price being self-betrayal. Or I could say what I felt, what I meant, and risk life as an anchorite. I mostly chose the latter road. What I never did was to wander life whining for approval or validation. What I surely never did was to go about fawning for love. And so, having been the stranger in other times and other places, I was braced to be the stranger in Venice. I'd set out to be delighted. For if I, myself, were not delighted, what delight would I have to give? To be already full is the one and only way a body can aspire to and help sustain another one's joy. Any other one's joy. Fernando had his job; my adjustments, I would make alone. Many of my pleasures, I would take by myself. Five days each week were mine to

engage. Out to greet my new city, I could be garrulous, innocent, gauche, lips too red, voice too soft, bungled manners,
bruised language – all of it was mine. I could *decide* things.

I'd thought, you see, that one of the best things about going
to live in another country would be the chance to be ten years
old again. Or for the first time. Everything fresh, untested.
Learn to speak and think and dream in another language. To see
how the new people sip their tea, break their bread, treat each
other. Not just passage through, not a wander among the
natives but setting up with them. I knew that to be at home in
the world was the way to grow rich. The way I wanted to be
rich.

And so, like crumbs of old cake, I could flick away the
fatigued snobbery of the pair of old contessas in chronic tweeds,
their long, dry faces attached to girlish velvet hairbands as they
lunched each day at Harry's on asparagus and unsparkling water
and their own brittle treacheries. Or, by the nature of my daily
presence, make friends in the market bars and among the farmers at the Rialto. Thus did I find my way in Venice.

Here and now in Orvieto, though, I follow my husband's
lead, take on the rule of his *bella figura* as though it suits me. He
doesn't see how the fabric of it strains on me. How clumsy I am
tottering about the periphery of the Orvietano silence. And
their whispers. I recite Rilke to myself. And then André Gide.
I must learn to see the beauty of life here apart from myself. A
common expatriate burden. Yet it's one from which, for these
past five years of living in Italy, I'd exempted myself. But I can no

longer do that. Orvieto is forcing me to pay expatriate dues as though I'd only just arrived from America.

Ah, but the merchants in Orvieto are gallant, hold the door for me as I exit with my packages. *Buongiorno, signora. Buona passeggiata.* It's because they are glad to be rid of me, I think. I am some raffish barbarian before whom they quail, screw up their faces, cock their heads to one side in preparation for the onslaught of what they anticipate will be my incomprehensible requests. I rattle off volubly, oftentimes using better form than they do, but still they don't speak *to* me, don't answer me directly. Rather, they speak to Fernando. With something like relief, it's only the good-byes they say to me. And when I browse for half an hour in a ceramics shop, say *grazie, arrivederci,* step back out into the piazza without having opened my purse, the patroness, arms crossed upon her Alpine breast, stands silently, chin pointed upward. If you buy you get a fixed smile; if you don't buy, the smile fades into a nod and then diffuses into a glance that floats fourteen centimeters above one's left eye. In a few short weeks, we've moved from the cultivated manners of the Ubaldini and the seeming deference of Samuele to these perplexing encroachments of indifference. Even Franco is shifty, gently turning his shoulders inward as we pass him on the street, a delicate shunning.

We tell each other it's a plight inevitable, considering our unique status, that over time the awkwardness will fade. And besides, enchanting as this life might be for the Orvietani, is it the life we crave for ourselves? Would it be enough for us, all this to-ing and fro-ing? Might it not take on the airs of *Much Ado About Nothing*? I miss talking to people who worry over heat and rain and olives and grapes, women whose shopping costumes include fluffy pink slippers and flowered pinafores, men whose hands are work-swollen paws that have, only moments ago, pulled small white potatoes from the earth, carried them home to roast over the kitchen fire. I miss people who work so they can eat, and I don't know if I can live here among all these large, privileged, insouciant children.

Would it have better suited us to find some replica of the stable, some broken place we might have made good? Was Redbeard right about the house with no roof? Am I regretting my contempt for it? Perhaps it's only a kitchen that I miss and hungry people around my table. As much, I fear we are country mice and that, for all its physical raptures, this town will not be our home as much as will the valleys below it. But surely we have not come here to be embraced by the Orvietani. Our peace doesn't wait upon their blessing. We've work to do, books to write, guests to care for, each other to love, our own lives to live.

Even Samuele, who I think might have sponsored our social initiations, even he stands apart. Gone back to bed. When we see him in the street, he barely breaks stride. The hand-kissing moments are history. He's matchmaking with someone else. And then one morning he knocks on the door in Via Postierla.

THERE'S BEEN A CHANGE *of plans. The work in Palazzo Ubaldini cannot begin until September. Unexpected difficulties on other jobs will keep the crew occupied until then. Nothing to worry about; they'll recover lost time by doubling the manpower once the project is begun. These things happen. Aren't you comfortable here? Of course, you can stay here for as long as things take to right themselves. You can stay here for years, if need be. I've seen to that.*

The last two phrases send me upstairs to my bed. I know that if I'd stayed a moment longer in front of Samuele's cold-blooded delivery, I would have bitten him. Why didn't I trust *my* impulses rather than everyone else's? Why did I sit, demure and erect, to be bamboozled by this somnolent noble? *You can stay here for years, if need be. I've seen to that.* His words are a sneer. A presumptious, arrogant taunt, and how I wish we'd spent our money to rent and furnish some small place where we could have lived and worked. Yes, the recurrent *taverna* dream. The *taverna* with the fireplace and the table for twelve. Who wants to live in a ballroom anyway? A ballroom with no floor. A metaphor for my life, is it? Or, by now, only resonant, poetic justice?

First we are used by the Lucci, asked to pay a fat price to live in a squalidly restored, heatless stable while they pocket the State's contributions for the proper reconstruction of the place, which had been legally intended as a center to promote tourism and the Tuscan culture. Hah. And now what funds we've been able to save from my book advances and our just-born business we've written over to another group of nobles, who, for all I really know, have used it to buy land in Costa Rica. I try to calm myself by remembering what Fernando had told me when we were trying to decide about Palazzo Ubaldini:

Listen, Italy is the most corrupt nation in Europe. Being Italian, I can acknowledge that. But when these sorts of arrangements are struck between individuals, they become far more than legal contracts. More like vows. The parties are joined in conspiracy. Everyone moves to the same side of the table. In fact, this may be the single form of collaboration that thrives in this land of individualists. Does any of this make sense to you?

It didn't then and it doesn't now. And all I can think of is that I'm a cook without a kitchen living in a fancy house creeping with mold. If it was true what Barlozzo had insisted about San Casciano, that it wasn't 'real life,' I wonder what he would call this.

I hear Fernando on the stairs.

'Has he gone?'

'Yes.'

Fernando lies next to me, holds me. A single touch from him and I am ripe fruit falling from a tree. I stop crying and listen to him.

'Samuele has given me his word that he'll make things right. Please remember that he's on our side.'

'I'm trying.'

And I am trying. But I'm missing the old Bombastes in me, with her congenital penchant for joy. The one who loved long odds and the danger of the wait. Winning by a nose and the thrill of the narrow squeak. The one who liked life sweet and salty, who suffered sea changes with the shrug of a buccaneer, who knew that, by turns never equal, life is grim and then it's marvelous.

Someone else is knocking on the door downstairs. Fernando goes to answer it, and I go to wash my burning face. I hear Barlozzo's voice.

I hug him, tell him he's grown fat in half a month, rather than the truth, which is that I don't know how he stays upright with so little flesh about his bones. I can't even offer to cook for him, and my tears start again.

Fernando is reading the mail, which Barlozzo has delivered. A letter from one group of our September clients. They've canceled. Kindly requested a refund of their deposit. The other piece of mail is addressed to me. From my publisher. My manuscript has not gone into editing; rather, it has been patently rejected: *Due to the revised mission of our company brought about by our recent acquisition, all properties not yet in production have been reviewed by our board with an eye to a different editorial list and, we are sorry to say, your book does not fit our present criteria. As per your contract, etc., etc.*

No house. No work. No book. I doubt there's much that's delicious about indolence.

7

Bombastes Is Back in Town

*B*arlozzo sits in the garden with us and we pour out the whole story of the Ubaldini. Everything from which we'd protected him spills forth in torrents. He is *d'accordo* with Fernando: there is nothing amiss here other than life, taking its own route, being willful. And as for the clients who cancel and a publisher who wants another sort of book than mine, these are even more ordinary digressions. Their solutions are simple. Write the refund check; stop trying to sell books without an agent. And go take a look at those hills out there.

Feeling I've been wicked and weak, I do these things. I go to a bar and telephone several trusted colleagues in New York, ask them to recommend an agent. The same name is proposed by three of the four I call. I dial the number of the named agent, who tells me that she will read my first book and appraise it, says

that I should post her the manuscript for the second one. She'll
need a few days of consideration.

I walk back to Via Postierla with freshened spirits and, upon
entering the house, find Barlozzo and Fernando in the *salone,*
barely distinguishable in the acrid mists of their cigarettes and
engrossed – both on their knees – over a map of Umbria.

'We're looking at the road to Trevi,' Barlozzo tells me. 'The
festival is this weekend, isn't it?'

'*Salsicce e sedano nero* – sausage and black celery, which really
isn't black at all but very dark green. And wide. It grows wild in
between the olive trees. The curve of a single stalk can hold a
half kilo of sausage stuffing, according to the official Trevi
tourism materials. Braised in tomatoes and white wine, drizzled
with oil and pecorino and then baked,' I say in my chef's voice.

'But black celery is not a spontaneous plant. At least not any
longer. It's cultivated from heirloom seeds, which cost the
earth. I've got some,' announces Barlozzo.

'In the ground or somewhere in your dreams?' I ask. How
does he just happen to have a few heirloom seeds for black
celery? Who was it who gave Jack his start with the beanstalk
anyway?

'In my truck. At least, that's where I think they still are. I
traded some wine for them last winter, with a man from Todi.
Forgot I had them. In any case, the thought of that Trevi concoction is not at all appealing. I prefer my sausage on the other
side of my plate from my celery, but every town has to have its
piatto vistoso, its show-off dish.'

'What you're trying to say is that you won't come with us, right?'

'I might be able to meet you there, since Trevi's not so far from the ruin. But today is Tuesday and I need to find my way to Friday before I can say yes to black celery. Or to you. Truth is, I still need to get through my winter, Chou.'

We go to walk with Barlozzo, wander through the Duomo, each of us lighting candles in different chapels. We present Barlozzo to Franco, who sits us down, brings us thick slices of roasted bread and a green porcelain bowl of chickpeas pureed down to velvet, stirred with bits of smoked pork and whole leaves of fried sage. He pulls the cork on a bottle of Falanghina and holds it half a meter high over great, chimney-shaped glasses, the wine so cold it pours down in fragrant icy puddles. Franco is in fine form, and his showmanship is not lost on Barlozzo, who roots into the curve in his chair, looks up to an arch of the ceiling – the ballroom floor – and traces a cross in the air with his glass, drinks to Franco, to us, to the Ubaldini, past and present. He doesn't need to say Flori's name. All the names are hers.

Back in Via Postierla, we sit on the terrace and pluck apricots from the branches of them Barlozzo broke from our trees. And just as we used to do, we read to one another, taking turns, this time, from D. H. Lawrence. *Sketches of Etruscan Places.*

'It's a fair book, but I believe he wrote it from a parlor chair by his fireside in Soho, never having set his boots upon the soil of Etruria,' the duke pronounces, distributing the collection of apricot pits among his pockets.

'Heartless scoffer,' I accuse.

'Always will be,' he promises.

I arrange a room for Barlozzo, put towels and cinnamon soap in the tiny bath, lay Fernando's old green robe on a chair. I light a candle, place a glass of grappa on the night table, and he barely protests as I propel him up the stairs from behind. *Buona notte. Buona notte.* Fernando is filling the tub in our room, opening the terrace doors upon the moonlight. Running here and there about the house, I feel as I used to when one of the children came home from school, that sense of the womb singing a *baby's-had-a-bath-and-the-soup-is-on-the-stove* sort of song. As though the house is properly full again. As though all the pieces match and the edges don't cut. And when I hear the water running in Barlozzo's bathroom, I creep into his room. I am Stealth filching vandalized clothes, rushing them down to the washer. Extra detergent. Double cycle. I plan tomorrow's lunch. I know he will neither stay long nor visit often, but still, he's here right now, if ultimately inaccessible. It's enough. Bombastes is back in town.

8

Umbria Is Italy Unmingled

A consortium of saints and serpents has commanded this land of Umbria for thousands upon thousands of years. Desolate, secretive, it's a place as sublimely conceived for the cavorting of gods and goddesses as for the austere contemplations of the mystics who walked upon it after them. The lands of Saint Francis are the same lands where brigands pillaged and the legacies of the sacred and the profane have long lived together in war and in peace. Chiaroscuro is the complexion of Umbria.

Because of the region's purely central position on the peninsula, Umbria is neither northern nor southern. Or she is both northern and southern, claiming and disclaiming allegiance at will. Umbria marks the beginning of the north as surely as she marks the beginning of the south, and yet, perhaps because she is the only region of Italy that touches neither a sea nor the borders of another country, most often she stands apart, alone. Umbria is Italy unmingled.

For ages, writers on Italy were tempted, gastronomically, to crack the peninsula neatly in two at some point near Rome, as though all that lay north of the invented line was washed in butter and cream and all that fell to the south of it was garlicked and oiled. By now we know that the culinary truth is far more complex than that. But there is a line – a philosophical line that seems laid down straight through Umbria's heart and that demonstrates her inherent comfort with both northern and southern stances and temperaments. To the north, the imprints of Austrian sobriety and discipline resonate, while the south reflects a sunny, cunning sort of languor. Umbria, sitting betwixt, reflects both. A very different place, even, from her celebrated Tuscan neighbor over the hill.

Tuscany and Umbria sit side by side, and yet Tuscany is, by far, the more beautiful sister. Long-ago hands grappled with the rock and stone of her, smoothing luxuriant earth into elegant, intimate proportions. With sympathetic mists breezing about pink sand hills, Tuscany is a tender, watercolored place christened in wine and oil, sitting prettily to await her company. Umbria is the rough one. Her land is less tamed, if tamed at all. The vines that drape her hills are pruned less artfully, and even the color of Umbrian sheep seems darker, of a more barbarous breed. Umbria is the one so ancient she can seem barely birthed, unfinished, still becoming. The melancholic one, older than time. The one who warns, *Take me as you find me*. And as there are differences between their atmospheres, I think, too, there must be between their manners. But the only Tuscans I've known with any degree of familiarity have been farmers. Until now, the only impressions I have of Umbrians are those so recently offered by the Orvietani. And between these two groups lies an impasse too vast to consider, beyond any regional measure. There is everything to learn. As I have always, I begin the learning at table.

WE DECIDE WE'LL sup at as many summer food and wine festivals as we can manage throughout both Umbria and Tuscany. We'll make the rounds like hungry pilgrims. *Sagre,* they're called. Fairs. Every region, every province, nearly every village and commune in Italy stages its own at one time or another in the year, whenever the food or wine to be celebrated comes into season. But it's the period of midsummer through September that marks the high point of the *sagre* calendar.

Rustic handmade posters and fancier ones printed on Day-Glo pink paper decorate the country roads like Burma-Shave signs did once in another part of the world. But rather than cheeks like a baby's hind ones, these promise ecstasies of the culinary kind. Apart from the three grand and glorious festivals that celebrate the grape harvest, the olive harvest, and the truffle-hunting season, there are *sagre* for gnocchi made with potatoes or ricotta or the wild spinach that shoots up along the riverbeds. Wild mushrooms, wild duck, wild boar, wild hare, suckling lamb, and suckling pig. Snails and lake trout. There is a *sagra* to celebrate eels – hacked still wriggling, chunks of them are threaded on oak twigs between fresh laurel leaves and roasted in the leaping flames of a lakeside fire. Chestnuts and hazelnuts and walnuts. Charcoaled sausages and cauldrons of thick yellow cornmeal. Small, plump chickens, split and grilled under bricks, their juice-dripping flesh smeared with a savory paste of wild fennel and set down with pan-roasted new garlic, whole heads of it, the cloves and skins still soft and unformed.

And farmers organize their very lives about these events, often their only respites from work. Pocket-size *locandine* – festival schedules – are published by each province and tucked into wallets and purses and stuffed behind the visors of trucks and autos and taped onto tractor windshields – delicious evidence of the small huzzah that awaits a man and his family at the end of each summer week.

Not to be confused, an Umbrian will tell you, with the festivals that celebrate the saints' days, these are purely gastronomic feasts, reprises of pagan sacrifices to the gods of the harvests. Older than memory and once staged only for each other, these are feasts meant to honor their own continuing survival. With the relative benevolence that came in the days after the last World War, the festivals were slowly expanded to include the people from surrounding towns and villages. Thus a new and somewhat exotic exchange of gastronomic patrimonies sprang up among the provinces. Two hamlets, bestriding neighboring hills and separated by the dozen or so kilometers that stretched between them, were often never breached in a farmer's lifetime, his own patch of earth and sky enclosing all the events of his own particular living and dying. And it was this isolation in clusters – small and tight – that raised up the fiercely canonical styles of cooking. There wasn't ever and isn't now any such thing as Umbrian cuisine. What the land gives up in the wild and what can be coaxed from its rich, fat soil may vary little within the region, but how each small society or fraction of a society works with these elements is what creates the complexity.

A single illustration can be seen in the eighteen communes of Orvieto – all of them situated within a twenty-five-kilometer radius from the town – in which one can collect no less than twelve ways to mix and shape and cook *umbrichelli,* the rough, hand-rolled pasta of the Umbro tribes. Further riffs on the theme are found, family by family. And all of it composes a kind of gastronomic *campanilismo* – an infinitely local pride – which, apart from enriching the culinary legacy of the region, cultivates competition. *The* umbrichelli *from Sugano are better than the ones from Alviano.* And so the *sagre,* whether in Tuscany or Umbria or any other region of Italy, have become demonstrations of homegrown expertise, the formulas and tricks passed down as scripture.

Yet as many are the interpretations of the dishes, the production of the *sagre* follows the same design, if some more elaborately than others. This is how they work.

Each commune designates certain indoor and outdoor spaces for the annual fair. Relative to the commune's wealth, tables and benches are fashioned from bits and pieces or commissioned by their own artisan woodworkers. There are always some sort of garish lights strung about doorways and in the trees for the event, and these are sometimes left to dangle throughout the winter, lit again at Christmas. There is some manner of cooking system, ranging from half an oil drum piled with wood to long, metal table grills fired with charcoal and vine cuttings. If the commune is rich enough, a kitchen has been installed in either a grotto or some unused farm building. In there, pasta is rolled and cooked, sauces are set to bubbling, bread is baked. Gossip is enlarged. Apart from all of these, there is always an open fire on some area of the premises, a great and roaring fire that serves no purpose other than to soothe their congenital desire for it. There is no proper *sagra* without it.

There is most often an accordian. A mandolin or two. Electrified, played exuberantly, beckoning dancers. Not until the dining is done and the wine jugs have been refilled for the fourth or fifth round does the music soften and the swaying and singing begin under the the seething leaves of the sycamores.

In minor-key laments about love gone bad, about loneliness and bad crops and hungry children, the singing is a tribal thrust against the miseries. A tango always breaks the spell. In pinafores and Dr. Scholl's, the ladies are the uncontested divas of the rustic flamenco, while the second string is made of grand-fathers who dance with their grandchildren, children who dance together. And without fuss or warning, the oldest couple in the village, walk or hobble, as they may, onto the grassy floor. There is silence then, save hushed exclamations of joy and pride from the field. The two hold each other in a comfortable pose, look at each other haughtily, tenderly, she seeing that boy, he that girl. They nod, and still in silence, they begin to dance. How they danced back then, they dance now. Or so it seems to them, and they dance all the better for it. Then slowly, softly, the music begins and that helps them, too, and they begin to smile and laugh and take risks with their turning and stepping – risk being a thing well trafficked in their lives – until the music is full, fuller than it's been for all the evening and everyone at the tables is on their feet, applauding and shouting, *Viva le sposi,* long live the bride and groom. Long life to the bride and the groom.

There must be relief, then, from the crying and the remembering, and so the fire and the wine are replenished and *tombola* – bingo – is announced, to the shrills of gamesters who will play far into the night. And as one, flushed with wine and sleepiness, walks out to the unlit car park or drives away down the hill or through the woods, every once in a while one hears *Tombola* ringing through the night. That's how the *sagre* are, generally.

One spectacular exception is the series of festivals staged in the red-brick serenity of the small Umbrian village of Città delle Pieve. Le Taverne dei Barbacane, they're called.

Set up in a great, long field inside the village walls, these are more folkloric pageants than farmers' picnics – the name, *barbacane,* signifies the small, rectangular holes left in castle walls, through which guardians might see the approach of an enemy. So minutely and magnificently conceived, festivalers are transported to a medieval garden. No trunkfuls of cheap velvet costumes are shaken out for the events, no pasteboard crowns. Rather, the villagers – elders to small, teetering children – wear hand-loomed linens and handmade boots and slippers as they go quietly about the business of the fair. The business of their heritage. Everyone has a job. There are the ritual fires and long communal tables, stone jugs of wine, traditional village foods; but instead of the raucous folly of other *sagre,* here the scene is placid. From a roofless chamber made of cypress trees comes the thrumming of lutes and the flourish of a harp. A shirtless cook strides about in chocolate breeches riding low on his hips above handsome brown suede waders, his handkerchiefed head betraying wisps of black curls; he is Puss-in-boots sashshaying back and forth behind the grills. Aprons kilted up over wide skirts, women tote baskets of bread or kindling on their heads, some while holding a fat squirming child under an arm.

But perhaps our favorite *sagra* is in the commune of Monterubiaglio. The festival of the fava beans. Traditionally, it's staged each Sunday from late March until the fava bean crop is finished, sometime in June. But this year, there are favas coming up even in August. Still in their pods, the beans are passed about from great baskets of them, set down with hefts of new, soft, white pecorino, a dish of coarse sea salt, a pepper grinder, bottles of good oil, and hunks of wood-charred bread, broken from great three-kilo loaves. Barrels of red wait nearby.

How voluptuously the diners gorge these humble stuffs, breaking open the pods, dragging the fresh, crunchy beans through the oil, the salt, grinding on pepper, their pocketknives ready to shave the new cheese, each of them tearing at the still-warm bread. Each of them quaffing the wine like water. Perhaps the oldest of the *sagre,* the ritual making of supper from a tangle of raw beans inspires its stories.

'Sometimes – no, most times – when it got to be March all the stores of dried beans and fruits and vegetables were gone. Used up over the winter. And nothing new was coming up yet in the fields. Nothing much but the fava beans. Now there was just enough grass showing through on the meadows for the sheep to graze, giving up the first milk of the season rich enough to make cheese. And that's what we did, we made cheese with every drop of the spring milk. No one waited for that particular pecorino to ripen, let alone age. We ate it as soon as it set. We ate it with the fava beans because that's what we had, those and our dose of daily bread, a thread of oil if there was some. We almost always had wine. That's what we ate in March, and so that's what we still eat in March. And we like them so well that we eat them in April and May and June and through the whole summer, for as long as we can. Tasted good then, tastes good now,' says the small man in a Sunday shirt and a shiny corduroy suit who sits next to us in front of the fava beans. He's called Neddo, he tells us, and the gentleman who sits beside him, a somber sort of Umbro with a long brown beard and furrows in his cheeks deep enough to plant potatoes in, is called Gaspare. Neddo tells us, too, that he and his sons work a patch of land just outside of Canonica, another commune of Orvieto. He says that he and Gaspare will guide us through the route of the best *sagre,* in Umbria, Tuscany, and Lazio, for that matter. They know them all. Which ones to avoid, too, like the ones where ignoble cooks recycle already emptied snail shells, tuck them in the bottom of a dish of full ones, making the portion look bigger. The memory of this treachery sets Neddo to snorting under his breath and the formerly comatose Gaspare to a long string of mumbled curses.

'That happened almost fifty years ago, and it was probably just a mistake. I can't believe you still remember it,' are the first words Gaspare says aloud.

Neddo ignores him. 'The only story I remember better than the snail story is one about a peach. Remind me someday to tell you that one,' he says, as though we're sure to meet again and our intimacies to grow.

'I beg you never to raise the subject of peaches with him,' says Gaspare, turning his black-olive eyes directly upon mine.

Neddo stretches his lips into a puppet's grin, and I can't help but think that this exchange over our paper cups of red wine, sitting on benches at the oilcloth-covered table under a pergola of wisteria, is the longest, most intriguing one we've had since coming to Orvieto.

And we so ride the homespun route of the *sagre,* each Friday and Saturday and Sunday evening finding us at table in another village. Often we see people we've seen before, couples and families on the same delicious pilgrimage, and sometimes we sit together; other times we wave and wish each other well. There are almost always Orvietani among the crowds, their pomp perhaps a little less swollen. Though one of them will gamble a discreet wave, a tight smile, they are mostly self-contained, arriving in large groups, sitting together, talking among themselves, and, as though a bus awaits them, departing as one. When we next see these people in town, they will act embarrassed and ours will be like the unmeant, morning-after meeting of strangers who'd been much too familiar the evening before. It hardly seems to matter. Especially when, on one Sunday at a *sagra* in Baschi, we meet up with Miranda-of-the-Bosoms.

It's Fernando who sees her first. 'Isn't that the lady from Civitella del Lago, from the *festa di Sant'Antonio?*'

She is unmistakable, a great bronzed bloom of a goddess striding among her flock. Like all the church bells chiming, even her laugh is big, and when she comes our way I stand up to greet her, but someone else steps up first. I sit back down to my supper.

Later, when it's dark and the dancing has begun, she appears without warning, says, 'I remember that you like to dance. Come with me, both of you.'

And so we do and so we dance and I ask Miranda why we never see her in Orvieto.

She says, 'I've quit my job to work for myself. I'm converting my mother's old *rustico*, summer kitchen, into an *osteria*.

Ten tables, I think. Perhaps a few out on the grass during the warm months. It's where my sisters and I used to preserve vegetables and fruits, where my father would go to sleep when it was too hot in Orvieto, where the whole family would go on Sundays all summer long. Much cooler up there. In the locality of Buon Respiro. Stop by someday. It's the shack all surrounded by orange plastic netting. You can't miss it.'

Miranda wanders away, looks back at me, flashing her goddess smile. Buon Respiro. She's going to open an *osteria* in a place called Good Breathing. I think this is wonderful. Maybe she'll give me a job someday.

ONE SATURDAY EVENING when we return home to Via Postierla from a *sagra,* I find a letter from the agent with whom I'd spoken several weeks before. She'll take me on, she's written. She read and liked my first book, sent out the manuscript for the second book to several publishing houses, and has already received an offer from one of them. Encouraging responses from one or two others. She won't accept the first offer at this point, but rather she'll wait, evaluate, and present her thoughts to me later in the month. She's also met with the rejecting publisher and convinced them to settle for the return of only a small percentage of my advance on the book. She sounds pleased, enthusiastic. She has enclosed her contract for me to sign. And so, from now on, she will navigate. Yes, she is my partner now in this writing life. And as if this were not news enough for an evening, more waits in the garden.

'*Permesso. C'é qualcuno?* May I come in? Is there someone here?'

Concetta and Ciro, two of the Ubaldini counsins, are calling from the the open door. Fernando welcomes them inside and I'm about to hurl myself behind one of the sofas, unwilling to be seen yet again in work boots and reformed curtains, but I rally, go to greet them, settle them all on the terrace while I try to pin up my hair and open Prosecco and find the rest of the good dried black olives we'd had with our lunch yesterday.

But I'm taking too long, so Concetta comes to help me. She puts her arm around my shoulder and says, 'Chou-Chou, *sono mortificata* – I am mortified by the delays. We all are, and when Ciro and I spoke with Lidia and Tommaso this morning, we agreed that we must offer you and Fernando a way out of this contract. Ciro is telling Fernando about it now. There is simply no recourse for us, or for Samuele for that matter, no way we can hurry the pace of the *geometra* and his crew. Our contract fell like all the others in front of and behind it when their current project was stalled. And please don't ask me why we can't just hire another *geometra* and another crew, because I don't know the answer nor would I be able to understand or accept the answer if someone was willing to present one to me. Chou-Chou, you must know by now that a small subterfuge, an occasional display of furtiveness, the very act of concealment or vendetta or conspiracy, you *must* have learned that these are vestigal needs and desires in this country, as necessary to an Italian as his bread and wine. Most of us satisfy them within relatively harmless expressions, while others do so perhaps less harmlessly. I don't know which is the case here, but we Ubaldini will not leave you and Fernando to feel the victims. Ciro has brought a check. If you and Fernando think it better to interrupt our *accordo,* we are most willing to oblige. To return your funds.'

Sensations smash, one fast upon another, while Concetta is saying something like *Take your time, think it all over, we'll be staying the night in Orvieto, not going back to Rome until late tomorrow — shall we come by at about five in the afternoon?* I nod my head yes and keep repeating, *Certainly, certainly,* though nothing has ever been less certain and I don't know whether it's thrilled I am to be so succinctly out of this affair or if what I'm feeling isn't despair.

I follow Concetta out to the terrace, where the gentlemen seem to be in a similar condition of silence. They get to their feet then, Ciro saying, '*Fate una bella dormita e ne parliamo domani pomeriggio.* Have a good sleep and we'll talk tomorrow afternoon.'

I pace the terrace while Fernando accompanies the Ubaldini to the door, refilling my glass, gulping Prosecco, thinking it would all be so perfect if it weren't so terrible. Fernando enters chuckling.

'How can you be so smug? What is there to laugh about when so much is at stake here?'

'Do you mean you believed them?'

'Yes, I believed them. Concetta was very straightforward. She doesn't want us to feel victimized by the delays.'

'And did she tell you that Ciro had a check in his portfolio?'

'Yes, she told me. She said they're prepared to break the contract if we wish, that they're all mortified, that—'

'And you believed that, as well? You are a pigeon. Here, come and sit with me.'

He pulls me down onto the scrawny cushion of his thighs and I can see he's in difficulty trying to keep from laughing. This seems impudent and close to cruel. I get up, go inside, closing the terrace door too hard, muttering, 'Italy and the Italians.' For universal emphasis, I say it in French and then in German before I say it again in English.

He follows me, sits down on the sofa across from mine.

'It was a bluff, Chou. A splendidly delivered farce. Ciro and Concetta came here this evening to help us understand how much we want to live in Palazzo Ubaldini and realize that the wait for it will not, in the end, thwart the pleasures of it. They divided and conquered. He, me. She, you. It was a magnificent success. Weren't you confused and torn when she said we could exit the contract? Didn't all the memories of our long search come crashing down when you thought we might have to take it up once again? And weren't the virtues of Palazzo Ubaldini immediately crystallized when you imagined it gone? Didn't you even become a little angry at their presumptuousness in bringing along a check? After all, which of us ever said we wanted an out?'

'Yes, yes I . . . yes. But I thought they were being their noble selves, stepping forward elegantly.'

'They were *indeed* being their noble selves, *indeed* stepping forward with elegance, but not at all with disinterest. Why wait for us to ring them and begin haranguing when they might put on their lamb's clothing and open the door back out into the wilderness for us? That the offer was unexpected, unrequested, gave it more innocence. The offer placed us in the position of power, however false. On the face of it, they gave us control. We could, ostensibly, tear up the contract and take back our funds and be on our way. Though I can tell you now that the offer to do that would never have been carried through on their part. But that doesn't matter right now. What they counted on was that we had no alternative plan. No hidden cards. But what they counted on more than that was our fresh recognition of the soundness of the original bargain, that the palazzo is wonderful, that we're paying a just figure to restructure it, that we can participate in the tastemaking of the restructure, that once our deposit is amortized, we'll pay only the agreed-upon monthly amount until we die or until we don't want to live there any longer.'

'Until we set off for Barcelona,' I whisper. 'Or Budapest.' But the whispers don't disarm his gravely delivered finish.

'They know that we know it might not be so simple to strike such a deal somewhere else.'

Now we are both quiet, Fernando resting from his labors as instructor. Me from mine as foreigner on the island of nowhere.

'So all this was scripted and staged? Why didn't you say

something? Why didn't you tell them that you knew what they were up to?'

'What would that have proved? Besides, they already knew that I knew. I think they weren't so sure about you.'

'But it's depraved. Senseless.'

'How can you say that when they've accomplished all they'd set their minds to? Did either one of us jump at the chance to exit? Did either one of us ask for the check and breathe a sigh of relief? The tip-off was the timing. If they'd truly expected us to consider their offer to renege, they would have set a different time frame. A few days – ten, maybe, or two weeks. Time to look about. But by tomorrow – which is Sunday, a day not chosen casually – what could we have put into action, had we wanted to put anything into action at all? At best we might have found Samuele, but surely he's been privy to this visit or is even its perpetrator. Power for the sake of power doesn't amuse most Italians. It's the intricacies of the opera that stimulate them.'

'But what would have happened if I had asked for the check right there and then?'

'Ciro would have said something impressive and perplexing, such as that he'd have to wait for Samuele to provide the contracts. Or he might have said that a paper check was only a figure of speech, that he'd have funds transferred to our account in a few days.'

'And then?'

'And then some other twisted trail of messages and post-ponements would play out until either we came to our senses or the Ubaldini attorneys sat across from us in Samuele's office to demonstrate that there is no exit clause in the original document and that, though Ciro and Concetta are most willing to stand by their offer, Lidia and Tommaso are not in agreement. The old warring-faction coin would be turned once again. All these events would take probably a year or so, and by then a date for the startup would surely have been fixed, or perhaps the work itself would be under way.'

'And you're telling me that they knew that you understood every oblique angle of this performance?'

'Yes, I believe they did. But why are you so angry? What harm has been done to you? To us? Italians say, "To keep things the same, change them. Stir the waters, make them cloudy. Then wait. You'll see how much clearer they become. If we want things to stay the same, everything has to change. Or appear to change." Giuseppe di Lampedusa told us that.'

Giuseppe di Lampedusa. As though an epithet from him is all it takes to set things straight. I hear Concetta's voice. *Chou-Chou, you must know by now that a small subterfuge, an occasional display of furtiveness, the very act of concealment or vendetta or conspiracy, you* must *have learned that these are vestigal needs and desires in this country, as necessary to an Italian as his bread and wine. Most of us satisfy them within relatively harmless expressions . . .*

'There was nothing evil about their visit or its intentions,' Fernando says. 'They could have brought us to the same conclusions by talking endlessly about the magnificence of the palazzo or how fair and just are the parameters of our agreement, but there is no sport in that. No risk. They are not laughing at us. Not at all. They are likely already on their way back to Rome, feeling twenty years younger for having perpetrated an intrigue and telling each other, "*Vedi, sono tutti tranquilli*. See, everyone is serene now."'

What with all we've learned about life in Orvieto, about the good of it and the less good, what with our wait for the work to be finished – no, even to start – looming out in the great unknown, why don't we just begin all over again? I test the words first in my mind. I say them aloud.

'Why don't we just begin again?'

'Because I think we've already found what we've been looking for. I admit there've been some surprises, but aren't there always? Try to remember how you felt that first day when Samuele's man – what was his name?'

'Nicola.'

'Yes, when Nicola opened that door for you. That's the sensation to hold on to. I admit that the route to Palazzo Ubaldini twists more than we thought it would, that it's longer.'

'Yes, and a few trolls live along its way.'

'They matter least of all. Show me a road with no trolls.'

A SILVER-WRAPPED parcel in his hand, it's Samuele who knocks on our door late the next afternoon.

'Ciro and Concetta had to rush back to Rome. They asked me to bring these to you with their regrets. Pastries from Scarponi.'

Far too elegant to gloat, Fernando will not look my way. He settles Samuele in the *salotto,* pours out a tiny glass of grappa. I sit across from them, the silver package in my lap. Surely this is the last act of the play, and I won't miss a word of it.

'*Sentite*. Listen,' he begins, interrupting himself with another sip. 'We are, all of us, so sorry for this "disorder" in our plans together.' Another sip. 'With, shall we call it, *influence,* from the Ubaldini, I have arranged it so that you will pay no rent as long as you're here in Via Postierla. For as long as it takes for Palazzo Ubaldini to be ready for you. We are hoping this small gesture will make the wait easier for you.' He drains the glass. Stands, reaches down for my hand, holds it in both of his for a moment longer than he might have. 'And now I must run. When there is news, any news at all, you will have it. In the meantime, *vivete bene*. Live well.'

With neither Fernando nor I having spoken a word, the sleepy Monaldeschi count retreats. I see that even the dispassionate Venetian who is my husband is confounded. An unexpected ending. Perhaps not an ending at all, I think, but the opening scene of the next play. Are we the beneficiaries of some other configuration of vendetta and conspiracy? It occurs that Barlozzo might be behind this sudden *gesture,* as Samuele had called it. But no. No, it's not Barlozzo. It startles me that I am beginning to think like an Umbrian.

9

She Says People Need to Be Together as Much as They Need to Eat

*I*t's nearly the end of September and the wait has no more shape than it did in June. Save a few days of the 'preparation' crew's hammering at the debris, enlarging it, nothing has been done in the ballroom in Palazzo Ubaldini. Nor has there been news from Samuele. Yet the other sides of life race all the same. There are recipes to test for articles and the newly resold book. My agent has succeeded in placing it with a prestigious publisher, and the contract that I've signed dictates the completion of both text and recipes by December 1. The text edits are minimal, but all the recipes must be tested. I must find a kitchen. Somewhere I must find a kitchen.

'I'll have to rent a kitchen. Yes, that's the solution. Rent a kitchen. Even though he's been so distant lately, I'll go to Franco, make an arrangement with him to use his on the day he's closed. After all, we're going to be living right upstairs from him someday. Surely he'll want to help us. I'll make a similar arrangement with two or three other chefs so that . . .'

We're stemming basil and drinking wine and Fernando has just lit the first fire of the season. My rambling delivery of this kitchen-rental idea is barren. I already know better. I know about the universal possessiveness of chefs toward their domains. I know about their fastidiousness. Their bedrooms they might share, but never their kitchens. The fire is smoking badly, so we take our sweaters and the wine and the tub of basil and go to sit on the terrace for a bit. It grows dark so much earlier now that if the smoke hadn't shooed us outside we would have missed the last light. It's all blue silence over the fields and in the valleys below the cliffs. Just a few meters to the left of us are the ruins of the fourteenth-century Albornoz citadel. Only a gate, the curve of a wall, and a tower remain, a lonely carapace among black-green parasol pines careening against the clouds. And tonight, as though the sky were stone and she were Fury, the sun heaves up Spanish wine in a ruby bottle, splashing fifty reds across her leaving. As there are always at twilight, people are sillouetted in shadow as they lean over the tower wall. Looking up and looking down, marveling at the scene. We hear the scream, faint, as from inside a well. Other screams, then, closer screams from the ones who are still standing on the tower. Looking up and looking down, tormented by the scene. Now it's the sirens' time to scream and nothing else much matters.

*

I BEGIN A CAMPAIGN among local chefs, but even the granting of time to explain my plight is denied. And from the few who will listen long enough to understand that I'm asking to rent their kitchens on their *giorni di chiusura,* the days when they're closed, I am turned soundly, unconditionally away. Mine is a foolish, empty route through a town sealed shut to any but its own needs and wants.

In a downhearted triage, I begin writing to magazine and newspaper editors, playing for time, asking for deadline extensions. Some agree. But I know that without the solution of a kitchen, my only proper recourse to ensure future assignments is to decline these. Still, the recipes for the book must be done now or I'll lose it, as well. There must be some closed restaurant, some unused commissary kitchen. I go to city hall, make an appointment with some midlevel bureaucrat, ask him if he might know of some abandoned but working kitchen that I can rent. Long-term. Short-term.

'*Ma, signora,*' he says, 'but, madam, the city hall is not an agency that aids refugees. You must visit Caritas or the Red Cross.' Black, dead Goya eyes stare out at me. He dismisses me with these two sentences, waving his hand backward in my direction, signaling me to leave him. The audience is finished. I am frozen, trapped somewhere in Kafka: an old woman who's come to beg a pension is slogged down dark, greasy stairs by a knavish commissioner in a plastic collar, onions on his breath. But the American girl rallies.

'Refugees? I am hardly a refugee. I have an Italian identity card, permanent permission to live in Italy; I'm married to an Italian and I am a passport-carrying citizen of the United States of America.' A force beyond my usual reason prevails now, and I repeat, if only for the pleasure of hearing myself: 'I am an American citizen who holds the state of Italy's permission to live in this country. I am a recent resident of Orvieto and I've come to you in good faith. For counsel, for direction. How dare you patronize me in this way.' I say this last as though a microphone were lodged in my throat.

The vice mayor – or to whomever belong the Goya eyes – seems splayed against his swivel chair by a rebellious wind. I turn on my heels, and though red and breathless with rage, I open and close the door with a skater's perfect figure eight.

A clerk is hunched over a crossword puzzle at a table just outside the door. Raising only his eyes, he mocks me: '*Buongiorno, signora. Buona giornata.*'

With this encounter, I have sealed my fate with the Orvietani as *the strange American woman*. I have just burned the title onto my chest with this encounter. Somehow Hester keeps surfacing in this story of Orvieto. I know this as I clump, wilted, down the marble stairs and past the open doors of smoky rooms, past two women who stand in front of their adjoining offices, each one with a cigarette held between the fingers of a hand poised on her cheek. Each one shaking her head at the other.

I call to tell my agent that I still have no kitchen, that I need another extension for the book. She says it's bad form to make a publisher wait inordinately. 'If we can't suggest a later date and keep it, it's best to let go,' she tells me. 'For the time being,' she softens the blow. I know it's the long, hunkered-down wait for which I must, at last, prepare myself. But not just yet.

'No,' I tell her. 'No, I'll meet the new deadline. Yes, I understand. Yes, I'll keep you posted. No, no phone yet. No, no e-mail.' I laugh at this last admission. She laughs, too.

First I will ferret out a stove from some part of this Etruscan town. Then I'll worry about e-mail.

'IT'S ALL JUST about ready,' says Miranda-of-the-Bosoms. 'I'll be opening for *Ognissanti,* All Saints Day. You'll be there, yes? There are only thirty-one chairs. Call me or stop by early in the day to tell me you're coming. *Prendiamo un bel caffè insieme.* We'll have a good coffee together.'

We see her at the *supermercato* in Orvieto Scalo, the postwar, brutally ugly commercial part of town that sits below and away from the *centro storico.* She pushes a cartful of oven cleaner and plastic wrap and cooking parchment and paper towels. Two five-kilo sacks of flour. I'm jealous of the flour. At this point, I suppose I'm even more jealous of the oven cleaner. And of her project. Here she is at the age when most people think about sliding into the praying-and-rocking stage of their lives and she's out and about, hauling sacks of flour and opening a restaurant. I wish I were opening a restaurant. She tells us she must run, that she has four more stops to make before a rendezvous with the painter back up at the new place. He's finishing up the last pass today on the dining room walls. Green, like the leaves of olive trees, she says. He'll need to have his lunch. Says she has to scrub the stove. Bought secondhand from a convent up near Castel Giorgio. Installed this morning. The nuns kept it anything but clean, she says. She'll be opening on November 1. All Saints' Day. Day after tomorrow.

'*Buona fortuna. Auguri, Miranda,*' we say. Good luck.

'I think I've found my kitchen,' I tell Fernando as I watch her rumble down the aisle, one hand steadying the flour sacks.

'Let's go to her opening and maybe you can take a look at it. If she's willing, the idea is good. But don't count on it just yet.'

Fernando keeps suggesting that we go back to San Casciano for a few weeks, use the Centrale's kitchen during its off-hours. Stay in an *agriturismo*. But somehow that notion doesn't feel right to me, and I'm not certain why. Too much like going backward, perhaps, though I know we would be welcome there. Maybe it's exactly that graciousness over which I don't wish to tread. I'd rather 'go home' to them in plenty than in need. Or in defeat. Invite them to dinner once we get settled. If anyone of them is still alive by then. No, going back to the Centrale is not the right thing at all. But I feel comfortable asking Miranda.

A copper sign swings from a wrought iron arm attached to the stones of a small, low house. Yellow light shows through two latticed windows upstairs. Like a pair of bushy eyebrows, boughs of pine are arched over them. Downstairs, there is a weather-worn wooden door and newly painted dark green shutters pinned back beside long, wavy-glassed windows. *Miranda,* the sign announces in delicate scrolls cut into the metal and backlit by a gas flame in an iron lantern. A sheaf of olive branches heavy with fat porphyry fruit and tied with a hank of rope is stuck to the door with a hunting knife. An ancient sign of welcome. A house invitation to travelers, passersby, a sign that here comfort waits. I see it and I remember something about pineapples being cleaved to the doors of sea captains' houses on Nantucket. Another ancient sign of welcome. *The captain has returned from his voyage to the South Seas. To the West Indies. And he awaits you.*

We open the door upon a card game. To a round table where six men in woolen berets and layers of sweaters shout all at once, light their cigarettes from the red ash butts of their previous ones in a kind of keeping of the flame. It's *briscola* they play, and the stakes are water glasses full of purple wine. They've already dined.

'*Sera, sera. Buona sera,*' they all say, hardly raising their heads to such people who would come to sup at nine o'clock, when every decent soul who's not playing cards should already be abed.

A length of faded, starched stuff is the doorway from the card room into the dining room, an opening so squat we must stoop as we hold the curtain and pass through it. There is little more room to stand on the other side of it. Split beams are set into a slouching, whitewashed ceiling, from which more olive branches are hung, so that one must continue the stoop until one sits, takes a place at a table covered with a green-checked oilcloth. On a stool or a bench or a caned chair. Over a grate in a small hearth, sausages are roasting. Miranda enters from behind a barely disguised bedsheet of a curtain. Wide polyester pants show below her pinafore and just graze new plastic clogs. She's fashioned a fresh white kitchen towel like a turban over her braids and she's a vision, the magic fairy of the burners, waving her long toasting fork of a wand.

'*Venite, venite, ragazzi. Benvenuti,*' she says, fairly pushing us down onto chairs at a table already occupied by two men.

'*Fernando e Chou-Chou, loro sono Orfeo e Luca. Buon appetito.*' And there it's done in an unlabored instant. The rabbit in her frying pan is ready to turn, she says over her retreating shoulders. Life seems so easy for Miranda-of-the-Bosoms. We shake hands with our table mates, wave them on with their pasta, and they, in turn, pour us some wine, offer us bread. The two men seem perfumed in milk and grass. A troupe of Miranda's grand-nephews and great-grandnephews – all sizes and shapes and aged somewhere between five and sixteen, perhaps – work the room. One brings more bread, refills the now communal wine jug, while another one sets down a half liter of water, as though in apology. And behind him, the smallest one sets down a plate of prosciutto, which the obvious team leader has hand-sliced from the haunch laid on a worktable near the fireplace. There is no menu, neither spoken nor written. One sips and waits in the dim, wood-smoked place. I am quietly enchanted by it all, feeling as though this were the home I'd been missing. The home that I didn't even know I'd been missing. Yes, here, exactly here is where I'd wanted to be.

Miranda comes forth then carrying a cloth-lined basket of fried rabbit, gold as sun-roasted wheat, sets it down at a table of five, each of whom is diligent over his own oven dish of gratinéed cardoons. And when one of the nephews brings them roasted potatoes, still in the pan and sending up the hot, moist fumes of wild fennel, I wish there'd been room at that table for us. But we're alone now, the two men having finished their pasta, said their good evenings. Their leaving charged the air with a yet richer smell of that milkiness, pleasantly sour. Fascinating men – exotic they were, but perhaps not so hungry as the rest of us.

We are served a deep basin full of pale, yellow pasta run through with wild mushrooms and their own dark, garlicky juices. Lost in pungent steams, I twirl and suck and chew the thin yellow strings, skate through the glossy sauce with the broken heels of my bread. I drink so deeply of my wine I can feel the small wet purple horns of it above my lips, but I barely have time to pat them away before the sausages, bursting from their charred, crackled skins, are set down and our own fried rabbit is brought with a small pan of those roasted potatoes. And more bread. More wine. Too ravished to speak, I flash a postcoital smile at my consort, and he every now and then gazes back, becharmed.

No one asks for and no one brings a bill. People just seem to know what their supper costs, leave wads of lire on the table as they go. I notice that some leave more than others and I wonder how things are calculated – quantity of food, number of dishes?

But no one seems to be thinking about it except me. No complications are evident, no one fusses over numbers. Can it be that people are paying what they *can* pay? But I noticed that our table mates left nothing. Has Miranda set up some sort of an honor system? Can that be possible?

The room is nearly empty now, the nephew troupe is washing up in the back. Miranda, still exuberant, carries out a fist-size round of new cheese — a soft, white solace from the feast. She eats it with us, sips some wine. Through her big, wide smile, she makes little purring sounds, hums, taps her feet as though inside these motions she could contain her joy.

'It's a wonderful place,' Fernando tells her.

I just sit there looking at her, saying the same thing with my eyes.

'Well, wonderful, I'm not sure. All I can say is that it turned out just like I'd wanted. You know, those men out there' – she tilts her head to the card room behind the curtain – 'and their fathers before them have been playing cards here since I was a girl. They've played by gaslight or candlelight or firelight, depending upon the season, for as long as I can remember. I knew all of them when they were old,' she says, looking at me. 'And I've watched all of them grow young again, if to varying degrees.'

'You think it's true? I mean, that we are born very old? That we grow younger with age?'

'Some will say it's a nice, neat excuse for not facing another truth but, yes, I think that if we work things right, we do grow younger. Think of the three-year-old and how he drives the miniature auto at the amusement park, how he grips the wheel clumsily, his back tense and a bit tilted backward in fear; now look at the eighty-five-year-old driving his three-wheeled Ape up the hill into town. He grips the wheel just as clumsily, his back is just as tense, just as tilted backward in fear. The very young and the very old seem to respond to life with the same kind of exhilaration and the same kind of fear. It's those in-between years, the ones that come after childhood and before old age, that confound us. Those are the brutal years.'

'So they're not just playing cards, waiting to die?'

'Maybe they are. Could be they're waiting to be born. Or waiting for nothing except their supper. You ask too many questions. All I know is that these men and their fathers before them have been here as long as I have. My mother's *rustico* has always been the "town hall"/card room/social club up here in these hills. On Sundays in the summer, each family brought their lunch and we'd all eat together under the chestnut trees. So when I began talking about fixing up the place, putting in a real kitchen, I raised up some discomfort among my neighbors. *Why is she going to change what's already good, what's been good for all these years? And at her age,* they were saying. But I fooled them all. I made it better without changing the things that were best about it. And every one of them helped me. Their wives, too. Whole families made the new roof; some of them even brought old tiles that had been saved from one place or another. If you look close, you can see the roof is made of different sizes and colors, but I like it that way. Same with the floors. I thought they were going to make them level, but no, they wanted to keep the slant, and so they did. The walls are straighter, though, and they made me a small apartment upstairs, so one of my sisters and her daughter and her daughter's sons and their wives and their children can go to live in my house in town.'

Miranda needs to talk. Like women who've just given birth need to talk, I think as I look at her, her kitchen-towel crown crumpled on the table, her face pink with triumph.

'You know, my mother and I used to talk about doing something like this, but we just never got around to it. I thought I'd better do it sooner than later. I mean, *when,* if not now?' She laughs and all the church bells ring again. 'Would you like to see the kitchen?'

Fernando says he'll just sit by the fire and wait. 'Go on, darling. Go to see the kitchen.' He crosses his fingers behind Miranda's back. Blows me a kiss.

'It's all settled and *she's so happy,*' I nearly scream out to Fernando – in English – as he sits watching the *briscola* boys.

'*Piano, piano.* They're concentrating,' he warns me. 'Wait until we're outside.'

'I've paid the bill. I left thirty thousand lire.'

'What do you mean you *left* thirty thousand lire. Was that enough?'

We've reached the car now, and each of us gets in. Closes the door. Fernando lights a cigarette. I ask for one, too: my warning to him that I'm about to say something difficult. He puts his between my lips. Lights another one. Looks at me hard.

'When I asked Miranda for the bill she said she didn't want to bother with bills. Said she'd opened the place not as an *osteria* but as a *circolo*. People are supposed to "subscribe," you know, like to a country club. Pay an annual fee. But she says that's rot and she'll ignore that part of her permit's regulations. Anyway, she's let out the word that supper costs fifteen thousand lire. A whole supper with wine, water, antipasto, *primi piatti, secondi piatti,* cheese. Everything. But if people dine here every night, they leave a little less. If they have only pasta, they leave even less than that. If somebody doesn't have any money, well, she says, they can eat anyway. That when they do have money, they'll catch up. She says that some people will come just to drink wine, eat *bruschette,* a few slices of prosciutto. She says people need to be together as much as they need to eat. Does that sound familiar?'

'Yes, it sounds familiar.' He says this with a tinge of be-grudging, and in a voice an octave higher than his own. My exuberance, when he is not the cause of it, tires my husband.

I go ahead anyway. 'And I've got a job, Fernando.'

'What is that supposed to mean?' He's more alert now.

'Well, not a real job, but in return for Miranda's allowing me the use of the kitchen after she's finished serving supper, I'll do the final cleanup. Have things ready for her when she comes downstairs in the morning. She says I can begin my work at about nine or so in the evening. All in all, I should be about three hours. I'll be finished by midnight. Just twice a week. She says it will give her nephews a break, and also she seems to be intrigued with the idea of tasting what I cook. We'll make some sort of lunch out of the tested dishes the next day – you and I with Miranda and whoever else happens to be there setting things up for the evening. Once you've had a chance to think about it I'm sure you'll agree it's a good thing. I'll have a kitchen, Miranda will have some extra help, and we'll all have some fun.' I speak in an animated rush, trying to settle his eyes on mine, but I can't. Rather he looks above and to the left of me. Out the window and at the moon.

'I suppose we could try it but why can't you get your work done in the kitchen early in the morning, before she starts her cooking? If she doesn't serve lunch, she probably doesn't begin using the kitchen until noon or so. Maybe later. Did you explore that possibility with her?' What he doesn't say is that he's embarrassed that his wife will be working as a kitchen maid.

'No. When I told her about what *I* needed, she told me what *she* needed. Or, I guess, what she would *like*. It didn't seem fitting that I should counter her. And besides, this isn't a forever arrangement. I can finish the recipes for the book in ten or twelve sessions. Six weeks. By then, maybe another plan will have unfolded out of this one and I can continue to use the kitchen. Then I can go back and start again to query the magazine editors. But what matters right now is that I have a place where I can get to work. Honor the new deadline for the book.'

'I agree, but having to work until midnight—'

'Listen, she said the card games go on at least until then, that she comes down about that time to send them home, turn out the lights. It's not as though I'll be there all alone. You'll be there, won't you? You'll have your choice of joining the *briscola* boys or prepping for me. Or you can do both. You look great with purple teeth. And you've nearly become a Norcino with your knife.'

I see he is not complimented by my reference to his being a pork butcher, but still he says, '*Va bene*. Okay. This is good. Not what I'd expected but nevertheless, *good enough*.'

He's quiet then. And so I am. Both of us letting the pieces of the evening fall freely, collide, settle into some kind of form.

'Yes, we'll take the nine-to-midnight shift in a kitchen in a converted shack next to a wheat field, in front of a sheepfold, at the edge of a pine forest in the thriving hamlet of Buon Respiro. Yes, that's exactly what we'll do,' he says more to the moon than to me.

10

Besides, They All Have Something of the Ass about Them, Chou

At Miranda's there is a smokehouse. At least that's what the narrow wooden building out behind the *rustico* has always been used as in her time, she says. She thinks it was once a field chapel, though, a place where farmers and shepherds came to pray of a morning or an evening. To light a candle, leave the offering of a wildflower bouquet or a few stalks of new wheat. And in a way, it still feels like some kind of church to me as I sit inside it, threading apples on a string. It's getting close to Christmas, and Miranda wants to decorate her place with garlands of dried lady apples. Since Barlozzo has taken Fernando out to shoot pheasant up near Collazzone, I've come to stay here for the day. It's warm in the smokehouse, though only heaps of flickering ash sit in the great, deep hearth dug into the ground. The man who keeps the fire is late today. Yes, this

131

could surely be a church with all the haunches of sacrificed beasts hung from the rafters, wood smoke swirling about them. Another kind of incense. Curls of it bursting from the chimney, a portion for the gods. I sit here on a bench piercing apples with a smooth wooden needle strung with butcher's twine, making triple knots between each fruit. A bushel of them. I hang them, then, festoon them over the door and the long windows out in front of Miranda's while she's inside rolling pasta for tonight. Our working together has gone well over these past weeks. We'd begun to tell each other how sorry we were to see it ending until we began saying, *It doesn't have to end at all. Let's do more together*. There's a good sentiment grown up between us, an unlikely pair of women – a local goddess and stranger – who've found it easy to laugh together. To be quiet, sometimes, one with the other. And as I learned from Florí, I don't ask why or how.

At some point, the richness of Miranda's friendship overtook my impoverished rank as exile up on the rock. Sped right by it so that I hardly notice the reserve of the Orvietani anymore. And when I do, I understand that they're only being themselves, just as I am. Days and evenings spent in Buon Respiro bring fresh perspective to life in town. Oddly, and not so oddly, I notice how much more at home I've begun to feel, even settling into some slim affection for the antibiotic friezes in Via Postierla. And I no longer wake up wondering if this will be the day when the work on Palazzo Ubaldini will begin. When I think about that, if I think about it at all, it's like thinking about Christmas. Sooner or later it will happen. A person's sanctuary, if it's real, will go where she does. Even make its way up onto Orvieto. But surely Miranda rethrew the stones for me. The nostrum of work has been part of the cure. But Miranda-of-the-Bosoms herself has been, too. She and her stories.

Removing her smock and her apron, adjusting the straining seams of her dress, preening her dazzling brown breasts like the most beautiful bird in the yard, she sits down at the big marble table in the kitchen when her evening's work is finished and as mine is just beginning. Her thimble of whiskey or a pot of fennel tea beside her, she begins unraveling some tale. One time she tells me about Etruscan tear jars.

'Every woman, every man, every child had one. You can see them in the Faina museum up in town, but they look like this,' she says, getting up to reach for a vial-shaped terra-cotta vase that holds a single dried rosebud and stands on a shelf in front of a small, silver-framed photo of her mother. 'When an Etruscan cried, he held the vase up to his eye, collecting the tears in it. Tears fall from the soul, they believed, from the melting of the soul, and so to lose tears was to lose one's soul itself. Then they would crush violets or rose petals and scent the tears, make a kind of perfume of them, use the potion to annoint the people they loved. Thus giving up their soul for love.'

I can't help but think I could have used a bit larger container than that tiny little jar at one time or another in my life. A twenty-liter amphora might have served me well. Makes me wonder, too, where all that melting soul of mine ended up. Left dripping on the torn leather seats of trains, on my babies' cheeks, on satin sheets and silk shirts, on the pointed tips of my dancing shoes. On handkerchiefs, often not my own.

One winter evening when I've finished my own work and before I've set to scrubbing down the kitchen, I decide I'd like to put some bread to rise overnight. I want to set some simple cornmeal dough in the big brown-speckled bowl I'd seen in the pantry. Cover it with my apron, leave a note for Miranda to shape it, bake it when she comes downstairs tomorrow morning. I think she might like that. I am inspired by her stash of coarse, stone-ground cornmeal, the stuff she uses to make polenta, the kind of polenta that must be stirred, always clockwise, while it plumps and squeaks over a low flame until the stick or spoon or broom handle used to turn it stands up straight in its middle. Thick as yesterday's oatmeal. She stores this cornmeal in a fat terra-cotta jar stoppered with a cork to keep it safe from tiny creatures, winged and footed. I have some of my own bread flour and a few pinches of baker's yeast left from another evening's trials with Sicilian *sfincioni,* a kind of onion focaccia. And so I begin. Rinse the dust from the old bowl, wipe it dry. Dissolve the yeast in barely warm water with a whisper of sugar. Dip a small white soup dish into the polenta jar, into my flour sack, then. Sea salt, a tilt or two from the oil jug. More water. A soft rendition of 'You Do Something to Me.' By candlelight and firelight in my friend's kitchen I am making cornmeal bread. Cornmeal bread for Miranda. In my note, I draw a primitive design of a loaf with a topknot, a shape I'd learned to make years ago from a French baker in Biarritz. I write her the barest details of my history with this particular kind of bread. As well as those with the French baker. And when Fernando and I arrive the next evening, wend our way through the dining room, we see people tearing off hunks of golden yellow bread from the beautiful rounds of it that sit on each table. Beautiful topknotted rounds. As I pass by him, one man says to me, 'This American bread is good, signora.'

I thank him very much and don't dare to tell him about the Wonder kind.

'So which bread will you make tonight, Chou?' Miranda says in greeting, flashing her great goddess grin.

And that was how I came to be the official house *fornarina*, lady baker, at Miranda's. We sat later that evening and figured out the costs of house bread versus bought. If I wouldn't get too fancy, she said, wanting herbs she'd have to buy rather than forage or flours like rye and whole wheat, which we'd have to order from a supply house, if I would be content to just make a few basic breads, we'd not only stay in budget but save a bit. But she said that what she liked best about having her own *fornarina* was that the *rustico* would smell like it did when her mother and her aunts and her older sisters would make bread on summer Saturday mornings. She liked that idea best of all. The old brown-speckled bowl, the one I'd found among the battery in her pantry, was the one her mother had always used for bread. When Miranda had come in this morning, seen it on the marble table, looked under the apron and spied the dough, risen round and smelling like the first smell in the world, she said she could feel her mother's smile.

Now that the recipe testing was finished for the time being, Miranda said I could put the bread to rise in the morning if I preferred. But I'd already grown accustomed to the night shift and told her I'd like to continue coming by when she'd finished for the evening. We kept agreeing with each other at every point, but still, I could see that some part of things was causing distress for Miranda. She was worried about my compensation, especially since she knew that I wasn't worried about it at all. I understood her well enough to leave her to fret as she must. Meantime, I set about the rifling of her oven pans, appraising the shapes and sizes. I'd set some grape skins out to ferment on the back ledge of the stove so I could make a *biga,* a starter, with natural yeast. From a pile of them Fernando found in the wine cellar, I'd scrubbed enough bricks to line the oven.

'Shall I make some tea?' I ask the still-fretting Miranda, but she shakes her head no, asks me to come sit by her.

'I propose that my *fornarina* and her consort dine in my house each evening. I have no money to pay you, Chou, but if you and Fernando would become nightly guests, everything would seem more fair,' she said.

'Why don't we just keep that idea a bit flexible. We'll know we're welcome, and sometimes we'll be here. But perhaps sometimes we'll be somewhere else. I think it feels better that way.'

In the evening while I'm putting the bread to rise, she sometimes pulls a chair up to the worktable, says she'll just sit with
me for a minute, catch her breath. But mostly she stays, watches
me, talks about what she'll cook the next day.

'When Palazzo Ubaldini is finally ready, the first thing I want
to do is to have a dinner party. No, not just a dinner party.
More like a feast. Yes, a feast that everyone will remember,' I tell
her, my hands flying through the flour.

'Who's everyone?'

'I don't know yet. Seems as though I've a long time to think
about it. But you'll be there and Barlozzo will and, well, I'm not
sure who else. People from town, people I've met here.'

She's laughing her church-bell laugh now, as though I've just
told her a fine joke.

'You can't put people from here at the same table with people
from town. You just can't. Not one of them would be comfortable. Not one of them would consent to such a thing. It's not as
though we don't know each other or even, sometimes, like each
other. But we don't sit at the same table. Except maybe at fairs.
Even that's never planned or desired. It's only something that just
happens and is endured. I've worked for so many people up in
town — cooking their suppers, scrubbing their floors, washing
their underwear — and each one of them is related to five hundred other people, so that you'd have to go a long way to find one
who doesn't know me as Miranda the maid. And not one of
them is going to the same party I'm going to. Not one of them is
going to sit next to me round a dinner table. Except for Tilde.'

'Who's Tilde?'

'Even though you don't know her name, you must have seen Tilde hundreds of times up in town. She'll be coming back for supper one of these nights and I'll introduce you. I used to work for her about a million years ago. She's the only person I know who moves among us here as well as she does with the people up on the rock. Truth is, she's more alone than she is anything else. You'll meet Tilde. And who knows? She might be a candidate to sit at your feast.' She proposes this with a glint of sarcasm.

'Are you trying to say that she's indiscriminate about where she dines?'

'Not at all, especially since she likes dining here with me. Rather than indiscriminate, I'd call Tilde impious. I'd even call her brazen. She knows how to please herself and that's what she does, what she's always done as far as I know. Tilde has earned her titles and her rights, and you, my love, have not. You still don't understand how things are done here, Chou.'

'Will you tell me about Tilde?'

'No, I won't. Just be patient. The only thing I'll tell you is that she's a fascinating creature. And now let's decide the menu for this mythical feast.'

Whoever she is, I like Tilde already. *Impious, brazen, fascinating.*

Miranda is rattling off orthodox dishes. 'If it's in the spring, you'd just have to make *coratella* – suckling lamb intestines braised with tomatoes and new garlic – and a nice dish of *puntarelle* – wild grasses – which I'll gather for you from the hill-

138

side behind the smokehouse. Boiled, shined with an anchovy sauce. *Scottadita,* tiny little lamb ribs and chops grilled over a hot grapevine fire. Suckling lamb sealed in *coccio* with butter and onions and left over night in the embers.'

'But whose feast is this? I'll decide what I'll bring to the table.'

'To your thus far *fictitious* table. With guests made of straw who sup on vapors. Ah, you're a funny little person, Chou. Will you cut me a piece of cheese to take up to bed?'

'WHAT MADE YOU decide to put together this *circolo* – I mean, at this time in your life?'

We're ensconced in our usual positions in the kitchen: me with my flour; Miranda sitting, slapping head after head of purple garlic with the side of a cleaver, scraping the smashed cloves into a five-liter jug of *olio nuovo,* just-pressed oil, in which she's already stuffed shredded leaves of sage, the roasted seeds and the dried flowers of wild fennel, rosemary leaves chopped fine as powder, and a handful or so of crushed hot, very hot chiles, the completed potion of which she'll set in the dark pantry for a week or so, shaking it hard every time she goes back there to fetch one thing or another. She calls it *violenza,* violence, and uses it to sauté vegetables, to gloss potatoes before she tumbles them into the roasting pan; she massages it over loins of pork and the breasts and thighs of her own fat chickens and drizzles it over charcoaled beef and veal just before delivering them to the table. 'It's good for everything but lamb and

wild birds and the aches and pains of most men. Though I have,
and more than once, rubbed it into a cut or a scrape, disinfect-
ing the wound better than straight alcohol could and leaving a
much more pleasing perfume on the patient,' she tells me.

'Are you trying to say *at my age*?' she asks me now, laughing
and slapping the cleaver. 'Surely wasn't for profit. I think what
I wanted to do was to finish up my very good life by saying
thank you.'

She said she didn't want to be the upstairs-and-downstairs
maid until she could no longer carry the pail and the mop. She
wanted to end that before she had to so she could begin this
other, this – 'yes, I'll go ahead and say it: this last part of my life
while I'm still strong.' Perhaps the strongest she's been in years,
she says.

'All I need is to pay the taxes and the maintenance on the
place. As far as *things* go, I have enough of them. Enough to
sleep on and sit on and enough things to hold all the other things
I have. I'd like a new dress twice a year – one from the market
and one store-bought. And new shoes, too, if I can. Get my hair
all fixed up once in a while. Go to the dentist. But everything
else I want is here.'

'Do you ever think about getting married again?'

'Of course I do. Everytime I see Luca or Orfeo, I think about
it. Mostly Luca. Or the man who brings me wine from Baschi,
or even when I look at some of those fool card-playing widow-
ers out there. Sometimes I think about it when Guerrino, the
wood man, is out piling up logs. And I think about it again

when he comes inside and sits at the bar and drinks a glass of wine, and then I think about it after he's gone and left that clean smell of new wood in his wake. More than I think about marriage, I think about men. Does that surprise you? Age has relatively little to do with libido. That's a secret among some of us older people. No one ever talks to us about sensuality. Desire. And if we are audacious enough to marry at some moment in our sunset, the act is tallied up to latent idiocy or convenience or economics. To one person needing the other one to carry and fetch. Children are wont to think a late marriage a disrespect to them, since the new partner might be chinking away at their rightful legacies. No one ever thinks that old people's coupling might be for something purely intuitive. Or inspired. Our fires may be banked, but they're not always spent.

'It's sad, isn't it, Chou, how anagraphical age becomes a sort of identification at some point? How it sets down new rules and acceptable behaviors. It's like going back to being a teenager. *You're too young to do this, too immature to do that.* For folks past seventy or eighty, the adjectives change. *Aren't you a bit old to be considering such a move? Why don't you just sit back and enjoy yourself rather than behaving like some ancient fool? Here, let me change the channel for you.* People want our lives to be over before they really are. Oh, I don't say they want us to die, but they just don't want us to be any trouble. They want us to be good and quiet and generous. They want us to sleep through the afternoon and go to bed early just like they want their babies to do. Always trying to make somebody be still. Why does everyone stop talking to old people? Really talking, I mean, and not about glucosamine or rice pudding. They're convinced that we can't hear over the noise of the past or see beyond the light of the television, when all the time it's we who see it all.

'*Noi vecchi vediamo la bufala tra la neve*. We old ones see the buffalo in the snow,' she says.

Buffaloes are white in Italy. White as snow.

'Pardon me, Chou. I've strayed from your question, and I'm sorry. All you did was ask me if I ever think of getting married again, and the truth is that I do. The greater truth is that I never would.'

'But why?'

'I don't know. It's too late or not late enough.'

'But which one would you choose? Of all the men you know, which one would choose?'

'None of them. I had a good marriage. My husband was a great beast of a man, kind as a baby deer. Worked and laughed and slept and ate and drank with the exhilaration of a passionate man, and all the while he held me up like a china doll. Or at least that's what I thought he was doing. And most of the time, I still believe, he did.'

I'm lost. I wait for her to show me the way.

'You see, Nilo's dying was made of two swords falling. How could it be that such a man could go off one morning, big and sweet and crushing my lips with his coffee-stained mustaches, telling me he loved me just as he always told me. How it could be that he never came back? That he could be stacking bricks, sending them down a line to be counted and wrapped, readied for shipping, all the while talking to the man working next to him, and in the time it took for that man to turn around and talk to the person next to *him* on the line, then turn back to Nilo, Nilo was already dead. Slumped in a heap right on the spot where he'd been standing and laughing two minutes before. That was sword number one. The second sword came after the mass, the funeral mass.

'I was standing there in the church, surrounded by my sisters, when this child – this small, thin boy with skin so white the veins showed through it, and eyes like big dark holes burned into a sheet – walked toward me, shackled me like a prisoner. Toe to toe, eye to eye. And in that moment, the vague sensations of the morning – and those much older than the morning – broke like glass. Ice falling hard and fast from a mountain into a ravine, and I knew it before he told me. Standing there sober as Abraham, I knew it was true before he could say it: "*Sono figlio di Nilo.* I am the son of Nilo." I think the boy neither expected me to speak nor even wished me to. It was his own statement he'd come to make. To say it out loud. So that he'd be real. I understood that even in the first moment. Yes, that was the first thing I understood,' she says, as though she's understanding it all over again.

'And behind him, not so far behind him, stood a girl. I looked over the boy's head at her as she stepped closer. "*Io sono l'altra.*

I am the other one." At first I thought she meant that she was the other child, for she was small and delicate, too. And so young. White-skinned, red-haired, just like the boy. But what she meant was that she was the other woman. The other wife. Her gaze made that clear. Even though I kept trying to make her eyes slide off mine, she held them there until she was certain that I understood. So discreet was this exchange among the three of us, so intimately delivered and received, so free of anything like bitterness or cruelty, it seemed more like something hard that had to be said and then held inside a caring family. Which, in a way, I suppose we three were. Like specters, then, the boy and his mother dissolved into the crush of the others, so swiftly and leaving no trace of their having been there that I began to think I'd imagined them. Imagined them not only then in the church but much longer ago than that. Certainly I have since then. Sometimes I think I see them even now, even twenty years later. The two of them as they were that morning, my fantasies not compensating for the passing of time. He's still about ten and she still seems not much more than a girl. But when I get closer, it's never them, of course. No matter how much I will the boy and the young woman to be them, they never are.

'Oh, Nilo had given me all the signs. He did everything he could apart from sitting me down and telling me outright. All the times he'd stayed away, never constructing lies around his absence, never apologizing for it, only saying he had "things to do over in Acquapendente." That was the town where he'd grown up, where he'd worked for years, where most of his old chums lived. Acquapendente was where he still went to have his confessions heard. He left me free to wonder about the empty spaces he'd leave, to ask him about them. Neither of which I ever did. I'm still not sure, but I think I *did* know. Don't you think we always know?'

'I think we always know. And I think we always tell. Each in our fashion.'

Yes, in our fashion. What I don't tell Miranda is that I also think that as a race, we have a genius for disguise. Each of us is a secret to the other. Beware the simple person, who is rarely so. For most of us, it is exquisite to conceal. A lover; a bank account; a thought, recurring, flickering; a single afternoon at a white wicker table midst the languorous dancing of figs, pendulous as milky breasts. Another black skirt. One more reading of *the close shave.* Sometimes I think the lie intoxicates more than the reason for it. A human condition.

'For all my robustness, Chou, I've a frail spirit, and no one understood that better than Nilo. His was the sin of omission rather than of the lie. He was nothing more than "stained." Most of us are, you know. I've always been wary of the claim to immaculateness, which I believe is the sign of a false heart or simple stupidity. I've made my peace with Nilo, but what I still don't understand is why the boy and his mother ran away. Days after the funeral, when I went to Acquapendente to try to find them, they'd already gone. Of course people there knew who I was describing, knew the circumstances, as well, I think. But if anyone with whom I'd talked knew where they'd gone, no one was saying. If the boy and his mother had wanted me to find them, they would have left a trail. If they'd wanted anything from me, they would have never gone away.'

'Did you ever hear from them or about them in all these years?'

'Not a word. And I've been sorry about that fact more than I can tell you. Rather than being relieved at their vanishing, I grew to feel the loss of them as a kind of third sword. Another kind of betrayal. I wanted to know the boy. Help him if I could. Tell him wonderful things about his father. Look for traces of Nilo in him and praise them. I wanted to help her, too. I don't think they had any family at all – at least that's what the people of Acquapendente told me. In how many different sorts of life I have imagined them, Chou. There've been times when I could hardly stay upright for my worrying over them. As though it were me who was the mother. Mother to both of them. It's the strangest thing.'

Not so strange for a goddess, I think. She's quiet but not at ease. She prepares herself to say more.

'We knew that I was barren before we married, and Nilo seemed just fine with that. But he was thirty then, and by the time he was forty maybe some other sense of wanting to be a father, needing to have a child, maybe some other desire took on more light. Or maybe he just fell in love with *her*. Maybe it was as simple as that. Love is made like a pearl. Layer upon layer of suffering. I don't think the easy part is the beautiful part of love.

That's why I don't regret loving Nilo. I think despair grows from regret, and despair never did anybody any good.

'Rather than feeling cheated, over time I began to think that I'd gotten everything I'd ever bargained for from Nilo the first time he kissed me. The first time he kissed me and I kissed him back, that was everything. That longing, that sense that you could crawl up and die, smiling, curled up inside the other person. You can tell love by a single kiss. I'm sure of that. But I'm also sure that we can't know what pleasures are going to turn on us, become pain. When you tuck that truth in your pocket, the pleasures themselves – even the very smallest of them – get to seeming complete, round. Whole. Unconnected even to the next moment. We can't know what we'll be happy about later on. Or sorry for. Or what we'll remember backward or upside down. If we're smart, we forget. Only that, of course, which we should forget. Knowing what to forget is as important as knowing what to remember. It's the same motion as harvesting wheat. Know what to keep and what to refuse. There's a great delicacy in that, Chou. Sometimes people insist on mixing the chaff with the good stuff, boiling them up together, but all they ever get is a pap that sticks in the throat.

'But just as any fresh wound will do to a body, Nilo's death and Nilo's truth left me unguarded. And profiting from my teetering state, fear took over. Set up to stay. I was and am victorious over despair, Chou, but fear is still with me. I cover it up with my prancing and joking. And now with my cooking. But it's fear more than any other thing that's kept me from being another man's wife. So the answer is that I would choose none of them.'

She looks at me for the first time then, and I see that she's well. Talking about sentiments enlarges them. Makes them better or makes them worse, and surely Miranda has come back serenely from her talking. She is better for the telling of her story. She's even laughing now, a quiet, rascally kind of laugh.

'Besides,' she says, 'they all have something of the ass about them, Chou. Every last one. Come over here and hug me, Chou. Hug me and then cut me another piece of cheese.'

IT'S TEN-THIRTY NOW, maybe closer to eleven, and Miranda's just gone up to bed. And because I stayed so still while she was talking, I've yet to mix my bread. Fernando's gone out back for some wood so he can lay the fire for tomorrow. The *briscola* boys keep yelling for him: *Fernando, get out here please and take over Erichetto's hand since he's playing a thieves' game. Fernando, we are in sore need of arbitration. Will you please oblige?* He does just that, and a contented silence is resumed in the card room.

When he comes back to sit with me I ask him, 'What do you men talk about out there anyway?'

'Not much of anything. Scoffs and jests. If they talk it's mostly about the weather – how it is, how it was, how it used to be. How it won't ever be again. Weather takes up a lot of time in men's conversations. I suppose it takes up hardly any time at all when women talk.'

'No, not much time at all about the weather.'

'Some of the men talk about things they did when they were young. The global fishing-and-hunting coming-of-age stories. The one that got away. The even bigger one that got away from his father.'

'I guess men are the same everywhere. I mean in the way women are the same. Men talk in the abstract, rarely tearing through the skin of their self-imposed constraints. Dance around the hard stuff as though it were poison jelly. They'd rather roll around in a bed of thorns than talk about emotions. They use substitute words and phrases for love and pain and fear, as though they were talking in code. Yes, I think that's what men do. Most times, I think that's what they do.'

'I never even got to the substitute words. I just stayed quiet. Quiet until I met up with you.'

'You stayed quiet for a while even after that.'

'I know.'

Fernandino, your presence is needed here once again.

He goes back to the *briscola* boys and I get to kneading my bread, slapping the dough on the cold marble of the worktable, thinking about Miranda's story, thinking about my own, thinking about how much more we're all alike than we are different. That truth always startles me. Umbria. South Dakota. The Ukraine. Twelve minutes of slow, rhythmic meter in the quiet of a nighttime kitchen. Moments spent with flour and water and the spores of grape skins. A fistful of salt. The cracked, chipped beauty of Miranda's mother's bowl. Dark, wet air sidles in through the open kitchen door. A rogue breeze teases the candle flame, which is my only light. *Slap, slap,* the dough sounds on the marble, and I think how many of the beautiful things in life have this same cadence. The rocking of a cradle, *woosh, woosh.* The suckling of a hungry baby, the creaking springs of the lovers' bed. The clicking of the beads of a rosary. I wonder if a few drops of a melting soul aren't what make a really fine loaf of bread. I think it must be so.

11

I Preferred One Waltz with a Beauty to a Lifetime with Someone Less Rare

The benevolent winter surrenders early, so that by February trees bud. Grasses sprout, and women with kerchiefs tied about their red, high-boned faces and sweaters under their pinafores bend to the hills and meadows up near Miranda's place, digging, scratching, pulling up wild shoots by their roots, tying small nosegays of the dark green stalks with kitchen string, cutting the string with a knife and heaving the little bundles – a stash of emeralds – into the old pillowcases knotted to their belts. They work as country women have worked since the time when the Furies went to sleep. Competing with the sheep, it seems, when some woolly thing prances over to graze where they are digging. Miranda is out there with them most mornings, again just before sunset, and even when the women work different patches of a hill, they still talk to one another, shout gossip and recipes back and forth. One of them asks who will help her to pin up the hem of a new dress that afternoon. Sometimes they sing.

The book has been finished and sent to the new editor, who — unusually, in the eternal volley of the publishing process — made the most minor suggestions and passed the manuscript into production. A trickle of magazine work is beginning to come in, and we've booked two groups for touring in late April. All in all, an honorable collection of small feats. Miranda has given me carte blanche to use her kitchen when I need to test recipes, and I tend to my bread-baking duties mornings or evenings, according to the path of the rest of our life. Apart from kitchen time and sleeping and writing and telephoning time, washing clothes and dusting the picture galleries that hide the mold in Via Postierla, we are always outdoors. Ten flats of white pansies we plant near the back door, white impatiens along the flags of the walkway, and hydrangeas of a strange powdered-silver color beside the house. Tomato plants and herbs fill the Deruta urns on the terrace. Despite our trying not to be, we are at home in Via Postierla, that sense of its being an interval, a holiday house, long gone away.

Like the ladies up in Buon Respiro, we forage, too. For wild asparagus, thin and brown as hop shoots, or *barba di prete*, priest's beard — a long fat-bladed grass — or the silky transparent cress that grows by the Tiber and, more profusely, by a rill where we eat our lunch, bathe our feet in the riffles of water breaking on the stones. Our toy boat is a bottle of wine, which we float, chill in the icy water, its neck tied with a string, the other end looped into a bracelet on my wrist. The wine tugs at my arm like an old trout caught on a line and I move along the bank to its will, my face to the sun, guiding it away from the bigger rocks sometimes, performing this foolish rite only because it's what Barlozzo does and because when I do it I seem to miss him less.

We rinse the cress, eat it out of hand, wolfing it. I push the small peppery leaves into my mouth with the back of my fingers, catching the errant ones and sucking them from my palm. More decorously then, I lay leaves of it across our bread and cheese. What we don't eat right there on the spot, we take to Miranda to add to her collections, but no matter how much is gathered, the almost barbaric hungers of her diners make scant work of the tonic weeds.

'We've all been living mostly on flesh and pulses for a few months now,' Miranda says. But in springtime we eat wild spinach and dandelion and chickory and wild onions and wild garlic, all of them spontaneous and just born from the earth, all of them boiled and squeezed, then fried in good oil with garlic and hot chiles and taken with bread torn from a fine crusty loaf. Yes, that's what we eat in springtime. *Il rinascimento annuale per il corpo,* the annual rebirth of the body. 'That's what weeds do. Weeds are medicine. A person has to eat what's ripe.'

Just as we'd learned by living among the rural Tuscans, we notice that here, too, the average Orvietano farmer lives well until he dies. Until she dies. And that's most often well into their nineties. Literally, *well*. This truth has its tenets. Hard physical labor in the outdoors, which begins in youth and continues through the eighties and is always tempered with intervals of rest — most notably, *il sacro pisolino,* the sacred post-lunch nap. But above all, it's the *Eat what's ripe* commandment that rules, the only constants on the table being bread, wine, and olive oil. Eating or living in any other way but this one is unthinkable, as undesirable as a February strawberry.

EACH EVENING ON our way up to Buon Respiro, we stop at the *belvedere,* the lookout terrace, stepping from the car to lean over the wall, to gaze upon Orvieto on her throne. Bewitching and divine. I look to the black-and-white-striped walls of the Duomo and think, *There, just a few meters from that magnificence, there is our home. There is Palazzo Ubaldini.* Riddles seem fugitive from this distance, chased away by a thrill.

If we're hungry, we go directly to Miranda's and our supper. But often we prefer to wait, to share what's left from the pots and pans with her and the nephews a bit later. These nights are just too lovely to stay inside. Racing against the sun, we leave the car in Miranda's garden and go to walk in the bluish light of the meadows, find our seats on a broken stone wall, the toneless droning of the sheep riding the air in accidental chorus with the moaning of the wind. It's time now. Riding on red silk plumes, the sun shimmers, flames, her light falling away fast as the brown edges of burning silk, until all that's left is a cold jade sky. The darkening always comes too soon. I'm never ready for the dark. We walk then, taking care to stay far away from the roof-less ruins of a castle where a fire is always lit. It's the place where Orfeo and Luca – the beautiful men with whom we sat that first evening at Miranda's and who smelled of milk and grass – lay down their heads of an evening. Shepherds, they trade fresh cheeses or foraged grasses and mushrooms for Miranda's *umbrichelli*.

In the dining room one evening, we'd watched them as they'd flavored their pasta themselves, taking a rusted grater and an unwrapped chunk of hard yellowed cheese from their sacks.

'The pecorino they pawn off on me is too young for these fellows,' said Miranda as she passed by them, shaking her head at Orfeo and Luca, turning to heave vine cuttings and dried laurel leaves onto the fire, setting thick chops on a grate over the crackling, dancing flames.

Other guests had sniffed appreciatively at the sharp, footsy scent of the shepherds' private cheese, and so the one called Orfeo passed it to them, hand to hand, along with the crusty grater, the *pft-pft-pft* perfuming the little room like a cheese-making hut in August. There seemed a more absorbed attention for Miranda's good pasta then, followed by the quiet hallelujahs of bodies consoled once more from their hungers for food and repose taken among the wood smoke.

But the contained pleasantries of dining in the same room with Orfeo and Luca at Miranda's do not give us license to trespass upon their working and living territories, and so we stay well apart from them on our sunset walks. But not so far that I can't watch them, rapt as I would a pageant. From somewhere else in time, they seem. Luca must be seventy. Tall, broad, handsome as the king of the gypsies. The cape he wraps around himself is large and long and he wears it like a penance, stoops under it, constantly adjusts it as he sits or walks. Hides in it. Orfeo is younger, fifty perhaps. Pale eyes like sea glass ornament the dark skin of him, pulled tight and smooth over high, wide bones. Black as a crow where it hasn't gone to gray, his hair is bound in a tail with some strip of cloth, and a long woolen scarf is twined about his neck, caressing the small pointed beard on his chin. I would wear his clothes. Washed, perhaps, but I would wear his clothes. Orfeo seems a shipwrecked prince who'd swum to shore in velvet vest and leather breeches twenty years before – four hundred years before – and has worn them ever since. The two of them are engrossing creatures whose life it is to coach the great ragged flocks across the meadows, goad them inside the walls of the orphaned castle, soothe them like children unready for sleep. Back outside, under the stars, they set a fire for warmth and, judging from the lingering perfumes of it, for the concocting of some stew or soup over its flames when their accounts at Miranda's have been used up for the month. But they are always finished with their meal by the time we come by, sitting, drinking red wine from a two-liter bottle, passing it between them like a rhyme. They seem to wait for us, or so we think, and we begin to venture closer to them until it is, unspokenly, established that we'll sit together around their fire.

At first they'd pass the bottle to us in turn and we'd drink from it, I less thirstily than Fernando. But one evening soon after our soirées began, Luca pulled a cloudy tumbler from his sack, a single, small chip on its rim, and it – never washed in anything more than the wine itself – was designated as my own. And when I'd finished my wine he'd take the glass from me, throw the dregs over his shoulder, saying, 'For the angels,' and place it gently back in his sack for the next time. Theirs was a hospitable refuge in that Umbrian sheepfold, and in the dark blue hours that make the heart tender, we four talked well and long by the fire and under the stars. And we always ate bread.

From a day-old or older two-kilo round they kept in a plastic sack hung from a nail in the ruin, Orfeo would saw thick slices, clutching the loaf to his chest. He'd roast the bread on a torn wire screen propped over the flames and the cinders. Turning it with his fingers, he'd squeeze thin threads of fine green oil from a wineskin over the charred bread, dole out a piece to each of us, a diamond cutter handing over a lustrous stone. We'd sit there, one of us working the fire, one tidying things, Luca going off every now and then to check on his charges, to deliver a fatherly whack to the unruly ones. Loping back across the field then, fixing his cape, settling himself down, he'd look into the fire and recite Pablo Neruda or Giovanni Pascoli. And Fernando would step on the last lines of the poem with one from Virgil. Verse after verse of the Aeneid. Afterward or sometimes during the recital, Orfeo would take up his mandolin, strum the untuned strings in a kind of *rasqueado,* his ear bent close to the small wooden thing, and invent tranced sounds. And when the other two men were quiet, Orfeo would sing, too, a *triste* lover making lace with words and the small delicate spaces between them. Sometimes he'd quiver the strings, making the noise that the blue glass tears of a Venetian chandelier make, jingling in a breeze.

Though my penchants to feed them were awakened on those nights, I knew that my carrying any sort of supper to them would be wrong. An intrusion upon Miranda but more upon them and their private feasting, upon their own arrangements for the taming of their hungers. More than once we'd seen them — as we'd passed by on our way up the road to Montefiascone — in some detached pose on the edge of a patch of garden, fingering a few tomatoes or a fat, yellow squash, plumping their shoulder bags, operating in some middle sphere between forager and pica-roon. And I'm sure that one stood guard while the other wrung the neck of more than a single chicken in the time that we knew them, swiftly pummeling the stunned, limp bird into a sack, the last flurry of her feathers rasping against the rough stuff of it. How would they explain the sizzling of a domesticated bird over their fire should we stop by with some potluck of ours to add to theirs? Not everyone yearns for rescue from his own ways and means. No, not everyone does. Barlozzo taught me that.

I conceded bread, though. I'd bake a fat, thick-crusted loaf for them twice a week, wrap it in a kitchen towel, slip it, un-announced, into their plastic bag, none of us acknowledging or ignoring the humble gift or needing to.

In their eloquence, rich as cream, Orfeo and Luca barely

talked about themselves. Where were they from? Did they own the flocks, did they live anywhere else but under the sky? Had they always been shepherds? Nor did they ask questions of us. Our pasts. How we came to be here. But, once, looking at the fire rather than at any one of them, I risked, '*Siete sposati?* Are you married?'

Though the question was plural, only Orfeo answered me. And only in his fashion. Holding up his bottle, he said, 'You see this wine, Chou? Rough and coarse as it is, I will drink it to its last drop. But if I had something, shall we say, more precious, I would drink less of it. My father would say, *With a good wine, it's enough if you'll just pass the bottle by my nose.* It's the same with women. Yes, wine and women are the same. I preferred one waltz with a beauty to a lifetime with someone less rare. I had my waltz. And now I have this.' He spreads his arms as though to enclose the meadow.

To them and, after a time, to us, nothing else seemed to matter save our being there together. Four muddied ghosts we were in the red light of the blaze, passing the evening in a shepherds' salon on the meadows beside the ruins.

12

Wait until Midnight If You Can

A nd as our evenings with Orfeo and Luca widened the circle of comfort Miranda drew around us, so, too, that spring, did Orvieto's market and more than a few of its repertory players.

Sprawling over Piazza del Popolo on Thursdays and Saturdays, it is a ritual event attended by locals of all ages and stations, as well as the farther-flung citizens from Orvieto's communes, neighboring villages and hamlets. These arrive by lopsided truck or bicycle or *moto* or in three-wheeled farm wagons – Ape – which boast the space and power of toaster ovens set on wheels. In one mode or another, everyone comes to the fair.

Passed down from generation to generation – not unlike the licenses of gondoliers in Venice – the permits for the square footages on which the farmers set out their wares are sacred. In new violet light seeping through the night fogs, the farmers transform a car park into a lusty scene just as Brueghel would have liked it. Everything smells like damp earth. It clings to the farmers' boots and the wheels of their barrows, crusts the potatoes and the beetroots harvested an hour before, when the moon was still high, and it stays, eternally, under the jagged, hard nails of the farmers' beautiful hands. Though in a few moments these men and women will become competitors for the lire to be passed about this morning, now, as in the privacy of a back stage, they are all of a company. They meet to embrace, to ask after one another's families, to lament the rains or praise them, to flatter each other's bounty.

'Our earth is so black it shines copper in the sun, dyed as it is with all that Saracen blood. It's rich so we don't have to be,' says the farmer called Gaspare, whom we met at the fava bean supper last summer. His *banco* is laid with neatly tied bunches of just-pulled onions and garlic and long, snaky peppers, pale green and yellow ones and bouquets of asparagus looped about their girth with white string, a pink rose at the center of each bundle. He has daffodils in a bucket, and lilacs, towering branches of them, wobbling and spilling from another, larger bucket, and making a frame around his head as he talks to me. 'We make do with what the earth gives up. It's always enough to keep us. If a person has more than he needs for supper and some to put by for tomorrow's lunch, he has too much. And with too much, you lose track of things. Too much to eat, too much money. It's all the same. What we can find and what we can grow is mostly all we have. Living off the land wants a man's cunning and his reverence. The rest is up to the gods. Except when the cooks take over. Hah, when they take over, well, you've tasted what our cooks can do, haven't you? They match the gods, miracle for miracle.'

'I'm a cook, too,' I tell him, already knowing I'm making a mistake.

'Bah, nobody cooks in America, do they? What with all those '*ambur'ger e ata dogha*.'

I know when to defend and when to smile. I flash a full grin and turn toward the cheese man, whose table is across the way. I ask for a kilo round of *marzolino,* a soft, white pecorino aged only a few weeks, and then for a wedge of a much older one. 'To eat with honey,' I tell him.

He chooses for me, hacks a fine, gold piece from the great wheel of it, trims the hard crust from its heel, and weighs the cheese.

'You pay for the cheese, not the rind. Can't eat the rind,' he says, 'though I do. I boil it in my soup. The rind enriches the flavor of the vegetables and softens almost to melting. I cut it with a fork, *veramente un boccone da prete,* truly a mouthful for a priest,' he tells me, knowing I'll want to try the rind in my own soup. In fact, before I can suggest that I would, indeed, like the rind, he's already wrapping it, handing it to me along with the parcel of cheese itself. He is Parsifal in jeans and boots, informative, polite, honest, having sacrificed the price of a rind of cheese for the sake of chivalry.

Down at the end of the market, by the Via della Costituente, there is a table set up in front of a San Rocco. So lovely is its mistress, she seems the living part of the church's old stone facade, a beatific angel wrapped in a long gray shawl. Her hair, still brown and wavy and knotted in a chignon, is a strange young frame around the sun-crinkled face of such an ancient. I walk the few steps to her, avoiding Gaspare for the moment and any further maligning of American food. I want to see what the lady has to sell today. The queue is long before her, and I'm happy to stand and look at her. She is perfumed like the mushrooms and field grasses and just-dug turnips she weighs out on a handheld balance. I think she can't read or count because everything seems to cost 2,000 lire. Her customers call her Tomassina. All her wares she has arranged into a still life, so that when she sells a rose, she pulls another one from a vase, lays it beside the red-veined lettuces. Where the other one was. And when she sells an egg – wrapped singly in newspaper, the ends of which are twisted like party favors – she must replace it, too, her customers waiting as she takes another egg from a basket below the table, unfolds a quarter page of newspaper, rolls the egg in it, twists the ends. Tomassina is a gentle priestess saying mass. When an old man asks if she has radishes today, she bends to part the folds of her tablecloth, putters about her stock, comes up laughing: '*Ecco*. Behold.'

She dangles a dozen or so pink radishes by their leaves, each earth-frosted shoot small as a thumbnail. Both she and the old man are enchanted by them. In the other hand she holds a cauliflower upside down, its long leaves drooping like a spaniel's ears. She lays the radishes carefully on a lettuce leaf, freeing her hand to pull back the leaves of the cauliflower, revealing a head small as a baby's, white as a camellia, a mother unwrapping the swaddling from around her new son.

'*Vedi che meraviglia?* See what a marvel?'

On another market morning, Tomassina, resplendent in a fresh white linen pinafore over her long black skirt, thick black stockings and black rubber boots, is tying the leafy stems of artichokes into sheafs so beautiful I want to take one to Miranda to hang on her front door. An American man with Ralph Lauren logos on his pants and shirt and jacket and hat – blue plastic flip-flops his single fall from fashion – is speaking very loudly to Tomassina, volume being the preferred method of communication for a certain sort of traveler. He is asking her how to cook artichokes. I sense she understands the question but is choosing to ignore it, calmly selecting six artichokes from her great tangle of them, fanning them out on her worktable, tying them round and round with the string while Ralph, with a now growling crescendo, repeats and repeats his question. Posing it in various ways. He adds mime. First he makes a stirring motion, then, bringing his fingers to his mouth, he makes a chewing one. Tomassina won't even look at him. This must not be the level of service that Ralph ordinarily commands since he turns around, eyes rolled back to white, and bellows, 'Doesn't anyone here speak English?'

I'd been about to try a rescue, to translate Ralph's question for Tomassina, but his petulance seems out of place. He's in Italy, and in Italy people speak Italian. I stay quiet. Ralph takes his artichokes, if perhaps a bit too gruffly, from Tomassina's small brown hand. And, also a bit too gruffly, he lays 2,000 lire on her table, leaving it for her to gather up rather than putting the bills directly into her hand. He might not have known that to throw money at a person is not as respectful as it is to place it in his hand. A symbol of civility.

A few moments later, while Tomassina is tying up my artichokes, she says, 'We don't have recipes. We cook from memories. We watched and listened to our mothers and our mothers' mothers, just as all the other women in a family had watched and listened before them. Rather than learn how to cook, we *inherit* the way we cook and bake, our methods being birthrights, like the color of a father's eyes, the jut of a mother's chin. Like the past itself, which nourishes us at least as much as the food. And the rest is instinct. There's not much left of life that is inviolable, but I'd say that how we cook still is. Stuck in history like a sword in a rock. *Grazie a Dio*. But how could I tell a man like that about *instinct*?'

She asks this looking up at me with hands clasped as in prayer, shaking them up and down, a gesture that says, among ten thousand other things, *There is nothing left to be said*. Tomassina had not only understood the man's questions but perhaps had understood the man himself.

One morning I arrive at her table as Tomassina is taking cherries, fat as walnuts and chastely pink, from a pasta strainer and placing them on a small, unpolished silver tray. I ask her to choose a melon for me – for my lunch – from the small pyramid of them built up next to a newspaper cone full of dusty blue plums, which she'd laid down like a cornucopia. She dismantles the pyramid, pulling and pinching at the stem end of each melon, shaking her head, gazing at me once in a while, hopelessness rising. When she has inspected all of the navels of all the melons she looks at me, a surgeon with tragic news.

'I have nothing that will be ripe enough for one o'clock.' Holding up one in the palm of her hand, she says, 'Perhaps this one will be ready by eight this evening. Surely it will be ready by midnight. But *nothing* will be ready for lunch.'

Speechless in the light of her specificity, I simply nod toward the melon still resting in her palm. Tenderly she wraps it in brown paper and then in a sheet of newspaper, pleating the ends in intricate origami folds, making a cushion for the melon. She comes around to the front of the table then, opens my sack, places the melon in it. She looks up at me, then, 'Wait until midnight if you can.'

I need this woman in my life. I need to learn more about melons and much more about timing and patience and what matters and what doesn't matter at all. I have a midnight melon in my bag, its flesh ripening as I walk in the Umbrian sun, as I make my way past the dark, crackling veneer of a suckling pig laid on a pallet of herbs in the back of a shiny white van, past the man from Attigliano who's roasting chickens over an oak-fired grill on the bed of a pickup. And all the while I'm trying to remember what Gaspare had said. *Our earth is rich so we don't have to be.* And what Tomassina said to me as she laid the melon in my sack. *The less there is, the more important all of it becomes.* Yes, that was what she said.

On market days, it's in front of the *tabac* in Piazza della Repubblica that the farmers, with the stiffness of hardworking men in their Sunday clothes, gather. Basques tilted, faces scrubbed, they are costumed in vintage suits – always a size too small or too large – of corduroy or velvet or some garish striped wool. Wide, always very wide ties – the stains of hundreds of suppers ornamenting them like medals – are knotted carelessly over perfectly ironed shirts and tucked into belts strapped low beneath *la pancia,* a great wedge of which protrudes from between the straining buttons of their jackets. While their wives sell turnips, they renew their brotherhood.

On winter market mornings, the farmers troop inside the bar Sant'Andrea, rearranging the furniture, satisfying their need to sit very close together. And around a bottle or two of grappa. Often in dramatic conference over food, they talk about what they ate at supper last evening, what they're going to eat at lunch today. What they ate for supper half a century ago. What they did when there was no supper. Once I sit nearby – brazenly close, it must seem to them – to listen to their talk about the proper braising of pheasants. Though they'd never consider inviting me to their table, they seem to like having an audience. Some of them glance over at me once in a while, doff their caps, proffer a gallant nod. Others just look to see if I'm paying proper attention.

Three of the farmers talk at the same time, each one listening only to himself, while the rest take sides, give attention to their preferred speaker. There can be no consensus. When the trio finally quiets, a man among the audience, one whom I'd noticed for his silence and his black velvet suit coat and vest, says, 'All of you are wrong. I'm only sorry none of you has ever tasted a pheasant cooked in the one true way it was meant to be cooked. All other ways are blasphemous. Might as well eat the bird raw.'

So authoritively does the man in black velvet speak his indictment that, rather than raising jeers, it provokes his chums' consideration of their purportedly sinful pasts with pheasants. The man in black velvet, the table in his thrall, tells the formula like a story. A father reading to his sons.

'The birds must be hung for not less than ten days, complete with their feathers and innards. But where they're hung matters very much. Though you could hang them in the barn, it's better to hang them in the cellar. Close to a tapped barrel of your best red. The adjacency of the birds to the wine and even the wine to the birds proves magical. Both will be better than they would be alone. Truth is, we leave our bread to rise in the wine cellar, too, letting the dough breathe in all those spores swirling about the wine. Helps it to rise and to take on the flavor of bread *come una volta*. Bread like it used to be. We let the bread and wine have their own communion before we have ours. And I'll tell you a secret. I stand by the cellar door when my wife brings the bowl of dough downstairs at night before we go to bed. She doesn't know that I wait there while she arranges things, covers the bowl with an old sheet or a blanket, or that I listen while she says good night to it, talks to it as though she were tucking in a baby, tells it how wonderful it's going to be when it's all grown up and baked out back in the oven. It used to make me laugh, but after all these years I've grown to like her little ceremony. But more than my liking it, I can tell you that there's no better bread than hers. None.

'So I've sort of taken on her ways with my birds. I go to visit them each day, talk to them, tell them I'm going to turn them into the most glorious dish. And even when I'm doing other things, I think about those birds hanging there, think about how, each day, their flesh becomes riper and riper. And when the day comes that I go down to talk to my birds and I can barely breathe for the stink of them, then I know they're ready for me. I pluck them and clean them, wash them in grappa, stuff them with a handful of smashed juniper berries. Then I pound some lard with rosemary and sage until the paste is nice and smooth. I heat the paste to sizzling in a stew pot and turn the birds in it until they're dark as nuts, take them out, wrap them in thin slices of pancetta, lay them in a *coccio,* a terra-cotta pot, dose them in that red wine with which they are now so familiar, cover the pot, set it over the embers of a dying fire. Then I go to bed. After I listen to my wife's chatting with her bread.

'The next morning, the aromas of herbs and wine and smoke and fat and melting flesh fill the house. But we don't touch the pot. We leave it to cool and rest until lunchtime, and then we eat those birds with our bread and wine, right from the pot. Two forks, two knives, napkins, bread, and wine. That's how to cook a pheasant. And that's how to eat one.'

WHEN THE WEATHER IS FINE, the ensemble settles itself on the terrace, the *grappa* waived for pitchers of red. A man called Fausto, a self-appointed chieftan – the way Barlozzo was in San Casciano – holds court. In a shrill Mussolini bray, he opens one morning with '*Come siamo ridotti*. How we've come down in life.'

He pauses. Adopts the hands-clasped-in-prayer-and-moving-up-and-down gesture. His upward gaze and high, tortured keen provide emphasis. Though no one seems immediately sure to what spiritual, political, or cultural deficit he refers, the precinct quiets. Waits.

'Italy, be ashamed of yourself,' he whispers hoarsely, a Franciscan friar in agony.

'Soccer has become the sport of *femminucce*.'

Femminucce is a word difficult to translate; it refers to men who comport themselves in a mode traditionally considered feminine. A distinctly uncomplimentary handle no matter at whom it's pointed.

'Yes, I repeat, our national sacrament, our games – descended from the Romans, nay, from the Greeks – have been reduced to feminine *tussles*. There are no more Italian men who play soccer. None. All we have left are *prime donne*. Let me tell you the story of a single day lived by one of these *poverini*, poor little things. He wakes up to an hour of body massage and a session under the sunlamp. Then the hairdresser comes to blond his hair, cut it, braid it, *arrange* it, while someone else buffs his fingernails. By then it's time for *il sarto,* the tailor, who pinches and tucks and drapes him like the Sun King. On to the studio for camera trials, to check how the broken nose – a discotheque casualty – looks on-screen. *GQ* and *Vogue* are coming to shoot him.' He says this last with appropriate hand mime.

That an Umbrian farmer would know *GQ* and *Vogue* seems wildly peculiar to me, but I will come to understand that television news programs inform and instruct these people on a much larger world than their own. Fausto takes a breath, sips his morning red, permits the crowd a moment to shout in consent with him. Now he holds up an imaginary cell phone, changes his voice to suggest one of the *femminucce* speaking with his mother.

'I'm exhausted, Mamma, absolutely exhausted, and still they want me to come to practice sessions. I'm a star and they expect me to get in there and *play.* It's just not possible. I'm calling my agent right now and my surgeon and my aromatherapist. And I have a headache. I need to rest, Mamma. What time are you bringing my dinner? Don't forget the sweets. *Ciao, ciao. Devo scappare.* I have to run. The pedicurist is knocking. *Ciao, ciao, mammina.*'

Roars of laughter fall, *piano, piano,* into silence until, as if obedient to some covert signal, the praying-hands gesture is assumed by all of them. They rise and step into the piazza and, in tattered formation, arm in arm and four abreast, they stroll

171

the square. One turn. As though blown backward by a lenient wind, their bodies move at a slant, in the breathless shuffle of portly men, no longer young. Two turns. Three turns and then they stop again in front of the *tabac*. Another discourse perhaps, one more round of handshakes and hugs, a quick run back into the bar for another tumbler of red, then unembarrassed, moist two-cheek kisses. *Ci vediamo, vecchio* – we'll see you, old man – riding the air, a *rondello* of birdsong, as they mount their Apes and their rickety trucks for the journey back down to the valley. After all, it's only Thursday and they won't be together again until Saturday.

These men are charmed by one another. By themselves, sometimes, as in Fausto's case. But surely all of them are charmed by the events of their lives, by the same things today that charmed them yesterday. And longer ago than that. Country people seem to live life in its most embraceable form, their days and nights made mostly of work and rest, food and wine and love. A peek or two at the television. Surely the emphasis on these fundamentals shifts and slides person by person, but by choice and by chance, life among them seems lived in long stretches of contentment. Contentment being something apart from happiness. Bigger than happiness, embracing pain alongside joy. The farmers stay fresh, astonished by life, even though it's composed of reprises and encores. Especially since it's composed of reprises and encores. But these are not the same as routine – which is the route one takes through a day and a night with eyes closed. Hauling stones, they call it here. Rather, these reprises and encores create the rhythm and ritual on which they thrive, the comfort and balance that boundaries suggest and that keep one from the jagged edge, they say. Or help them walk that edge with dignity. Remember when Monday was washday and Tuesday was ironing day, on Friday one changed the linens and on Saturday one bathed? And what about the historical American hash houses that served lamb stew every Tuesday, short ribs on Wednesday, meatloaf on Thursday and baked haddock on Friday? It's this sort of symmetry that shapes the life of the farmer. Certain that what they have is best, that their own well-practiced traditions are extraordinary, they are stimulated by *continuance*. After all, the counterpoint theme of a farmer's life is long odds.

Are there longer odds than those that nature throws down? What greater gamble is there than betting on the weather? Or the fickleness of the gods? A farmer's life is thick with suspense. Can he get the wheat inside the barn and close the door on the storm? Can he pick the last vines before the hail falls, big as plums? Will the price of tobacco hold long enough to pay for the new tractor? A farmer will tell you that his life is quickened by the unexpected, and he'll tell you, too, that it's what's good about his life. The thrill of fear. And when things go bad – and they will nearly always go bad – it's the suffering that lets a man know he's alive at least as much as the easy times do. It's because of those long odds that ritual matters so much. A man needs to count on something. And perhaps it's these two sides of a farmer's life — ritual and risk — that help him live as deliberately as he does. Each meeting with his friends, each supper at his own table, he treats as a potential ending. Everything he does, he scents in 'last time.' Last bite of bread, last sip of wine. Last story. Last kiss. Another way to say what Tomassina said: *The less there is, the more important all of it becomes.*

13

Sleep Well and Rise Early to an Exuberance of Bells

June marks the first anniversary of our still-empty wait for Palazzo Ubaldini. On the day itself, each of us determines, silently, not to observe it. Not openly. While I'm still in bed, Fernando, a thick brown towel twisted at his waist, comes to me with a nosegay. Three dozen roses – tiny, just flourishing, crimson, their stems trimmed short and sashed around with a wide red velvet ribbon. Homage to Gaspare's bouquets of asparagus centered with a single rose, my roses are studded with asparagus, tight points of dark green spears sprouting above red buds.

'*Buongiorno, amore mio,*' he says grinning, sitting on the edge of the bed, holding out the flowers, baring his delicious overbite below his mustaches.

'*Ciao, piccolo. Ma cos'è?* But what is this?'

Fernando still embarrasses me with his tendernesses, which,

though they've been a part of my life for six years now, always take me unaware. I think they always will.

'What sort of florist did you visit in that costume?'

'I have my cache of mysteries, too. Hurry, the tub is full and we're going to Rome. You must wear something extra beautiful. And no work boots.'

'We are? I must? Any particular reason?'

'It's a Saturday in June, 1998. A Saturday that will never pass this way again. Let's go to eat artichokes and spaghetti carbonara in Trastevere and let's walk and walk all afternoon.'

'Wonderful,' is all I say.

He drops the towel, vaults over the rim of the tub. Makes room for me. Later, as I dress, I consider telephoning Samuele or even Concetta with some sort of affectionate taunt to mark the day, but I fear the taunt would be heard more loudly than the affection. The truth is that Fernando and I had betrothed ourselves to the Ubaldini a year ago and then – fast upon the bluff, the noble farce, the Goldoni *commedia,* whatever it was that Concetta and Ciro had acted out on that evening last autumn – we'd renewed our vows, said 'I do' a second time. We'd accepted both the unknown length of the wait as well as the Ubaldini offer to pay our rent in Via Postierla for its duration. Certainly their arranging for the interim expenses has softened the year's passage but, as much, I think I've made a passage of my own. I seek less – and less often – to penetrate Italian wiliness and not at all its particular Umbrian interpretation.

Time has a less perishable quality in Italy. Or a more perishable one. Either way, here time's very spinning out is beyond any
mortal manipulation of it, and rightly so, I think. Rather, there
is indulgence here for however time flickers by. After all, hasn't
time gone before us and shall it not go after us? Who are we to
subdue its course? *No, no, it wasn't that date when I'd said I'd call but
'around' that date. How long until I deliver the finished work? I'll
deliver it as soon as it's done.* And so where the irritation was, I am
now benumbed. I am no longer astonished by the oddness of it
all, though, as yet, I have not fallen into passivity. I tell myself
over and over that life is a crafted thing, not a willed one. We
hardly ever climb the stairs in Palazzo Ubaldini anymore, hardly
ever slip the long rusted key, ridges down, into the lock on the
paint-chipped doors. Hardly ever lean into the still, deathless
quiet of its rubble. I have discarded the notion of control and
allowed myself to be seduced by the beauty of the wait. I tell
myself that control is like breaststroking in a long, sweat-
smelling chlorine pool with my hair contained, commanded by
a rubber hat while surrender is like floating, backstroking,
plunging my arms into the blue-black waters of a midnight sea.
I choose surrender.

Anniversaries inspire looking back, and so I do. In the six
years since Fernando and I have been married, we've lived three
in a concrete bunker of a beach house on the verges of the
Adriatic Sea, two more in a subtly restructured stable beside a
sheepfold in a medieval Tuscan hamlet, and, this last year, in an
Umbrian hill town, in a molding, partly subterranean, once

Dominican cloister next to a crumbling castle-cum-suicide-leap. While waiting for a phantasmal crew to restore an abandoned ballroom in a medieval palazzo that sits fifty meters from Italy's most splendid Gothic cathedral. An abandoned ballroom that we've seen only from its doorway. All in all, things go well, I tell myself, plaiting my hair into two long ropes, coiling them, fixing them into a pastiche on top of my head with long tortoiseshell pins. That we seem to be always lodging somewhere, staying awhile rather than being 'at home,' that we continue, as we did in the stable, to live by our wits – hand to mouth, pan to mouth – inventing the next step as we dance it, still, I would say that yes, things go well. After all, how many people live a life they can hold up to the sun?

Iridescent powder on the face and décolleté, a smudge of milk chocolate on the eyelids, metallic pink on the lips. Mine is the right life for a gypsy, for a wanderer. An everlasting beginner. And the right life, too, for her consort, who seems to have taken to the wandering. And to the beginnings. I look back through my life, through my thoughts and my troubles. I hear myself saying, *I'd thought, you see, that one of the best things about going to live in another country would be the chance to be ten years old again. Or for the first time. Everything fresh, untested. Learn to speak and think and dream in another language. To see how the new people sip their tea, break their bread, treat each other. Not just a passage through, not a wander among the natives but setting up with them. I knew that to be at home in the world was the way to grow rich. The way I wanted to be rich.*

I take my good black boots from their flannel sack, rub them to a gleam with an old washcloth, pull them on over bare feet, zip them up to the knee. They feel good. One pair of Gucci boots in a lifetime. I step into a long pewter silk skirt, the same silvery color as the hydrangeas in the garden. Pull it up over my hips. Good, still fits, if just. An old black Gigli jacket with a peplum. I fasten on every pearl I own. Two ropes. A single Australian freshwater beauty strung on a thin black ribbon. A two-strand choker. The long baroque drops in my ears. I find my shawl. I look in the mirror – really look at her, looking at me. She might be a Georgian serf in jewels lent by a czarina. Is she, perhaps, just a little sad? She would not leave the roses at home. She would take them, and so I do.

As we tool south down the *autostrada,* I continue the anniversary musings, aloud now, and Fernando joins in with his. Still we do not mention the significance of the day but, rather, tell each other that a straighter, shorter path to the ballroom in Via del Duomo might never have been strewn with the gifts we've found along this other one. We would never have come to know Miranda as we have. And without her, neither Orfeo nor Luca. Nor this famous Tilde, who most recently has joined Miranda's small legion at table each evening. And through Tilde, we've met a man called Edgardo and two sisters, Magda and Beniamina. And through Tomassina, we've come to know the farmer Neddo, whom we'd met earlier at one of the summer food festivals. Yes, it's true, we tell each other: had we gone directly to Via del Duomo, we might have been so occupied with all the settling in that we might have missed getting to know these people. The wait, we agree, seems always less like time lost than time found. Upon a contretemps we've built this era of our life, in quiet reciprocity with people sympathetic to the past, people who imprint the smallest things with grace. A fistful of radishes, a melon, a rind of cheese, a barrow of artichokes, an old story, the made-up words to a made-up tune.

WE RETURN JUST after nine that evening from Rome, park the car behind the Duomo and walk up the steep steps into the piazza, where, rather than the usual strollers in search of a post-supper gelato at that hour, we find hundreds and hundreds of people wandering about in the sultry air of twilight. The crowd is quiet, anticipatory. For what are they waiting? For whom? I hear drums. The far-off beating of drums and the crowd hears them, too, and cheers rise up from every quarter: *Ecco i tamburini*. Mothers take their children in their arms, whispering, '*Senti, li senti, tesoro? Ecco i tamburini*. Do you hear, do you hear them, my darling? Behold the drums.'

Eight boys in black breeches – red toques pulled down low over their foreheads, drums slung across their chests – enter the piazza from the Via del Duomo and mount the steps of the cathedral to face the people. There is silence.

One of them unfurls a parchment and shouts to the crowd: 'Tomorrow shall honor the miracle of the blood, the miracle of Bolsena. Be ready, *popolo*, be ready, for the celebration is upon us. Sleep well and rise early to an exuberance of bells. Gather here in the piazza for the bishop's blessing at seven after which the procession of the faithful shall begin. Be ready, *popolo,* the celebration is upon us.'

The boys in black breeches begin the beating of their drums again, pounding rhythms across the piazza, up and down the *corso,* up and down the Via del Duomo and over and across every alleyway and twisting lane in the town. 'Be ready, *popolo,* the celebration is upon us.'

Nearly every town and village and city in Italy stages some form of annual procession to celebrate a scene from its past – sacred or profane. Most are simple, folkloric parades that serve to please the townspeople and offer opportunity for a sanctioned fracas, a bit of robust showmanship, complete with the wearing of costumes sewn from humble stuff. In Orvieto this is not the case.

Along with its historical earthly riches, Orvieto boasts a miracle. A Mother Church-endorsed miracle.

In the year 1263, a Bohemian priest, in crisis over his faith – particularly concerning the question of transubstantiation – set off on a pilgrimage to Rome. One Sunday morning, the priest stopped to say mass on the shores of the Lake of Bolsena, which lies a few kilometers from Orvieto. Raising the host high above the altar cloth, he watched as the wafer bled. A sign. The priest brought the cloth and his story to the clergy of Orvieto, where, in flight from Vatican annoyances, Urban IV was then in residence. As if he'd caused it himself, the Pope embraced the miracle as salvation for his troubled reign. So began the three hundred tortured years, interrupted by plague and invasions and, once in a while, by peace, of the construction of Italy's most splendid Gothic cathedral. A marble-and-basalt monument encrusted with golden mosaics, a tribute to a miracle. And for these past five hundred or so years since the Duomo's completion, Orvieto has been 'awakened by an exuberance of bells' – a jubilant, half-hour-long clanging of every bell in town – on the feast day of *Corpus Domini*.

The morning proceeds with a solemn procession, *il corteo storico,* the historic cortege. Half a thousand people march in it, each one of them costumed in faithful reproductions of medieval dress. Brocades, heavy with gold and silver threads, loomed and stitched by a hundred hands, are the stuff of their tunics and robes. Every strata of medieval society is represented – the artisans' guilds, the governors, the soldiers, and the warriors, their swords catching the sun, their legs tightly stockinged over boots and spurs, their faces dour, implacable even as a mother shouts to her damask-robed son: '*Amore della mamma, ma quanto sei bello,* love of your mother, but how beautiful you are.' I will learn that this son of hers has been marching in the procession for eighteen years, yet still, each time he does, she is stunned by his appearance.

A man who is an artisan wood-carver and whose shop we pass nearly every day on a *vicolo* behind the bank is costumed as *il capitano del popolo,* the people's captain. Symbol of benevolent government. Proud, high-boned face, silver beard resting on his chest, hair brushed back straight and tumbling past his shoulders, a black-and-gold cape swinging over a velvet tunic and breeches. He carries a plumed helmet and looks straight ahead as he marches. Ahead, or is it backward where he looks? The crowd screams, *Bravo, bravissimo,* and applauds him and one begins to understand that these are not men masquerading as other men for the sake of a parade; rather, they are themselves, bristling with the roots and fiber of their own blood and bones. Over and over again among the ranks, a spectator can see how a cape, a headdress, a posture can transform a man, change his twentieth-century face into a medieval one. How these people look like the portraits of their ancestors. And I wonder, How must it feel to march to the pounding of the pages' drums in the Sunday-morning light of the town where you were born, where your father and his father and ten generations of your fathers before them were born?

The young woman who slices pancetta for me at the *salumeria* walks in the procession. In the shop where she works, a white cloth cap cradles her hair and a pristine linen smock is buttoned to her throat. But this morning her red-gold hair is loose under a corona of poppies and wild roses wound in blue satin ribbons. She is dressed as a shepherdess in a dress and bodice and apron, all in shades of yellow.

'Tiziana,' I say too loudly and without thinking as she passes, and Tiziana smiles, if barely, thrilled, I think, with her transformation. A band of angels, fat and rosy and none of them older than three, walk holding each other's dimpled hands. Their grandmothers walk behind them and hold hands, too, brown-stained hands linked in an ancient sisterhood. One tiny angel, the tiniest of all, is fatigued and dawdles apart, waddles in her pink silk dress and silver shoes, tilts over the cobbles, restoring her balance if not the position of her halo of baby's breath. A small, fresh hope for Orvieto. Hands clasped in prayer, there is showing between her palms a thin sliver of pizza, which she bites delicately as she goes. A small succor for the trek.

Standing in the piazza that Sunday morning – standing there as we will on the *festa di Corpus Domini* for years and years hence – we tell each other that to live a few meters apart from this celebration would be reason enough to wait for the Ubaldini ballroom. We don't talk about the insignificance of our own small crisis of faith, surely more mine than his. No time to talk at all as even the sky poses for the miracle.

Clouds, black and fierce, dance about the sun like chariots racing, while thunder, lit by lightning, pounds and cracks until everything is still except for Bach pouring out into the piazza from the great organ in the church, while the two-hundred-voice chorus sings as though it's the last day of the world. Now come the famous fourteenth-century tapestries that depict the scenes of the Miracle. Stitched to gilt poles and streaming with thick silk cording, these are held aloft by black-suited *cavalieri*, and the crowd grows silent as they pass. In rough cloth vestments thirty altar boys follow, swinging censers with the force of a child's faith. Breathless with the joy of their mission, they swing the vessels high over their ringletted heads, trailing frankincense mists, making a path for the treasure of the procession. The altar cloth itself. The cloth of Bolsena, visible through the glass of a gold reliquary, is held high in proof, perhaps more in triumph, and the crowd is in rhapsody. At last, then, and under a canopy held by his priests, shuffling old feet over the cobbles, the bishop, small, frail, holds the *ostensorio* with the folds of his purple robes while thunder explodes again and the chorus and the organ duel with the force of it, so that all of the sounds seem to descend from the sky. The music is fortissimo now and beyond jubilant as it swells to a yet higher crescendo, and then the sun breaks and, like broken seabirds, winds screech and rain falls but no one runs. No one runs for cover or even moves much, save to throw his head back to the benediction of the soft plashing drops.

14

Most All of Us Abide in Ruins

I am alone in the Via Postierla these days, since Fernando has been going up each morning to work with the duke, who has, at last, asked for some help. When he'd rung our *telefonino* a few weeks ago, all he'd said was 'Fernando, *bello mio, è ora*. My beauty, it's time.'

I thought Barlozzo could use my help, too, and so I accompanied Fernando up to the ruin for the first few days, brought baskets and bags of lunch. The place was full of *operai* who were laying old tiles in a palette of burnt and bleached reds and parched pinks, in small and large squares and rectangles and lozenges, creating a mosaic of his undulant floors so that the sprawling, smoky rooms seemed those of a poor man's San Marco. Other workers had installed the plumbing fixtures Barlozzo had bought in a salvage depository somewhere near

Orte. In an *antichità* up there he'd found a white marble sink for the kitchen and fixed it with a bronze pipe for a faucet. A claw-foot tub nearly long enough to hold him, legs stretched out, fills more than half his bathroom. A sort of stone birdbath he's rigged to the opposite wall, the small hole in the bottom of which drains into another deep, spouted receptacle below it. A long, narrow wooden table is next to the birdbath, and on it sits a large blue-and-white pitcher, a fat square of Aleppo soap, his razor, a comb, a toothbrush, a box of sea salt, a brass candle lamp, and a biscuit tin for his matches, from the lid of which a woman smiles, her unbound Titian hair tumbling about her white dress, her parasol tilted against the sun. From a nail pounded into the wall hangs a piece of natural jute, big as a bed-sheet, which he must use as a towel. He says he prefers to carry water from the tub to his 'sink' than break through a perfectly good wall to run a pipe.

'Don't need that much water for a shave, anyhow,' he says.

He has mantels for all his fireplaces, even old hearthstones, some of which he bought in broken pieces and laid back together, a savage Humpty Dumpty putting his world in order. He's painted almost every room a somber brown, the only color the depository had in quantity. Salvage from a hotel that closed before it opened. But with white ceilings and the half-meter-high baseboards, also painted white, with the sun and the wind and the shadows splashing through uncurtained, unshuttered windows, the daytime color is warmed to sherry, an old syrupy Oloroso. From the fathomless detritus of the outbuildings, he has resurrected an immense and rusted iron chandelier. Rubbed to black with olive oil, it rests on the *salotto* floor, to be hung, someday, where a single bulb on a cord still swings. The only electric light in the house.

I'd begun sweeping in some of the rooms, scrubbing floors and windows in others, but I'd never get even partway through a task before Barlozzo would catch up with me, shoo me away.

'If you wash those floors once, you'll have to wash them forever. I'm not going to wash them.'

'Never?'

'Never. I'll sweep once in a while, but I'll never wash. It's just not necessary. It will take years and years before they're dirty enough to wash, and I probably won't live that long, so I'm not going to worry about the floors. It's enough for me that I've *got* floors without worrying about washing them.'

He had similar thoughts about his windows, saying that he didn't buy newspapers and if he did, he'd rather burn them for heat than waste them in polishing windows that were going to be rained on in an hour anyhow. And talk about waste, did I know how much vinegar it took to clean a single window?

'Much rather pour it in my mineral water, drink it down nice and cold. Better to clean my own pipes than to clean a window.'

The kitchen he has painted like a ripe, red plum. A concession to me, he says, to my penchant for color. His way, I think, of saying he wants it to be my kitchen, too. The mantel he's set against the small kitchen hearth is, I think, the most beautiful one in the house, white marble gone to yellow, bordered and beveled in black basalt. The mantel shelf, also black, is wide, and on it are stacks of books and two yellow pottery pitchers.

'Those are very old, Chou. Belonged to my mother's mother. There used to be one more, but I haven't found it yet. I will, though. Someday we'll use those again for wine, don't you think?'

Next to the hearth, Florí's quilt is folded over the cherry-wood armchair just the way it was always in her little *salotto*. There are piles of books and canning jars and stacks and stacks of dishes and platters all along one wall – legacies of Florí and his mother, both their presences somehow felt – soon to be transferred to the shelves he's putting up nearly all the way to the just-oiled beams of the ceiling. Great black iron hooks stud the beams, awaiting haunches of beasts and ropes of figs and strings of chestnuts. Now, though, a single, small dried sausage swings in solitude with a handful of wildflowers shriveled to bronze. Just outside and to the right of the kitchen door are stairs. Long, steep, and lichen-covered, they lead to a fruit cellar. Over its door there are grapevines, somehow still thriving and thick as a man's wrist, gnarled and twisted into an arch. Once inside, two more steps lead down to thick flat slabs of stone dug into the earthen floor. I wonder how many squash and melons and potatoes and apples were thumped and tumbled across those stones to wait in the dark for a woman to venture down there, holding a candle and kilting her skirts, to gather in her apron what she needed of them, what she had of them.

Barlozzo hasn't much in the way of furniture, nor is it his intention to acquire such. He has the bed where his mother birthed him, the same one in which she died on that night after the war.

'But it doesn't haunt me. No, not at all. Her father built it, she was born in it, I was born in it. She died in it. If I'm lucky, I will, too. It's part of me,' he says, running his long, skinny hands over the curves of the time-darkened, unstained wood. 'Most all of us abide in ruins, Chou. Our own or the ones we inherit. Ruins being the continuum. To my young self, the ruins of my family seemed inviolable. I believed there was nothing for me to do but accept them as my due. But I'd be damned if I would pass them on to yet another generation. I wanted all that pain to die with me. That's why I never married Florí. But I was wrong. If we two had made a life together, maybe had children, I think we might have done some fine restoring of those ruins. I think, together, we might have put the demons to sleep, if not banished them altogether. Of course, the metaphor of this old place – how it was, how it is now – can't help but animate all these thoughts. By fixing the house I feel like I'm fixing other things. At least making them better. But I get so tired, Chou. Do you understand that?'

'I do. I understand that.' How I love this old man. I can see and feel the new part of him struggling up through the dark of those ruins, aiming toward the light. But I know that the greater part of him will stay undercover, unconsoled. Unconsolable, closed up in his own wilderness, cherishing his grief while the residues of ghosts nest among the eaves, settle in by his fires.

He has his mother's kitchen table – streaks of white enamel paint clinging to the rough chestnut legs of it, a brown marble top – and the armoire, immense and deep and wide, where she kept all the jars of preserved fruits and vegetables. Even though there's nothing inside it yet, he keeps the doors open wide. As though he can still see what was once there.

'It's wonderful, Chou; nothing matches, so everything does. I am seventy-six years old and this is the first home I've ever made for myself. Not a moment too soon, don't you think?'

'I think your timing is perfect.'

Apart from the tour of his realm and the few moments of rest he'd allow himself every couple of hours or so, when we'd sit and talk – in his truck if it was raining or out on the crest of a hill when it was fine – I saw little of the duke and barely more of Fernando during those days. I found myself taking long walks just to keep from being underfoot in what was clearly a men's work in progress, and on the fourth day, I decided to stay in Via Postierla. If we'd had another car and I'd had a license to drive it, the best plan would have been for me to cook supper for everyone and arrive at the ruin just about the time the troops were finished for the day. Stage a party. But there was no other car. And no driver's license for me, anyway. Instead, Fernando would head back to Orvieto by about seven and burst through the garden door just before eight, where I'd be waiting with cold wine.

We'd bathe and dress for supper then, but Fernando would be too tired to get back in the car and head for Miranda's. As much as we both loved being up there, we'd forgotten how much we loved staying at home. Or at least staying put. Before this period, months had passed since we'd sat together with the candles and the wine, absorbed in our own comfort, talking and laughing or staying quiet, gazing at each other like fresh lovers. We'd have the strangest, simplest dishes, sitting cross-legged in front of the marble table by the unlit fireplace, breezes off the terrace sassing the drapes, squandering the candles. A platter of tomatoes from Tomassina's garden stuffed with a pesto of *rucola,* which I make in an old marble mortar with a wooden pestle bought from an artisan in the Via del Duomo. I pound two whole heads of new garlic down to a cream, add the warm flesh of a few just-boiled new potatoes, some broken walnuts, tear the dark, peppery leaves of *rucola* into the mass, and continue the rhythmic pounding, pummeling. Parmigiano from the itinerant cheeseman in the market I grate directly into the mortar, then pound and pummel it all a bit more. I buy olive oil from Emilio, whose shop sits across from Palazzo Ubaldini – the best oil of my life – which I drip into the mortar from a flask, stirring and beating all the while until the sauce is emulsified, shined. Thick as pudding. It takes a good arm. And a good tomato then, its hat whacked off, some of its heart cut out, the juicy crevices of it barely salted. Dollop the sauce in without much attention to neatness, piling it to excess, letting it fall as it will over the sides of the fruit and onto the trencher of good roasted bread I set it on. The tomatoes get their hats back and the platter of them goes to wait, giving the elements some mingling time. The wine must be very dry and very cold. The glasses chilled. Hungers must be high; company, splendid. I guess it always comes down to that: who's on the chairs more than what's on the table. In our case, who's on the floor. We feasted away those summer evenings as two voluptuaries will, never minding what else was or wasn't or might never be. We'd go to walk afterward up through the town, stop at Pasqualetti for pistachio gelato, go to sit on the steps of the Duomo, lean back on our elbows to look at the sky.

'Did you know that Michelangelo came here to look at the Signorelli frescoes before he began to work on the Sistine chapel?' I ask the Venetian.

'Yes. But even if I didn't know it, I would feel it. The great hulk and power of Signorelli's figures would bring Michelangelo's to mind.'

'So right here, right here on these steps where we sit now, they once walked. Don't you find that startling?'

'Probably not startling in the way you do, though I wish I did. I'm more startled that we're sitting here together. And that you can still make me feel timid and that, in a few minutes, we're going to walk down that hill together and that we're going to sleep together so closely in that yellow bed of ours that I won't be able to hear my own heartbeat for yours. That's what I find startling.'

Sometimes we walk the few steps to Palazzo Ubaldini, bless the stones of it or chant encouragement up toward the windows of our future. Mostly we just wander back down Via Postierla, prop open the doors to the little terrace so we can see the stars from *that yellow bed of ours.*

I send Fernando back off to Barlozzo by seven each morning, sometimes earlier. And by eight, Miranda is tooting outside, come to take me up to Buon Respiro to make the bread. If it's a market day, we first walk up to Piazza del Popolo with our sacks. We're always so happy to see each other, as though an epoch had passed since the day before, and both of us talk at the same time almost the whole way. While I'm at work, she is too, having rearranged her schedule somewhat to avoid the heat later in the day. When the bread is set to rise, I help her with the day's prep or we just sit and talk. We bake one small loaf for us to eat together. The bread still burning hot from the oven, we tear at it like foxes, slaver it with apricot jam and eat it between deep drafts from bowls of warm milk and coffee. I am tempted to stay the day with her, knowing she would like me to, but as loving and seductive a woman as she is, I sometimes feel too much like her surrogate, her vice regent of the ovens. As though, along with her kitchen, she'd lent me her life to wear while I went looking for mine.

I hitch a ride back up onto the rock, back to Via Postierla with someone or another, or Miranda fakes some forgotten errand so she can take me herself. I tidy up the house, which takes three minutes, clean the bathroom. Head for my little office, where the mold thrives especially. I write and read, sometimes sleep, though I don't like to during the day. Daytime sleeps leave me disturbed, somehow, feeling as though I've missed something, which of course I have. Once, though, when I nod over my book, I dream of Tina Turner. I'm sure it is she. Walking up by the Duomo, she was all alone, just sauntering along. Wearing a pretty summer dress. I am behind her, and when I catch sight of her, I walk faster, come up even with her. She stops, looks at me, and I begin to applaud. Pounding my hands together with all my might. I just applaud and applaud and cry and cry and Tina smiles with all the pain and joy there is in the world. When I wake up my face is wet and salty and pages 77 and 78 of *The Confessions of St. Augustine* are decorated with all these little teardrops. From my melting soul, Miranda would say. That was one time when I was glad of a daytime sleep.

When my consort's arrival is near, I put supper together. Fix my hair, change my shoes. Lay out our things for the bath. Cut flowers for the table. There is something of Penelope and Ulysses about us. When we awaken in the morning or when one of us comes in from the garden. When he goes away. Mostly when he returns. By this time he's called me at least twelve times throughout the day, Barlozzo having gifted him his own *telefonino*. Compensation for his labors.

'I knew I'd get precious little from him if he was always

riding up and down the highway, looking for a telephone,' the duke snarled at me on that first day of work.

I keep our own newly acquired cell telephone in my skirt pocket, and so we are connected across the curving Todi road. Across the purling Tiber.

Sometimes I don't work at all, don't write, don't read, but go to walk up in town. I've come to know every alleyway and back street of Orvieto over this year, and these long afternoons remind me of my Venetian days. In fact, since that era, these are the first stretches of time I've spent without Fernando. I like having the chance to miss him. I go to the bookstore or to col-lect what I'm lacking for our supper. Mostly I go into the shops to listen to the discourse, to watch the play. Am I mistaken or can it be that when I'm alone the Orvietani seem more accessi-ble? Three degress less chilly. Do they think me more vulnerable without my cavalier? More vulnerable, hence more tolerable? Could that be so?

Basking in the new sliver of light brought upon by a few extra nods as I walk up the *corso* or a smiling *'Buona sera'* when I least expect it or a half bow from a gentleman who's removed his hat while he holds the door open for me into the *farmacia,* I begin to wonder if it was – if it is – me, myself they'd rebuffed. Rather, could it be – could it have been – my nationality, entire? World antipathy to the American colossus? Who said that? And who said that there is a world desire to see America 'get theirs'? More than a single someone said that, I suppose. Were the Orvietani only 'giving me mine' for nothing more or less than my citizenship? A subtle show of racism? And now that I've been here among them for more than a year, is all that falling away, dry brown petals scattered by diminishing winds? Perhaps.

A more difficult consideration presses. As much as I know that I possess the means to invite intimacy, I know that I possess the means for its sabotage. Have I been perpetrating my own separateness and blaming them? Have I been plodding about in heavy shoes when I could just as easily have disarmed them, taken my ease among them so they might begin taking theirs with me? Did I counter their haughtiness with my own? Did I go about all this with the same progidious gravity as I did with the avoiding society of my childhood? Had I forgotten the big secret that I'd discovered back then? None of us are very big and all of us are small.

15

I'd Like to Have Hair the Color of Hot Copper Wires

Really?' I ask the duke.

'Yes, really. I'd like for us to go to Florence together. Stay overnight, two nights, maybe three. I've never stayed in Florence. Never once. In fact, save the times I accompanied Florí on her visits to the clinic, I haven't been there for years. Now, don't start excavating for motives. I just want to be in Florence, and I'd like to be there with you and Fernando. I could use some time away from the ruin, and I believe you two could use some time away from yours. Any word at all from the Ubaldini?'

'No. No word.'

'Well, you're passing the time well, living in a good enough place, working. Let life shape itself.'

I give a silent scream against the notion of letting life shape itself. Even though I know it will anyway, whether I *let* it or not.

For reasons not shared with us, Barlozzo says he'll meet us in Florence. He wants to take the train from Chiusi rather than drive up with us.

'We'll take the train, too.'

'No, I'd rather take the ride alone. Got things to sort out, and trains are good for that. Now you, if you'd be so kind, will plan everything. Just like you do for your guests. Choose the hotel, find us the right places for supper.'

'I'll bet you've never been to the central markets at seven in the morning—'

'I've never been to the central markets even at noon.'

'Or eaten stewed veal tripe stuffed in a crusty *panino* from Nerbone?'

'I do not like *lampredotto* no matter who's cooked it, and don't think my wanting to be in Florence with you means I want to eat every foolish thing you want to eat.'

I change the subject. 'Can you get yourself down to the Porta Rossa by late morning?'

'I'll be waiting for you at eleven.'

'May I ask what you're going to pack? You do have something more decent than your "eternity" pants, don't you?'

He chooses not to answer that question, and I choose not to ask it again.

'Where the hell is the Porta Rossa?'

I proceed to tell him the history of the hotel, the location, about the man in the car park across the way whom I've known for more than twenty years, the story of the maid's room where, to save money, I'd stayed with my children when they were little. The plan is set.

'And as for your Florentine wardrobe,' I say, 'why don't we go shopping while we're there? All of us. I haven't had a new dress, a real store-bought dress, since Venice, and Fernando needs shirts. At the very least, he needs shirts, since most of his banker's pinstripes and white-on-whites with the round collars have been donated to the rag pile. Yes, it's perfect. On Saturday afternoon, we'll shop.'

I expect grief from both of them about the shopping idea but there is none.

'I would like that, Chou. You do know where to go and all?' Barlozzo wants to know.

'Yes, I think I do.'

'I want something English. Something tweed,' says Fernando.

'I thought you needed shirts,' says the duke.

'I don't always want what I need.'

'I understand that sentiment,' the duke replies.

It's just after ten on Saturday morning, nearly an hour in advance of our meeting time, when Barlozzo knocks on our door at the Porta Rossa. Just arrived ourselves, we're unpacking overnight cases, opening windows, calling Buca da Mario to make reservations for dinner.

'Are you ready?' he wants to know, exasperated, as if we'd kept him waiting. He rushes us out the door, down the elevator, out onto the street, stops to enclose us, each one under a long, skinny arm, holding us that way, saying not a word.

'Okay, the plan is that we'll concentrate on one of us at a time,' says Fernando. 'Let's begin with you,' he says to Barlozzo.

We take the duke to a shop in the Via della Vigna where I'd bought Fernando a navy blue blazer years ago, for our first anniversary. The duke enters before us, makes a slight bow to the *commesso,* the salesperson, who makes an even slighter bow in return. The Florentine shopping duel begins.

Restraint is the rule. It is not necessarily written that the *commesso* will ask if he can be of service. It was you, the client, after all, who walked through the door. Name your business, then. In the meantime, the *commesso* is content to stand, hands clasped behind his back, head cocked in mild defiance; to wait.

Barlozzo plays well. He is also silent, arranging himself in the old velvet confines of an armchair as though waiting for his tea. Unrefined as Fernando and I are, we actually look at the merchandise, risk fingertips to a jacket, then to another one, remark over their beauty. The other two teeter between disdain and diffidence, in unspoken accord that buying and selling is not how they might have chosen to spend this morning.

'Desidero un paio di pantaloni in pelle,' says the duke when he's ready to speak. I desire a pair of leather pants.

The slightest arch of an eyebrow betrays the *commesso,* but his recovery is brilliant.

'Of course. With your long and elegant structure, you will do well in them,' the *commesso* concedes.

201

In a tone harsher than the one he assumes with the duke, the *commesso* assigns the task of fetching the leather pants to his assistant, who appears from some unknown region of the shop, bowing and mumbling his way to another unknown region. Nearly all the merchandise available in these tiny boutiques is hidden away in *magazzini* – above- or below-deck storage areas – all of it splendidly arranged, cataloged, findable. The interval is passed with weather discourse, an intimacy quite acceptable now in this second act.

The assistant returns with four pairs of glorious leather pants. Barlozzo rises, pinches gingerly at the stuff of one pair, dark gray they are, with deep front pleats, the prize of the lot. He refuses the offer to try them on, asking if there might not be something in a more vibrant color. This perplexes the *commesso,* since all the traditional colors are represented in the selection he holds before the duke. Very dark green, chocolate, and black along with the gray ones. Another command is volleyed at the assistant. This time, the *commesso*'s Florentine lisp – so like the Castilian one – is more evident.

Like a maître d' with his napkin, the assistant returns with a pair of yellow leather pants hung on his arm. Not exactly yellow the way forsythia is yellow or daffodils are but yellow leaning toward saffron. Yellow with something of orange in it, which renders the tint at once quiet and assertive.

'Will they fit me?' is all Barlozzo wants to know.

'*Certo, certo, ma un minutino per provarli*. Certainly, but a half minute to try them . . .'

The duke ignores the idea of the *minutino*. 'A jacket. In linen. Double-breasted.' Now who is commanding? One would think that Saturday morning at eleven was Barlozzo's usual hour to order clothes. The *commesso,* his Dantesque nose seeming less cruelly drooped over his smile now, deigns to respond himself rather than rely on the assistant. He threads through a rack and pulls out a jacket the color of well-mixed cappuccino. With a creamy satin lining and nautical buttons, it's wonderful. This time, the duke is willing to try it on, and when he does, all it needs is to have the ticket snipped. Even the *commesso*'s awe is sincere. The duke is Gary Cooper dressed as Fred Astaire, preening through several half turns. I know that Fernando fears I'll step right up and begin dancing with him and that's why he holds me from behind by both shoulders.

'Please select a shirt and a foulard. And will you send the package to the Porta Rossa?' He is handing the *commesso* his credit card.

I didn't know that foragers carried credit cards, or that they wore saffron leather pants with foulards and cappuccino linen jackets. Of course, neither the duke nor the *commesso* has ever mentioned money. That would be talking truly dirty.

'There, that didn't take long, did it?' Only the slight sheen on the duke's upper lip declares his excitement for his purchases. Or is it for the intemperate sum he knows he must have spent for them? That we stare, openmouthed, at him he finds pleasant, his intention to shock splendidly achieved.

'I think you've just spent more for those clothes than you did for the ruin,' says the banker in Fernando.

'Perhaps I did. But I, too, am a ruin. Shouldn't I sometimes work on the restoration of myself?'

Having decided that my shopping foray should be the final one on the docket, the duke announces that Fernando is next. I know that before Blueberry Eyes can settle even on a pair of jeans, he must touch and ponder the stuff of hundreds of them, stroke his chin, hold his forehead in dilemma, fancy one pair and then another, favor none of them before finally plumping for several pair. And I know, too, that he will do all this after having sworn that the last thing he needs in the world is a new pair of jeans. That we three shall now embark on the trail of 'something tweed' for Fernando seems suddenly daunting.

'Wouldn't you two prefer to wander about without me? You know how I stop to look in every window and how I like . . .'

The duke reads me.

'Since my selections were so successful,' he says, 'I was just going to suggest that I take over as Fernando's adviser so, *cosa dici,* what do you say, let's meet at five back at the hotel?'

Fernando begins to dispute the idea, but I put my mouth on his, kissing him hard, wishing them a beautiful afternoon, then leap into the Via Tornabuoni as the light turns green, calling over my shoulder and the screams of the traffic, '*A più tardi, belli.* Later, my beauties.'

Fernando yells, '*Dai fratelli, all'una e mezzo.*' He wants to meet at our stand-up lunch place at one-thirty.

'*Ci proverò, ma se ritardo non aspettatemi più di tanto.* I'll try, but if I'm not there, don't wait more than a few minutes.'

Hah. It's a morning in October, I'm in love, I'm healthy, I am tooling about in Florence, I love my children and my children love me, Fernando is happy, and the duke seems well enough, both of them off on a lark, no bread waiting to be pulled from the oven, no story on deadline for the afternoon post, and a small velvet pouch stuffed with my lipstick and a wad of lire is strung across my chest, pulsing against my heart. First stop is Orsanmichele.

Under the Longobards in 750, this little church was dedicated to Saint Michael the Archangel, and somewhere in time, the Florentines began calling it Orsanmichele, dialect for Orto di San Michele, the Garden of Saint Michael. After a life as a convent, then one as a grain market, it was, once again, consecrated as a church, for me the most beautiful in all of Florence. I light my habitual eleven tapers, one for each of the eleven souls whom I count in my beloved circle. The last one I light is always for Fernando. I am alone in the church and follow the procession of large white candles that lead to the altar, the thin, tremulous flames of them making a path in the gloom. A single yellow beam slants across the first pew and I go to sit there among the echoes of chants, in the breath of incense burned.

Back out in the sun, I head for Gilli in Piazza della Repubblica, take a table under the canopy and ask for *un sorbetto di mela cotogna,* quince sorbet. The waiter is new this season.

With his thick blond hair caught in a ponytail, if he would trade tuxedo for velvet breeches, a Ghibelline prince he'd be. He sets down the ice in its silver dish, a long-handled spoon shaped like a tiny shovel he tilts against it. A glass of water. I remember another silver dish.

A long-handled spoon shaped like a shovel was set beside that one, too, and I used it to excavate the depths of vanilla ice-cream that had been scooped and smoothed flat over a ladle of thick hot chocolate fudge. The scene of the debauch was Ferrucci, on the north corner of Warren Street. The price of it, twenty cents. Maria would give me a dollar every Friday evening when she took me with her to the butcher and the grocery store, which smelled of salted fish and rotting cheese and where a man called Angelo would give me a scoopful of wrinkled olives in a paper cone. I was good enough at division to know that, with what Maria gave me, I might go to Ferrucci five times a week, should I surrender all other purchases. I'd perused that part of the neighborhood where I was allowed to walk alone, acquainted myself with options. Penny candy at Stearn's. End cuts of pizza with two sides of crust from Perreca. Doughnuts from Vita Rich. A slice of pink-and-green-and-cocoa-colored spumoni from Civitello. I'd quickly ruled out all commerce with Civitello, though, when I'd learned that they were deadly competition for Ferrucci, sitting right across the street as they were and taking almost all the wedding and first communion and confirmation business for trays and trays of sponge 'peaches' stuffed with chocolate and glossed in demure pink icing. Alberto had explained all this to me early on.

It didn't take long for me to decide that I'd rotate visits to the other gastronomic palaces and keep Ferrucci as my only constant. My Saturday-morning ritual. I knew that five hot fudge sundaes could never taste as good as one and so I waited, Saturday to Saturday, to turn the handle on the glass door that set the bell tinkling and Alberto shuffling out from the bakery behind the shop. He'd be wiping his hands on a small towel, which he'd then fling over his shoulder. I'd always feel shy at first, wishing I was a customer come to buy two dozen of those small pistachio pies or a pound of cookies rolled in sesame seeds or something important enough to take him away from his pastry brushes and his fat bags of frosting. But I would tell myself that surely he'd needed a break.

As I remember, Alberto never smiled but he always said, 'Hello-little-lady-and-how-are-you-this-fine-morning?' as though the greeting were all a single word. I liked the sound of it. Another language. Even though they lasted for only the Saturdays of a single summer, I think he looked forward to my visits almost as much as I did. In his own humble way, Alberto possessed what I would come to understand was a rare human benevolence. He could make a person feel that she mattered.

I would climb up on the stool like I was mounting a horse. One leg steadied on the chrome rung, I'd fling the other leg over the black leather seat, all the while holding the edge of the counter like a pommel. I'd settle into my saddle, arms on the counter, elbows out flat, and just look around. The place was heaven. I'd study the bottles of syrups and liqueurs lined up on marble shelves against the mirrored wall behind the bar, exotic elixirs meant for ladies in veiled hats tilted over Breck pageboys rather than for me in a yellow striped sundress with legs decorated in mosquito bites. Even though I did wear Tangee lipstick on Saturdays. Alberto never asked me what I'd like to have, understanding about the loyalty of my desires. Like a Wazir fingering his potions, he'd slowly set things up for me. First he'd turn up the heat under the tub of chocolate, stiring it with a wooden paddle, its bittersweet smells making me swallow hard. He'd wet the silver dish under cold water, shake it dry, ladle in the chocolate, and, working more quickly then, scrape a pallet of ice cream over it, covering it completely, smoothing the ice cream so it was exactly flush with the silver rim of the dish, the white looking so pure and innocent and all the while hiding the hot thick fudge underneath. Alberto made a perfect job of it. He'd place the silver dish on a big pink plate with a doily on it, put the little silver shovel, facedown, beside it, and then slide the package along the counter so it would stop directly in front of me.

I don't think Alberto and I talked much. I knew then that he was a friend of my father's because Maria had told me so. I wanted Alberto to tell me that I looked just like my father. I wanted him to tell me that if someone asked him, 'Which one is C.'s daughter?' he could surely pick me out of a crowd. At least that's what the lady in the insurance office on State Street said when Maria and I were waiting our turn to pay her monthly premium, and at the electric company when we went to pay the bill, and it happened again when were coming out of church one morning and a man named Mr. Barnes said I'd cut C.'s head off. I asked Maria to explain that and she did, laughing so hard she cried. I didn't cry, though, because I thought that looking like someone meant that you belonged to them and I wanted to belong to C. more than anything else. But Alberto never would talk about my father. He never did once, not even when, while I was sitting up in my saddle watching him fix my sundae, I'd slowly turn my head this way and that, hoping he'd get a really good look at my profile. I thought that if he looked at my profile surely he'd tell me, 'You know, little lady, you just have to be C.'s daughter. You just have to be.' But it never worked.

Finally, I'd give up on the posing and get down to business. As soon as I picked up my silver shovel, Alberto would busy himself with straightening up in another part of the shop. He'd leave me to concentrate on the ice cream, on how it tasted against the warmth of the fudge. Cold against hot. Shivery hot. Sometimes I would try to taste the ice cream by itself, then the fudge alone, then both of them together. I ate deliberately, scraping the silver shovel upside down against my tongue, thinking about things. Wondering if someone who loved you, really loved you, would *always* love you. If they would love you even after they'd gone away. And thinking about how strange it was that the taste that lasted longest in my mouth was the one of vanilla. Like when I'd sipped from the small brown bottle of it in Maria's pantry. I always thought about C. when I was up there in my saddle in front of the silver dish, wondering if I would always love him the way I loved him now. I would just sit there, quiet, until the vanilla taste in my mouth faded away. But I was sure that my love for C. would never fade. I knew that about myself and that felt good. Something to count on. The last few spoonsful were nearly liquid and I'd scrape my shovel against the dish, shamelessly, delicately lick it. Then there would be the ceremony of the Vichy water.

A small green bottle with a blue and white label, Alberto would stand it on the counter, holding it with one hand, slipping off its cap with the opener he'd pull from his pocket, letting the bubbles fizz and spew as he poured out a little of it into a metal cup misted from having sat in the freezer. He did this so that, just as I was surrendering the now polished silver dish, I could reach for the water.

'It's nice and cold,' he'd always tell me, standing there in his paper hat with his powdered-sugar smell, waiting for me to drink it, making smacking sounds as though he were swallowing it for me. He never charged me for the Vichy water. Years later I learned that Vichy was my father's favorite. Alberto was surely pouring the water for his friend.

My carnal and solo visits under Alberto's care helped form me, set the pace for a lifetime of banqueting, as often frugal as decadent. Mostly Lucullan. I think it must have been those

Saturday mornings at Ferrucci that taught me to be comfortable dining alone no matter where in the world I might be. Even in my own home. Often when I'd be cooking elaborate suppers and serving them charmingly to myself, I'd think of that sturdy girl astride the black leather stool, solemn, industrious with her silver shovel. How changed am I from her as, here and now, I sit in a Florentine piazza with *this* silver shovel? Just as I knew I would way back then, I still think about C. Still love him and that still feels good. That little girl held tight to the Fates, trusted them entire. So do I.

I walk down the Via Calimala to Guya and look in the windows, as I do always. I'm about to proceed until I remember that today I am flush. I can buy something. I see a skirt I want to touch. Satin in the palest gray, it's long and full. There is a shawl or a scarf or some such length of fabric wound about the neck of the hanger. I step in, ask for the skirt in my size, and there is head shaking and the clucking of tongues among the three saleswomen.

'È *terminato, signora, mi dispiace tanto.*' My size has already been sold, and they are in collective grief for me. I understand that this is yet another reading of Florentine commercial restraint. They stage this operetta to spur my desire for the dress. I play my part.

'I'm so disappointed. It's exactly the skirt I've been looking for. *Ma, la prossima volta.* But perhaps the next time.'

Rather than looking about for something else I might like, I prepare to leave, foiling the next scene, in which they would have shown me ten skirts and six dresses they knew I didn't want, all the better to convince me that it was the pale gray satin or nothing. The act speeds up as one of them says, '*Ma, Alessia, guarda un po'in magazzino, solo per sicurezza.* Look a bit in the storeroom, just to be certain.'

While Alessia goes to feign her search for the skirt whose existence and whereabouts are precisely known to her, the other two engage me in discourse about how quickly that particular skirt flew out the door, how they only buy one in each of the three most popular sizes and—

'*Eccola.*'

Alessia holds up the skirt and the three Graces claim a miracle.

So certain am I that it's mine, I buy it without trying it, racing out the door, almost sorry that I crimped the game. Normally, I stand still for the entire cultural show, which must begin with a quietly spoken no, proceed with a funereal face, which is suddenly illuminated by some forgotten box or rack or room where the desired object waits. Only for me.

Little more than an hour has passed since I left Fernando and Barlozzo and I want to visit the hairdresser. The afternoon is young.

For years I'd heard about a place called Contrasts. Tucked behind Piazza della Signoria, I recall, and so that's where I head. Once there and in audience with the colorist, I hear myself saying, 'I'd like to have hair the color of hot copper wires.' He barely breaks a smile, assuring me that mine is not the most immoderate request of his morning. Like the duke's first pair of Florentine leather trousers, this is the first time I will change the color of my hair.

He says, 'First we'll remove your natural color. It's much too dark as it is and won't accept a lighter color. After that portion of the process is complete, I want you to promise me that you won't look in the mirror, that you'll sip your tea quietly and continue to trust me. Then we'll apply the copper color, wait half an hour or so, rinse, shampoo . . .'

He tells me and then he tells me once again, repeating every half step of the litany in the calmest of voices, all the while looking directly into my eyes, clinically studying my skin, shining first one light, then another on my face. So successful is his preoperative discourse that I would permit him to remove my tonsils were they still in place.

I have had my back turned to the mirrors for three hours. Almost three and a half. There has been more than one softly exchanged consultation between the colorist and the stylist. I sense they are pleased. One of them begins to massage my hair with a foam, with more of it, much more of it, and then with a gel. Simultaneously, two people dry my hair with diffusers. Still I have seen nothing. They turn off the machines in unison, turn my chair around to face the truth. Just as I'd asked for it, I am running my hands through hair the color of hot copper wires. It is my own hair. These are my own long, curling copper wires. I think I love it. And then I realize that I hate it. I look again and I love it more than I hate it. The calm voice of the colorist is telling me that, as he'd thought it would, this color suits me better than my naturally nearly black hair.

'You have a redhead's pale skin, signora. Your dark hair was an error of nature. Some unfortunate collision of your DNA. Like a bad nose. I compliment you on your instinct. You were meant to be exactly like this.'

He proceeds with a succinct treatment of European history as it applies to shades of skin and hair, summing up with his suspicion that I am of Russian or eastern European heritage – Hungarian, Czechoslovakian, Polish – a lineage over which, once upon a time, a red-haired Norman crossed. As though he doubts that I know much of anything about it myself, he never inquires about my descendency but, rather, informs me of it. I fumble about with my purse and my sweater. I can only imagine what he might have been able to tell me if he'd been the one to take my tonsils.

The staff assembles at the door to shake hands with me, to tell me the pleasure it's been to receive me. I am an awkward, postmenopausal Match Girl as I step outside. I've left the gray skirt behind, and as I turn back to fetch it, I see the colorist coming toward me, package in hand.

'*Ciao, principessa,*' he says very quietly, redeeming me from the awkward, postmenopausal Match Girl, exactly as he'd intended.

I want to try life as a redhead alone for a while before trying it with Fernando. Surely I want to try it for a while without Barlozzo. I decide that they must be napping back at the hotel by now. I make myself walk more slowly. With coquettish nonchalance, I look in every store window, peeping at the redhead. Back at the hotel, the concierge tells me that *i signori* are still out. I imagine the duke languishing by now, his old papery fingers numb with their fondling of tweed. I see Fernando pressing his wrists to his temples.

I bathe and step carefully into the skirt. Tight, very tight about the hips and the derriere, the heavy satin falls then into lush folds, just clearing my bare ankles. I pull a thin white T-shirt over my head. With long, tight sleeves, it fits like a leotard. I'd packed my good pewter sandals, bought long ago from a shop behind the Rialto. I turn my head upside down as they'd asked me to do in the salon and crunch my fingers through the copper waves. Pearls. Opium. Loosely, I wind the satin shawl twice about my neck, letting the rest of it fall behind my shoulders. Where can they be?

I walk out the door and down the Vicolo Porta Rossa to the corner of Via Tornabuoni. I absorb myself in the shoes hung from branches of cherry wood in the window at YSL. When I turn away, I notice Fernando and the duke twenty yards distant, walking away from me. They must have strolled right past me. Surely they are heading back to the hotel. I go there, too. But when I arrive, they are nowhere to be found in the lobby, and the concierge repeats his previous message: '*I signori sono ancora fuori.*' I wander about the lobby, picking up maps and sitting down and standing up again, looking to the door, then looking away from it. Maybe it wasn't them at all. Then I hear

Fernando's voice asking the concierge if *la signora è in camera*. I turn toward Fernando as the concierge points to me.

'*Sei tu?*'

'*Certo sono io.*' For a moment I've forgotten about the copper wires. The new satin skirt.

He comes to me. Touches my hair, stands back, all the better to look at me. He pulls me close, saying nothing at all. Barlozzo is already gone.

Rather roughly he escorts me to the elevator, then to our room. He still has not spoken.

'If you hate it, I can change it. It was just something I've always wanted to try and today, well, it seemed like the right moment. I don't know – I felt sort of free and wanted to do something girly and foolish and . . .' Saying all this rekindles the Match Girl and I feel the gathering of tears.

'I love your hair.' He turns me about and begins to unfasten my skirt.

'You do, you mean you do really, I mean you really do love it?'

I'm stepping out of the skirt, protesting. 'I'm all ready for the *passeggiata,* why are you . . . ?'

'Because there's something I have to tell you.'

'And can't you tell me with my clothes on?'

'It will be easier for me if we're lying down.'

'What will be easier?'

We are on the bed now and I look at Fernando for the first time, really look at him. He's pallid as new cheese.

'What is it?' I turn to face him, wounding his thigh with the heel of the one sandal I am still somehow wearing. He winces, curses.

'I have something to confess. You know how we always talk about seeing only each other? About how we notice other people but as though they were in shadow? There but not there?'

'Yes.'

'Today I noticed someone. A woman. I saw her and I felt just as I did when I first saw you. That same sensation of recognition I had when I saw you in Piazza San Marco on that winter afternoon, your long white coat dragging across the stones, your hair half falling down from its pins. That was a year before I met you. Before I found you again in the little wine bar. This afternoon I was shocked when I found myself in that same state of, I don't know, excitement or agitation. As though I was betraying you. I ignored it as best I could and the duke and I went to walk on the bridge. But I have to tell you that I kept thinking about this woman. And then when we arrived back at the hotel, the first thing I saw was her. She was standing in the lobby with her back to me, just as I'd seen her half an hour before as she was looking in a shop window. I felt nervous and strange and then she turned around, you turned around, and she was you. You were she.'

'And so, you chose me long ago, and today, you chose me again. I think that's what happened. Yes, I think that's exactly what happened.'

*

THE DUKE IS KNOCKING on the door and we are dressing, guilty as children behind a haystack while the dinner bell is ringing. I'm ready first and go to open the door to him.

'I was looking for my friend Chou. Have you seen her? Nice black hair pulled back in a chignon.'

'Fernando loves it.'

'Yellow trousers, red hair – we can get itinerant work as the family Pagliacci.'

Fernando exits the bathroom like Caesar entering the forum. He wears trousers of fine tan cashmere. Soft leather moccasins the color of whiskey set down by a fire. All today's spoils. These he wears in combination with his vintage navy blazer and his favorite shirt cut from rough white silk. He'd grown his hair somewhat longer over these past months and the lingering dark streaks of it are bold among white, all of it gelled now to a cinematic gleam.

Conspirators against the dull we are, I think, as I try to see us as others will. We are glamorous, glamour being a state of comfort with one's self. Surely we are better as ourselves then ever we could be as anyone else. Belonging to no other ilk but our own. I like us.

16

And Be Careful of Edgardo d'Onofrio

*I*t's nearing noon on a December morning and the sky seems made of woolly lambs sliding across pale blue ice. Miranda and I are collecting cones and fallen branches from the pines behind her place and as we walk I play the Who's Coming to My Mythical Supper game, partly because it's what I'm thinking about and partly because I know it makes her laugh her church-bell laugh.

'Let's see, I've got Barlozzo, Orfeo, Luca, Neddo, Tilde, Edgardo, and you. I've nearly got a full table with Fernando and me. You said I'd never find twelve, but I've already got six.'

'The only thing you've got six of is holes in your head. Don't you know who Edgardo is?'

'I know that he's a count. Or is he a baron?'

'*Il marchese* d'Onofrio to be exact. And Neddo's arch and

lifelong enemy. If either one of them knows the other one has been invited, he'll make a great girth around your house that evening. Besides, you haven't got a house. And you haven't got a table. Until you do, why can't my table be enough for you? You said you want to feed hungry people. Aren't there enough of them shuffling in here every evening? And be careful of Edgardo d'Onofrio.'

'He's harmless enough, Miranda. Every time we see him at Tilde's or on the street, he stops to talk to us, takes us to Sant'Andrea for an espresso. He's invited us to a *festa* on *fine anno*, New Year's Eve.'

'Bah. Don't be offended by what I'm going to tell you, but he's most likely invited you because he's sick to death – which I think he truly is, by the way – of that pack of nobles with whom he's spent his life. You and Fernando will be viewed as something akin to dancing bears, his latest toys. Edgardo d'Onofrio has invited you as distractions.'

'That may be so, but I'd rather be considered a dancing bear than Typhoid Mary, which, it seems, is how too many of the Orvietani see me still. Maybe I'm looking at Edgardo as a distraction just as much as he is at me. I'm hardly about to get my head turned, if that's what you're concerned about.'

'I'm not concerned at all. I suppose what I am is envious. Just a little envious. You must remember every detail of the evening and then tell me all about it. And the menu. I hear he eats exclusively *in bianco* now, in white. You know, like invalids do.'

This imagined supper around my imagined table in my imagined ballroom begins to take on the proportions of quiet obsession. The supper is a dreamy concoction that takes the place of another, now surrendered yearning – the one for a small *taverna* where I would cook a few evenings a week, where fifteen or twenty people would sit down at a communal table together for a simple supper by the fire. But the *taverna* dream has been retooled, softened into one for a single dinner. Or a series of dinners. Feasts and suppers around our own table, emblem like the sea captains' pineapples cleaved to their Nantucket front doors, that Fernando and I are, at last, 'at home.' I long for our place to become, in some ways, like Miranda's. Where people we care about come to feel better, where they like to be.

I could go into therapy and, after seventeen years, I might be fortunate enough for someone to tell me it's only a family I'm missing and searching for. But since I already know that is what I've *always* been looking for, I might save myself the trouble. Get right to it. Make a beautiful house, cook beautiful food. Fill up all my chairs with good people. That's what I want to do. Patience.

But every once in a while I wish my patience to *inferno*. Along with my dainty form of listlessness. Weary of my own acquiescence, of our being ballasted only by ourselves, I regress back to astonishment, exhaustion. I forget about the Miracle of Bolsena, I forget about my resolve to surrender to the Ubaldini, and I tell myself that I don't like the shape this life is taking on by itself and that I think destiny could use a little help. The wait, the *commedia,* the manners, the illusions, the bowing. My heart goes loud and fast as wingbeat and, like a saber, I take up my irritation. Go racing to find the one with the delicious overbite. I fairly shout, 'Are you certain you don't want to fight this?'

'There isn't anything to fight. At least nothing very well defined, as things are defined in Italian terms. That is, *if* there are Italian terms to define anything at all. We could choose to set a case in motion to retrieve our money, but while we waited a century and a half for that to be resolved, if indeed it could ever be resolved in our favor, we'd have to find another place to live. Start again. You do remember that we've already had this conversation? But I'll do it, if you want. At this point, I'm beginning to feel something akin to a cuckold myself.'

'If someone would only give us a progress report.'

'You sound like a junior executive. There is no progress. And whatever information the Ubaldini may or may not have gathered over this past year, they've simply chosen not to share it with us.'

'Sometimes I think I'd settle for a monthly phone call from them, even if all they said was "No news yet." Do you understand? It's the void that disturbs. Surely they could at least have found a way to finish the demolition, carry out the debris, prepare the place for the work. Surely they could have done that by now.'

'The work is all of a piece. The crew that will reconstruct must deconstruct. At least that's what I think.'

I put the saber down. Go to kiss the mustache above the

delicious overbite. Every life is made, in some part, of madness. And as madness goes, I'd choose ours over most. We'll just keep waiting, plumping up our autoimmune systems here among the mold.

17

The Orvietani

Observations, impressions, stories told to me and stories told to them. Mostly by a fire.

About Tilde

Stick-legged body still unripe, hair blond and white and woven in a loose, thin braid, her face is made of gold-pleated silk. Her eyes are ice. Two small alpine lakes, frozen, rimmed skillfully with a cerulescent pencil, framed by straight, black, thick brows. Masculine brows between which a baby eagle's nose descends, hooked but delicately, like the profiles of Etruscans. What saves her crumpling beauty is her mind.

Thin cashmere sweaters, well-cut jeans, a vast scarf casually twined about her throat, she cuts the filters off French cigarettes, holds one – like Gloria Swanson would – to the center of her lips, fingers splayed, the back of her dark-spotted hand like a half mask over her face. She rides a vintage *moto*, black and beautifully kept, over the cobbles of the town above the farm where she was born. She is seventy-three. Perhaps she is a bit past the age to which she admits. People whisper numbers as she rides by. Tilde is her name.

'I was born low and lived high,' she said once. 'I'm a rare bird, at once a have and a have-not. I am Cinderella *and* I am the queen, you see, and so I can tell you the story from both sides.'

'THINGS BEGAN WELL ENOUGH. My father was a farmer. On their patron's land, my mother worked beside him. Sickly, small, I was sent early to the nuns, where I might be put to some useful if genteel task to earn my keep. To lighten the burden my belly would have caused at home.

'Trampled by a bull, my father died when I was ten, nearly eleven. Being hungry or sick with some other kind of emptiness, I was already living with grief. Like many children do, in one way or another. Always weeping for myself, I never wept for him. I'd hardly ever spoken to my father, nor he to me. Me, a scrawny, strange-eyed female, the single issue of his marriage bed. But I wasn't even that for him.

'My father's sister, tallow-faced and dying, tucked a sapphire ring in my hand and told me — when I was thirty and, to her thinking, beyond caring — that I was not my father's child. She said that my mother lay with another man. Not for herself but for her husband. She said that, as a woman will know such things, my mother knew she wasn't barren, that it was something in her husband, something in him that kept her womb a hollow. While my father cut tobacco, she went one autumn

225

morning to the noble's door, offering herself like a basket of red-cheeked fruit. Of course my father must have known. About himself, about her. About me. I am haunted with wondering who they all were. Who any of them were. And beyond that haunting, I stopped, long ago, wondering about myself.

'But I truly think that I was born when he died. I think it's true that when my mother's husband died, life began again for me. For my mother, too. She came to fetch me at the convent, packed my things in an apple crate, and all the way home she held my hand so tight it hurt. And how I loved that hurt. For three years afterward, we lived the life both of us never could have lived in my father's presence. Her husband's presence. Like a pair of wild turkeys streaking through the woods, we laughed out loud, laughed until we cried, sometimes collapsing where we stood, folding into a heap of giggling flesh and bones as though laughing were all there was. We worked long and well at our duties, fetching and carrying and stooping and breaking our backs and our legs as we were expected to. We'd sit at the long table in the *mensa* three times a day. We'd sit there with all the other workers and eat with the same rapacious hunger and then we'd walk awhile, stop somewhere to look at the sky, head home to wash ourselves and pull long white shirts over our heads and fall asleep on pallets we'd set down by our fire. Sometimes we'd stay awake for a while, though, lie there quietly or talk a little, wonder at the leaping shadows the fire made on the old crumbling walls, listen to the sounds seeping in from the other side of them, the noises of other people's love and, more often, their pain. And that's when she would tell me stories. She'd tuck me in the crook of her thin, strong arm and her voice would smudge the lines between the dark and the light. I'd barely breathe for my listening. All I have of my childhood was fixed during those moments before sleep, with those tales thrown by her voice and saved by a fire. But sometimes she'd climb up the worn stone steps to her bedroom and I'd stay alone by the hearth. She'd always wait until I was asleep – or until she thought I was – before she'd leave me.

'One morning I went up to wake her, carrying blistering chocolate in the cup with the yellow roses on it. Two biscuits. I stood by her bed, calling her in a whisper like I always did, already knowing she couldn't hear. I held tight to the cup with the yellow roses on it and called to her more sternly. I screamed and shouted. Surely if I screamed, she would waken. Surely there was time to wake her. She would never have gone without a word.

'"I shall always be your protector," the count told me, guiding me from the churchyard through the olive groves. "We'll have your things moved from the workers' quarters up here to the villa and you'll become even more a member of the family. Ah, Tilde, you're like a daughter to me. And you look so like your mother. So very much like your mother."

'Yes, of course. Like a daughter. He would be my protector and mine would be another bed for him to plague. She'd offered herself to him, hadn't she? And now that she was gone and her husband gone, too, what resistance could I pretend? I was next in line. And I knew if I stayed a night, I'd stay forever, and so I ran.

'Back to the nuns I'd go, even though I'd hated my life among them. Like a beaten wife, I would return. The nuns' righteous evil would be better than the count's hot, dry hands, I thought. Into the blue-stuff case she kept under her bed I laid the few things in my mother's armoire and those from the two drawers in the kitchen dresser where she kept our linens and a leather pouch with her savings. There was a thin gold chain tangled in a piece of white tissue paper. The chain she sometimes wore on Sundays. Inside the folds of my woolen coat, I put the biscuit tin and the cup with the yellow roses and I ran across the meadows, pulled the bell, waited for the Sisters of Mercy to welcome me home. I waited a long time, shifting the blue-stuff case from hand to hand. I rang again and waved up at the window where I thought I'd seen a face, heard the rattling of the shutters. But no one came. I waited and pulled the bell and waited longer, but the Sisters of Mercy never opened the gates.

'Upon my mother's death, I'd become full chattel to the count. The count whose gifts of fruit and oil and small white envelopes sealed with red wax the sisters would never risk for the sheltering of a skinny slave. By now they'd be sending some envoy to tell the count of my appearance there. I had to go. I had money for a train. I'd go to Rome. I'd find work, a paying job.

'That night I lay down in a stand of pines on the steeps between the convent and the farm, a few kilometers from the train station. Sleeping in my coat and covering myself with my mother's sweaters, I put her gold chain around my neck and ate biscuits and counted the lire in the leather pouch, praying and crying but all the while feeling something like fire inside me, something hard and ruthless in a way that I know now was nothing less than will. Incurable will. I doubt anyone up at the villa ever tried to look for me, for, if they had, I wouldn't have been so hard to find. I think the count with the dry hot hands must have thought me unworthy of a hunt. Why rouse himself from his pipe and his cups when there were, after all, other daughters of the house? His by blood, his by noble right.

'After two paid sleeps in a convent in Trastevere and bowl after bowl of thick bean soup from a *taverna* near Santa Maria, I was ready to begin. First, though, I needed a bar of soap. While the lady in the *profumeria* wrapped it, twittering with another customer, I broke off a piece of red lipstick from one of the opened tubes on display, held it loosely in the palm of my hand all the way back to the convent, rolled it carefully in a handker- chief and placed it in the leather pouch with what was left of my mother's money. Lipstick was to be part of the disguise.

'I'd reserved myself a bath and paid twenty lire extra for hot water. The soap smelled of oranges. I put on my mother's blue crepe dress with the covered buttons and the padded shoul- ders. Black lace-up boots and thick black stockings, my hair swept back with pearly combs, two dots of cherry red on my cheeks, rubbed hard, and then more of it slid across my lips with my little finger. There. I was easily eighteen.

'But the shopkeeps whom I asked for work were quite set

with help despite my costume. A thousand thanks, they said. Whether enchanted or amused by me, they all knew I was a lie.

'I tried at all the fruit sellers in Campo dei Fiori, but every *bancarella* was staffed by families. As were the bars and the *trattorie*. In a *pasticceria* near the Pantheon where I went to buy a ricotta tart for my lunch, there was a sign propped up near the pay stand. CERCASI APPRENDISTA. We are searching for an apprentice.

'It was simple enough to secure the job since I was willing to work twelve hours a day, six days a week for room and board and all I could learn from the master pastry chef. It would only be until I could find something else, I'd told myself as I was shown the room behind the kitchen. As I think about it, the room wasn't a room at all but a white-walled closet fitted with a clean white bed, a washstand, and a very large, dark-framed print of the Sacred Heart of Jesus, all of it drenched in the sugary perfumes rising up from the oven next door. And I loved that room. I loved it in a way I would love no other in my life.

'I don't know if it was me who had little desire to learn the business of pastrymaking or whether it was more a cleaning person than an apprentice that the job required, but all I ever seemed to do was sweep and scrub and polish. And as for my board, there was bread and coffee and milk in the morning, taken standing up at the worktable. Lunch was a bowl of soup from the endless pot of it brewing on the only gas burner where some syrup or another wasn't boiling. There was more bread.

Sometimes there were *bucatini* with big chunks of salt pork and tomatoes, or spaghetti with small, sweet clams. A broken pastry or two. Supper was much the same except on Fridays, when every Roman ate tripe; the baker's wife would carry down a casserole of it from her kitchen upstairs. Proud as if it were a whole fatted lamb. I was never hungry during those days of living in the bakery but I was never full either, which, of course, had to do with things more sentimental than physical.

'Used to working hard, I swept with a vengeance, washed the baking pans while they were still hot, heaving them to hiss in the pan full of soapy water. More for sport than appetite, I'd steal extra bread and almond cakes when I was sure no one was look-ing, wrap them in a kitchen towel, and stash them in my room. I was allowed to take the broken cakes that, when thrust too hot from their pans, fell to pieces on the cooling table. But some-times I'd break a few more myself, nonchalantly and with a rolling pin, as I passed through the cooling room on my way to the kitchen, eating those out of hand, passing by the baker with buttered lips stretched in a long, sly smile. If he'd had conquer-ing me on his mind, I think I saved him from the trouble with my brazen, full-mouthed promenades and my tapping of the rolling pin on every surface I passed.

'Since I had no money there was not much I could do in the evenings after work, even when I had the energy to do more than fall into my bed. But I would go to walk sometimes. I'd pass by the *caffès* and decide what I would order if I were rich. I'd have wine from a bottle, my own small bottle. *Quello frizzante,* the kind with bubbles, but better than the sour, salty *frizzante* the count would pour for us at the Christmas morning breakfast. And I would have Parma ham. I'd tasted it once at the convent, helped myself to a thick, rosy slice of it when the cooks were out in the garden gossiping. I'd folded it into a heel of bread and secured the little sandwich to my skinny thigh, under the elastic of my long black stocking. And when the house slept, I ate. Small, slow bite after bite, and I'll never forget the taste and the smell of that stolen supper. And so I'd have Parma ham with bread. I'd call for butter, too. Butter white as a lily, and what I didn't spread of it on my bread I'd eat with a fork. Then I'd have an *espresso doppio* in a glass with a silver holder and I'd drink it in a single sip so I could feel the hot, bitter strength of it down to my knees. I'd leave a tip for my waiter.

'But meanwhile I was still without money, and so I'd walk near the Pantheon or sit on the stoop of a closed shop and just watch the people pass. I'd walk as far as the Spanish Steps and climb halfway to the top, sit down, hugging my knees to my chin, and I'd think about my mother. About her and about a long table, candles, firelight, the perfume that laughter and hunger and bread and wine make. I wanted soup, a soup she would make for me. How I longed for soup in a deep white dish, a spoon – thin and silver – sitting facedown against the side of it, inviting me. I wanted my mother to say, "Will you help me here so I can get all this to the table?" I wanted my mother to say that.

'I was glad I was fifteen instead of eighteen, and glad I'd run from the count with the hot, dry hands and run from the Sisters of Mercy. And gladder still that I'd found the small white bed under the Sacred Heart of Jesus, but still I never stopped missing my mother. Perhaps what I really wanted was to be younger than fifteen rather than older; perhaps I wanted to be five and crushed against the breast of her.

'There was a boy who came to the bakery to clean in the evenings. He'd arrive just as I was leaving. He was the one who readied the place for the baker in the morning. Ugo was his name and he, too, was fifteen. We did little things to help each other. I'd save bread and cakes for him and he would bring me oranges he'd steal from the markets, and once a whole *salame,* which I hung, though not disrespectfully, next to the Sacred Heart of Jesus and cut thick slices from it to eat with stolen bread before I fell asleep. Ugo protected me and I did him, in my way, and we fell in love, protection being one of the first instincts of love. Now I had a motive for life. We whispered and laughed and began to talk about the future.

'As soon as he was twenty-one, we would be married, he said. And when the time was right, he told me, I would go to live with his father's family in Frascati, where I would help with the chores in a house where twenty-two people lived. Ugo would stay in Rome, work his way up to apprentice in the bakery, a real apprentice, learn the business well, and then the family would sanction our marriage, help us on our way. Perhaps buy Ugo a partnership in a bakery or even the license to his own shop. We'll see, he said. But then on that morning near

Christmas when Francesco came into the shop to order a cake for the *vigilia,* all that planning was put aside. Francesco looked at me and decided he would have me. And I looked at him looking at me and decided I would help him.

'You see, Francesco had vendetta on his mind. Yes, he did. He'd take a bakery maid for a bride and that would surely infuriate his family, assure them and anyone else who might have cared that his was a sham marriage, a cynical stroke of his noble humor. You see, the woman he loved was forbidden to him. The daughter of his father's enemies. The feud was another Capulet and Montague story, and when her father had learned of her attraction to Francesco, he'd given his daughter a choice. She could say her vows to Jesus or to her cousin in Bologna. And so the girl Francesco loved was married to the Bolognese, and he would marry a bakery maid.

'It never bothered me that I would be used as the instrument of Francesco's wrath. You see, I planned to use him, too. I didn't want to live in Frascati with twenty-two other people, no matter how kind and loving they might be. I didn't want my mother's life of work and supper and bed. I wanted bubbly wine in a green bottle and Parma ham and butter white as a lily. And more than all of that, I wanted to help the man I really loved. I wanted to help Ugo.

'Oh, Ugo was pale with rage. Ready to kill Francesco and me, too. But I held him, held his fists and afterward his body tight to my then sixteen-year-old self and I told him, "If I marry Francesco, I can help you. I can help your family. Marriage is nothing more than business. It has little to do with love and less to do with possession. You are my love and nothing and no one will ever change that."

'And so I married the noble Francesco. He was a good man and, in time, he became a good friend, inviting me into a kind of conspiracy. He wanted his privacy and I wanted mine. Normally in our culture, liberty would belong only to him, but he agreed to mine. Remember, I was sixteen. And I was beautiful then, beautiful and bold like a cat can be. He hired a woman to assist me not only in my toilette and with my clothes but with my *comportamento*. Half governess, half tutor, she taught me to read and write, to speak French. She read the classics to me until I could read them to her. I learned to play the piano, and when I was eighteen, Francesco set a viola da gamba, a cello, up against the great black pianoforte with a note that promised that if I'd learn to play it he would take me to Milano to hear Pablo Casals. The housekeeper, the majordomo, even the gardener and, most surprising of all, Francesco's mother ministered to me, worked together to raise me. We made a happy life with another kind of love.

'Almost all Francesco gave to me – and he gave a very great deal – I gave to Ugo, who, in turn, gave to his family. And always having accepted my love for Ugo, Francesco looked the other way when I would leave to be with him. Toward the end of Ugo's life, Francesco would invite him to stay with us for long periods. And when Ugo died, Francesco wept with me. Having known love once himself, he'd understood mine.

'But that didn't stop Francesco, in the very early years of our life together, from tapping his fingers on my door of an evening. I would always welcome him. First for duty and then for affection and, I think, some form of lust, I always having been vulnerable to lust.

'And when Francesco died – in a fall from a horse, exactly as he would have chosen to die – he'd left everything to me, as though I'd been, for more than forty years, a good and faithful wife. Which, in a way, I had been. I signed over the land and the palazzi in Rome to Ugo's brothers, to their children, and I came back to Orvieto. Bought the palazzo in town, the casale up in Buon Respiro. I came back and I stayed, even though the Orvietani called me La Maddalena.

'Some of them still do. Oh, they can be a hideous bunch up there on that rock. No matter, though. Truth is, when I sit of an evening on the verandah and think over my life, I raise my eyes to the gods. I got to have and I got to give, and there's nothing finer than that combination in anybody's life. I am strong and whatever tears I have are private. You'll see them shimmer sometimes but you'll never see them fall.'

'ALL OF US ARE MADE by a single event,' Tilde told me. An incident that sets the scene for all the scenes to follow. As though it were a costume, we wear the event. Pull it over our heads, zip it straight to the throat and right to the chin, and that's where we live. Inside the event, be it made of injury, be it made of joy. And when it's made of both, one sentiment always claims a body more than the other, the joy or the injury holding us till the end, making less of a life or more of it. I know that you'll tell me there were five events, a hundred of them in your life so far, all of which you're wearing, and I'll believe you. I will also believe that just one of them outdid all the others. Finding my mother dead was the event that shaped me. And since that happened to me so early in my life, it freed me. Nothing could hurt as much as that hurt and so I could do things, even contemptuous things, without worrying about consequence.

'Besides, all of it's fixed anyway, fixed under screw and seal. Most of us know that and yet we're still a race of intriguers, biting the insides of our hands, perpetually arranging, screaming across from one sea to another, shouting, Look here, this is how to make a life, when all of it's so much empty anguish. Another way to make the time pass. All of it's fixed, I tell you.'

'THE TRUTH HAS ALWAYS come easy to me. My truth, anyway. I've never suffered much thinking about what's real and what's true. Edgardo and I have talked for more hours about truth-telling in the past ten years than we've slept. He has absolutely no use for the truth. He says every time he tried it, he got nowhere. But I'm comfortable with the truth – scarred from it but still at my ease with it. Anyway, truth is singular as a thumbprint, and understanding this, I've saved myself from the folly of foisting my truth onto anyone else. Anyone at all. My truth is mine. Yours is yours. And when, rare as a yellow-clouded butterfly, two people come up with the same truth, well, it can prove dangerous as often as it can prove lovely.'

'YOU'RE THE TYPE who will perish from exuberance, Chou. I've never let myself be happy the way you can be happy. Mostly I have been exceedingly alarmed by happiness, understanding the perilous whimsy of the gods as I do. Happiness weighs the same as pain, when you think about it. If you think about what it takes to guard and hoard joy, keep it against the Fates, well, the bowls of cherries and the beds of roses take on another color. We're consumed either in battle against pain or in combat for the maintenance of joy. We fight off pain with the same stick we use to protect joy. Life is combat. Find yourself a good stick.'

'AND SO NOW there's no one. No Ugo. No Francesco. No one who waits for me. No one fixing the fire or looking to see me coming up the hill. I can buy cheese or not. Forget the bread. Who is there to care? No one. I am "at liberty." Why, there's nothing left even of my illusions, all of which I strewed about as I went, leaving one here, one there. Like alms in the market-place. Yes, I'm free.'

About Neddo

After that evening when we sat together at the fava bean festival the summer before, one of the first times I saw Neddo he had a tree limb stretched across the back of his shoulders, balancing the handles of two covered iron pots on each of the forked ends. He was carrying lunch to his sons at work on their land. In company with his attaché in the field – a brindled spaniel called Luna – Neddo would climb up from the stone house where they all lived, stopping once, maybe twice to put down his load, relight his pipe. He wouldn't permit anyone else to carry lunch to his boys.

He went, then, to set down his pots near a broken wall, arranging things the way he liked them. He uncorked the three-liter bottle of red that the boys had carried up in the morning and poured wine into a tin cup that was tied with string to his belt. Always ready. *'Buon appetito,'* he called out, and the boys came running. He handed each son a pot, taking off the cover, rhapsodizing over the day's feast, intoning hymns to Mary as he went.

'*Oggi, abbiamo uno stufatino di vitello con i piselli. Madonnina, quanto buono*. Today, we have a little stew of veal and peas. Little Mother of Jesus, how good it is.'

We've watched him many times since, carrying his pots on the tree limb stretched across his shoulders. Sometimes he'd bring beans stewed with red wine and herbs and a fine piece of pancetta that he'd left all night in the ashes of his fire. Whatever good thing he'd cooked for his boys, he always thanked the Madonnina for it. And he always had bread and cheese and some sort of fruit. Dried figs. Sometimes he'd have cherries or new pears, small ones, brown-skinned and hot from the sun. But his favorite fruit was a peach. After lunch Neddo would sleep, lay himself down somewhere near where the boys were working and, until the sun made shadows on the stones and curtains in the trees, he'd sleep the sleep of the angels.

Save his ritual summer wanderings up into neighboring hamlets and villages for the food festivals, Neddo – in all his life – had never ventured farther than this field where he'd been planting tobacco and harvesting it long before his sons were born. He'd never walked much beyond the meadow where he still sowed hay and still harvested what he could of it by hand, surrendering the rest of it to his sons and their machines. He kept a corner of a meadow to grow grasses for his rabbits, and I loved seeing him against the yellow luster of a sinking sun, striding that meadow like a warrior, swinging his scythe, high, wide, in rhythm with the wind.

Neddo says, 'There's no great secret to joy. Just divine what makes you happy. That's the first thing you have to know about yourself. Then set out to have or do or feel or be – according to that knowledge. Guide yourself. Keep your own counsel. Trust yourself. More or less, that's your job in life.'

There is a peace about Neddo, the quietude of a man on good terms with his passions. And we enjoy being with him. A few chance moments of walking through the market together or a rendezvous to climb into the leafy saddles of his peach trees, plucking all we can use of the blushing June fruit. Neddo sits among the wild-flowers and the weeds beneath the trees, spurring us on.

'Pick, pick those lovelies. Don't leave a single one for the birds to gnaw.'

The sun warms the fruit and the fruit scents the air and it's good to be in Neddo's orchards. We pick, filling baskets and buckets and carting them up to Miranda's, where we'll be boiling them into jam with long pours of black rum and a fistful of crushed cloves or canning them whole until all hours of the night. Neddo has almost three hectares of peach trees. A man fairly obsessed with peaches.

'THE BEST WAY for me to tell you why I like peaches so much is for me to first tell you about Edgardo,' he'd told us once when we were staggering under the weight of another load of the fruit. 'There is nothing moderate about him. He hates with the best of them. Even when he was young, he was like an old horse with a burr made all of hate stuck right under his tail.'

Edgardo saw the little boy that morning in the peach orchard even though the boy didn't see him. And Edgardo knew the boy's name was Neddo because he'd heard his own father calling to him from time to time. Inviting him onto the verandah for a glass of cool water shot with cherry syrup. Or, in winter, to come in by the fire for some hot milk. His father was affectionate with the boy, saying, *'Bravo, bravo, Neddo,'* all the time hugging him roughly to his side as he walked him back out to the garden or into the kitchen to find the biscuit tin. *'È carino, quel ragazzino,'* he would say to his wife at the lunch table. He's dear, that little boy. Neddo knew that was what the *marchese* said about him because one of the servants in the *marchese*'s dining room was his *zio* Michele.

But for Edgardo, the boy Neddo was no more than a field rat, a future pair of cheaply bought hands to work the farm. Never mind if the boy was of the fourth generation of a local family who'd always sharecropped for the d'Onofrio.

When Edgardo's father, *il marchese* Jacopo d'Onofrio passed away, rather than mourn him, Edgardo – the new *marchese* – celebrated *himself,* his fresh and sovereign status. He was sixteen.

So on that morning when the new *marchese* watched as the boy Neddo, then nine years old, reached up to pull a branch of peaches toward himself, burying his face in the leaves and the sun-fat fruit, inhaling the scent of them, he nearly shouted at the boy, who, like all the other workers, was not permitted to lay hands on anything growing in the fields or the orchards or in the woods – either cultivated or wild – without the presence of the overseer. Or else how could the bounty be counted and weighed and hence distributed properly? Standing still and continuing to watch, Edgardo steeled himself from screaming at the boy. The boy let go of the branch. But as it swung back into place, Neddo plucked a single peach from it, devoured it out of hand, dried his face and then the stone of the fruit with the tails of his shirt, put the stone in his pocket. Still Edgardo said nothing.

That night or one night soon after that, as Edgardo's household slept, the new *marchese* dressed himself with care, a cravat tucked into his heavy silk shirt, his father's hunting jacket buttoned over a handsome tweed gilet, also his father's. His hat he

pulled low, and at an angle. He walked the nearly two kilometers to the peach orchards and set fire to them. Watched the
trees burn to stumps. Had he set fire to the past, to his father's
reign? Could a small, hungry boy with a single sunlit peach have
so provoked him, or was it that Neddo and the peach provided
the new *marchese* with the means to a rite of passage into the
ruling class, an act of poetic injustice that would define his
reign?

The next morning Edgardo assembled his farmers and
announced that, because of Neddo's theft, no one would taste
peaches from his land ever again.

Later, when his mother asked Edgardo, *perché,* why, he
responded, 'It was my orchard and he is my boy. Would you
have preferred that I set fire to him?' *Zio* Michele heard that,
too.

After the Second World War, the tyranny of *mezzadria,* share-
cropping, at last collapsed. It was a time of great exodus. Of
farmers who would trade the miseries of veritable serfdom for
the fresh ones awaiting them in northern factories. Most
landowners preferred to leave their fields fallow, retreat into the
vastnesses of their rural villas or abandon their country lives
entirely to pout in the familial town or village or city palazzi,
which were less costly to heat and where the servants had
remained loyal. But some nobles did sell their land and for sums
just above a pittance. Neddo bought land.

A small parcel at a time, with lire borrowed from the bank.
He grew tobacco because it was a state-sanctioned crop and,

hence, one for which he would be justly compensated. Profits bought more land, restructured an old farmhouse, sent his sons to school in Perugia. And for all those years, he kept the old peach pit always in his pocket. As soon as he could afford to, Neddo planted peach trees. Flourishing under his care, he planted more of them. And now, in his relative dotage, he has established a ritual event among the *scuole elementare,* the elementary schools in the *comune* of Orvieto. *I Giorni delle Pesche.* The Days of Peaches. When the fruit is ripe, he invites the children, supervised by their teachers, to climb into the trees, to pick the peaches. He is especially fond of the third graders. The nine-year-olds.

Neddo invited us to supper once. And since then for the same supper many times again. Thick, rough-cut hunks of bread and deep white bowls of red wine. That was the menu. Over the years, it's never changed.

That first time we went to sit with him by his fire, he said grace and wished us *buon appetito* and started right in dragging bread through the wine and biting hungrily into the softened pinkish body of it. Every once in a while he'd pick up the bowl, take a long thirsty swallow of the wine, refill the bowl. Cut some more bread. We followed suit. And the more I ate and drank, the hungrier I became. I didn't know if the resonance of communion was intended or intrinsic. Bread and wine. The restoration of the body and blood. Over time I grew to think that this supper served to feed a purely organic hunger in him, as it did in us. He would tell us about how, when he could afford it, he'd bring a basin of mush made of bread softened in red wine out to the barn and spoon it to his mare or his cow, just as he'd seen the midwife spoon it to his wife. Body and blood. To restore a birthing woman, a birthing animal. And as we sat there wetting bread in bowls of wine, I felt stronger, knowing I'd been nourished better than I might be by any other kind of supper.

About Edgardo

Edgardo likes things to go wrong. A grievance between two of his servants. A war in Kosovo. Other peoples' troubles distract him from his own. His own so carefully packed away, dismissed or nearly so. Never inconvenienced by shame – shame being a sentiment belonging to the poor – Edgardo believes he represents the nobility as it exists today in his part of Italy. A self-stationed rampart against the encroachment of the present.

Edgardo says the nobility's sins are wholly acceptable to them, already justified and cleansed *al momento,* in the moment. Their stories and their sins, mostly one and the same, are private, spoken of among themselves around the safe haven of their own tables or behind the heavy brocade curtains of their beds. Stories and sins are passed down like sets of silver. Heirlooms.

He set fire to a peach orchard and lived for a long while in Paris, until his mother was finished with her dying and the rest of the family, with theirs. He is the last *marchese* d'Onofrio and, like the Scrooge of Christmas Future, he knows his passing will be mourned by no one. With nothing to risk, he is quick to hurt before anyone can hurt him.

Be it a shirt or a villa or a platter of oil-glistened roasted sardines, Edgardo calls his vision of beauty *michelangiolesco*. In the style of Michelangelo. At all costs, life must be chic. In the end, chic is all there is. To have dressed well, traveled well, lived well, to have outwitted *i volgari e la loro volgarità,* the vulgar and their vulgarity. A sweep that encompassed, at the point in his life when we met him, almost everyone but Tilde.

Edgardo knows Tilde's story, has known Tilde herself since she came back to live in Orvieto. Since she'd sent her maid to knock on his door one afternoon, bearing a note and a basket of figs. *As one pariah to another, you are welcome to join me for tea on Wednesdays at five. No need to telephone in advance.*

Their Wednesdays broadened to include a Sunday lunch, once in a while. A Saturday *gita* to Rome, a morning on horseback over his meadows and through his woods near Castel Giorgio. But Tilde is too fine a horsewoman for his comfort. More than Edgardo likes to ride, he likes to dress for riding.

And for dinner. In a beaver-lined dressing gown, a beret, and thick felt slippers, Edgardo sits at the table, rings for his servants with a small crystal bell, touches almost nothing of the ashen foods he insists upon for himself, urges upon his guests. His guests, who are mostly far-flung kith in loyal, sacrificial attendance on the last *marchese* of the d'Onofrio. 'Circling birds,' Edgardo calls them. 'They lurk about after dinner, measuring things. Measuring me.'

Miranda had, of course, been correct in her warning that Fernando and I would serve the *marchese* as a fresh curiosity. But he serves equally well for me. Just beyond his swank there is a lonely man, maybe even a good and lonely man, and though there are moments when I don't much like him, he commands my attention. I think he feels small the way people do who can see the end of things, or think they can. He seems always to be laying the way back and forth across his own seas, trying to find where he's gotten lost. Gone wrong. Gone wrong not for others but for himself. He always seems to be waiting, either for his life to begin or, more often, for it to end.

18

We're Going to Live in a Ballroom, Fernando. Isn't That the Most Wonderful Thing You've Ever Heard?

'*Mi senti? Mi senti, Marlena? Abbiamo cominciato e il capo dice che il lavoro potrebbe finire prima di Natale. Venite subito.* Do you hear me? Do you hear me, Marlena? We've begun the work and the foreman says all will be finished before Christmas. Come here quickly.'

I stand in the garden staring at the *telefonino*, calculating the chances that Barlozzo could imitate Samuele's voice so perfectly. Surely this call is some sort of joke. Can a two-year lapse be interrupted without warning? Two years of silence and mold and surrender and borrowed kitchens, relieved only by a farce or two. A silver-wrapped tray of pastries and countless little Umbrian vignettes. *We've begun the work and the foreman says all will be finished before Christmas.* That is what the voice said. Today is June 18. Can it be? Can it be that six months from now we'll be at home in the ballroom?

'Fernando. Samuele called and the work has begun and I could hear machines and pounding and shouting in the background and the crew is working and we have to get there right now.'

He is standing at the top of the stairs, looking at me, saying nothing. He comes toward me, takes me by the shoulders, kisses me hard, too hard, and pulls me behind him out to the garden, out the gate and up the hill. I don't think either of us says a word the whole way until we arrive at number 34 and see the frenzy made flesh.

One crew mounts the struts and braces of an intricate scaffolding, which rises from the courtyard up to the *piano nobile,* while another is laying an improvised floor in the *salone.* A third crew appraises the work of the other two. Samuele and the *geometra* confer in the courtyard, and when the Monaldeschi count sees us, he runs to meet us, wrings our hands in congratulations, pulls us tight to him and squeezes. Singularly alert and with both his high-tops laced and tied, Samuele seems the father of the bride, while the *geometra* might be taken for an undertaker with bad manners, and not a word of small talk precedes his pronouncements and caveats.

'I have ordered all materials and scheduled the crews for double and sometimes triple shifts. I will take you through the space in twenty days, at which time you will be free to measure floors and windows for eventual draperies and furnishings, and then again on November twenty-fifth, at the very latest, when the work will be, essentially, finished. There will be no reason for our communication at any other times but those. For any and all questions that may arise, I will contact Signore Ugolino himself.' With this last he bows deferentially to Samuele. 'Whether or not he chooses to pass along any reports to you shall be strictly his decision.' The *geometra* wishes a good day in our general direction and begins to climb the stairs.

'Signor Brienza,' I say, presuming to hold his sleeve, daring to detain him. 'But I thought we would be participating in the choices for the materials. Flooring, woodwork, doors, windows. What about the bathrooms? What about the kitchen?'

I look about for Fernando, who has engaged Samuele just outside the door, and I understand that he is dividing in the hope of conquering, but I could use some help in here.

'What about the kitchen?' I ask Brienza once again.

'I have chosen a kitchen that will be not only utilitarian but also quite attractive. And with the budget with which I was entrusted, there can be little choice about such things as floors and doors and bathroom fixtures, signora. Standard, no-frills economy. I can assure you that everything will be finished with care and good taste. No one, I repeat, no one has instructed me to inform you or Signore de Blasi, nor to consult with you nor to seek approval from you about anything. My job has been explicitly outlined, and I intend to execute it to the letter. Interference on your part will only lead to delays.

You do realize that this work is miserably behind schedule as it is?'

'Actually, I do realize precisely how miserably behind schedule it is.'

'Then I beg you to refrain from all interruption. *Di nuovo, signora.* Once again, madam.'

'But how can you call my wanting to be part of the decision making about the restructuring of *my own house* an interruption? You can't really think my request unreasonable, can you?'

He pauses. Looks over his shoulder as if to locate Samuele, who is still deep in what seems like playful discourse with Fernando. What can they be talking about while I'm lunging at this dragon?

'Here our intelligence differs, signora. Or could it be some difficulty you are having with the nuances of the Italian language?'

How convenient that an Italian – in all of his treacherous or even mildly roguish dealings with an expatriate – can always pardon himself with the tut-tut claim that the alien couldn't possibly have been expected to grasp the harmonious nuances of Dante's codified language, *poverino.*

'You see, it's all very simple,' he continues, as if to a naughty child. 'This palazzo belongs to the Ubaldini. And Signore Ugolino, there, is their agent. Both the Ubaldini and Signore Ugolino have hired me as *geometra*. In Italy, the title *geometra* signifies the person responsible for planning and overseeing the completion of each and every phase of a designated work. When the work is done, you, *gentile signora*, kind madam, will have the privilege of living here. As tenants of the Ubaldini. Now, is there anything further about these facts that I can help you understand?'

'No, nothing more at all.'

Brienza may look and sound like a beast, but it's suddenly clear that he is a soldier. It's the Monaldeschi count who is in charge here. I excuse myself, turn, and fairly leap upon Samuele.

I repeat my pleas. I repeat them all in a jumble and repeat them again, more calmly and one by one. Samuele waits. Even when I am, at last, quiet, still he waits. Then in a tone somewhere between grave and poisonous, he says there is nothing, nothing at all written in the contract that refers to our being consulted in the matter of materials and fixtures.

'I remember distinctly your saying that we could *participate in the tastemaking of the restructure,*' I push.

'I have no doubt that I said that and less doubt what it was that I *meant* by it, which is that you would be free to furnish the apartment as you wish. Often, after the restructuring of a noble palazzo, the owners rent the space *completemente arredato,* completely furnished, as befits the style of the property. But in your case, the Ubaldini have waived that option and so what I said is true: you will be free, with the approval of the Ubaldini, to bring in the decor and furnishings of your choice. Now that, and nothing more or less, is what was meant by your *participation in the tastemaking of the restructure.*'

'Are you saying that I must seek approval for my furnishings from the Ubaldini? That they will inspect my bed and my chairs to see if they meet with, what, medieval standards? And while you're saying that, are you also saying that I am to remain mute while Signore Brienza selects everything else that will go into my house?'

'*Ah, è qui che Lei si sbaglia.* It's here where you are in error. I think it's the term "my house" that we must reevaluate.'

'Do you accept the term "my money"?'

My left canine protrudes; in a spontaneous, vestigial gesture, I have just bared it to the count.

'Chou-Chou.' This is the first time he has used this intimate address, and it startles me, softens me, just as he knew it would. 'I understand your concern that your deposit should be spent efficiently, but a complete accountability will be presented to you at the end of the work. You will see how each and every one of your lire has been spent.'

'I'd like to *choose* how each lire is spent.'

'That's just not possible. At best, that would be counterproductive. Do you know how many palazzi Brienza has restored for the extended Ubaldini family alone? In Rome, in Naples, here in Orvieto? His judgment is impeccable. And his list of other clients is formidable. This means that we, you, profit not only from his expertise but also from his purchasing power. Brienza has his own warehouses where he stores basic materials, which he has acquired in immense quantities and, thus, at moderate prices. Enough stockpiled floor tiles to repave the Colosseum, for instance. When he receives a commission, he can get to work without the delays caused by gaps between ordering and delivery. He buys quality, if in various degrees, so that, depending upon his budget, he can pull from one stock or another.'

'I imagine he'll pull, as you say, from his low-end stock for our place.'

'Certainly he will not be pulling from his most luxurious materials. Perhaps it's time that we reevalute another point. The major costs of the restructuring of your apartment will be spent on just that – structural work. The subflooring, the re-inforcement of the walls and the load-bearing beams. All the hidden work, if you will, that renders an abandon livable. So you won't *see*, per se, much of your deposit in the form of *pretty things*. The compromise – the adjustment, shall we say? – was shouldered by the Ubaldini. You see, they might have waited for a tenant with a larger budget than yours, a budget that would have permitted their property to be outfitted more grandly. But their generosity, their instinctual affection for you and Fernando led them to disregard that eventuality.'

Each word – its impact and its delivery – feels like the bal-samic caress of a sage. The wisdom, the justice, the practicality of it all is set before me as an offering to an unwashed. I look at Fernando and he's looking back, timidly flashing the thin-lipped trout smile that says, *Let's get out of here now*. I am contrite, but not wholly. A small, final jab.

'So all of it stands to be a surprise for us. We will get to see the results and not the process?'

'Something like that. But I thought you would be so thrilled about the work beginning, about the condensed time frame. The Ubaldini specifically requested that you be able to take possession of the house before Christmas. They are behaving in an exceedingly solicitous manner with you.'

I should have known to be quiet. Next he will remind me that we have been living rent-free for two years. It's time for my submission. The trout smile quivers in fatigue from its long pose. My husband must be out of cigarettes.

I am about to hold out my hand to Samuele when he says, 'I'll tell you what I can try to do. Perhaps, given your *mestiere,* your métier, the Ubaldini might agree to your choosing some elements of the kitchen. The stove you'd prefer, et cetera. Should your choices put Brienza over budget, you would be required to pay the difference in cash. Would you like me to arrange that?'

Rather than giving Samuele my hand, I hug him about the waist. 'Yes, yes, that would be wonderful. Thank you.'

We say our good-byes to Samuele, but instead of starting down the Via del Duomo, Fernando heads through the doors to San Giuseppe, the little chapel across from number 34. I follow him into the cool, rosy emptiness.

'Congratulations. You really are Candide.'

'What are you talking about?' I want to know, stumbling across the kneelers and landing awkwardly in a chair in front of where he is already sitting. I twist my body around to look at him full in the face.

'Do you recall the magnificent farce played by Concetta and Ciro a year and a half ago?'

I don't answer.

'You, *amore mio,* have just stood still for the second act. And whether you know it or not, you just hugged Samuele, thanked him for getting more money out of us. "Should your choices put Brienza over budget, you would be required to pay the difference in cash. Would you like me to arrange that?" With a few lines of dialogue, he convinced you that, from the same font of their usual goodness and generosity, the Ubaldini might be willing to take more of our money. Only to please you, of course. So that you can have the kitchen you desire and who knows what else. I just wish I had foreseen this piece and so could have warned you. *Amore mio,* I'm sorry. I'm sorry for these last two years and for the presence of Brienza the buffoon and, more, for Samuele and his ruling-class elocution. You were nearly flagellant before him. I'm sorry. I'm just so sorry.'

As it will, Fernando's distress changes my own weather. 'But what does it matter? So I'm Candide. Don't worry. I'll take the kitchen Brienza chooses along with everything else. I'll drape and swaddle everything in velvet and silk anyway.'

He wasn't expecting the bravado of a turnabout, but I see he is relieved by it, jumps into the sport.

'I know, and you'll be throwing carpets down and crowding the floors with jugs of weeds and branches, so that even if they were made of dirt the place would be beautiful.'

'The Ubaldini can't stop me from doing that, can they?'

'No, I don't think they can. Nor can they say yea or nay to our personal furnishings.'

'So let's begin. Let's begin looking for furniture. Let's leave Brienza and the crews to their business. Yes, fine, that's what we'll do,' I hear myself say distractedly as we leave San Giuseppe and turn up the Via del Duomo.

But I can't help wondering; have I been besmirched or indulged? I still don't know. Pique and gratitude rub against each other until I ask, 'Please help me understand one last thing. Why would Samuele – or, I should say, the Ubaldini – take the trouble to lead us into temptation about upgrading things in the apartment? After all, the plan – the contracted plan – says that we'll be staying there for a long time. If not forever. Why would they concern themselves with anything beyond the proper reconstruction of the space itself? What would they care about the sort of kitchen we have? Or the height of the woodwork or the hardware on the doors? I think you're wrong about Samuele continuing the farce today.'

'Think again. Do you recall how many times we've asked ourselves how, why Samuele and then the Ubaldini – let's say – *embraced* us as they did? From the first meeting? How they just about took us over, set us up on Via Postierla? Patently seduced us? I think a significant part of our attractiveness to all of them was our history. A couple who met and married late in life; I who retired at forty-nine from a twenty-six-year banking life, you who are an obvious "artist" type, *insolita, spiritosa* – unusual, spirited, as Samuele has said so often of you. With our having lived in Venice for three years, two more in a Tuscan hamlet, and then that we were already searching for a place in Orvieto, we'd hardly have impressed them with our late-middle-aged stability. These facts – among others, I admit – placed us in a perfect light. We were the right candidates. We'd pay for the reconstruction, live in the palazzo until our funds were amortized – that is, if people with our vagabondish ways could stay put for that long. And then we'd be off to the next adventure. Of whatever else they were convinced about us, they sensed we would not be the sort of couple who would climb the stairs at number 34 and stay there until the end. Our end. Or even theirs. So, since they're counting on our sooner-rather-than-later departure from the place, why shouldn't we be encouraged to leave it in as elegant a form as our vanity and our bank account would permit?'

'Right. Straightforward, fourteenth-century speculation. Well, much to their potential and collective chagrin, I say let there be no upgrades. Even though I can hear Barlozzo calling the whole job *squalid,* just as he did when he first saw the stable.'

'The Ubaldini are not the Lucci. There'll be nothing squalid about the work.'

The Ubaldini are not the Lucci, I repeat to myself, and it recalls a thought that helped me get through the early days with Samuele. *His is another kind of device, the shape of which is not crooked but serpentine.*

'Let all of it be now,' Fernando is saying. 'The deposit they asked for was moderate, and so we'll have a moderately lovely apartment. It will be enough.'

Of course it will be enough. And besides, nothing is ever as we think it is. It's either worse or it's better. Or it's different some-how. We're simply not meant to understand any of it. Neither when nor how it is that we're supposed to take a turn at shaping things. And when we're supposed to let things shape themselves. We're not meant to know. These thoughts comfort and I lengthen my stride up the hill until I'm nearly breathless and the morning's news finally reaches my heart. I let go of Fernando's restraining hand and begin to run, turning back to face him and shouting, 'We're going to live in a ballroom, Fernando. Isn't that the most wonderful thing you've ever heard?'

19

Brahms at Eight O'Clock
from Across the Vicolo

A fantasy, a desire, if it remains aloof, can begin to torture. And so, to save oneself, one puts aside the longing. Smudges it over with the next dream. Another conceit. And that is precisely what had happened to us, willy-nilly, over these past two years of waiting for the ballroom. In defense of our tranquillity, we'd put aside the fantasy of living in Palazzo Ubaldini. We'd gone on to 'live well,' as both Barlozzo and Samuele had challenged us to, each in his own way, and despite the once in a while sense of backstroking through a midnight sea more or less toward Portugal, we did live well. And worked well and so gathered in some small progresses, both personal and practical. But what we hadn't done at all, at least not since the first months of the wait had passed, was to prepare ourselves for the fable to come true. For the remote business of it all to appear before us in the form of shiny scaffolding and thirteen Sicilians and Neapolitans in work boots with red wine in water bottles tucked in their tool belts, commanded by a blackguard who stockpiles floor tiles and is called Brienza.

And so we tell ourselves that now, if we are there among the hammering and the cement dust and the Sicilians and the Neopolitans and the red wine and the blackguard, witnessing the smallest transformations of the ruins, we will begin to believe what we'd already begun to disbelieve. That's what we do.

Early on we invited Barlozzo to come see the action, and, less than an hour hence, he was stalking the place, stepping over Brienza as if he were a bundle of two-by-fours, flashing long silvery eyes in princely disdain at the *geometra*'s sputtered warnings that visitors are not permitted on his work site. Barlozzo entertained the crew with stories of his own not-quite-so-ruined-anymore place and hoisted a proffered plastic bottle of breakfast wine with unfeigned gusto.

I felt the duke had come to bless us that day, if not with sainted water and incantations, with the simple goodness of his old lion's heart. And that blessing helped us to, once again, sign on to the fable.

It wasn't long before Miranda and Tilde made a visit together, and I think their entrance into number 34 and their exit as well was duly noted and pondered by our neighbors. And when Edgardo climbed the stairs, his Moravian majordomo in tow, carrying a basket of cheese and fruit, Brienza folded, a little too deeply, into a quick cringing bow.

'*Buongiorno, marchese. Che piacere.* What a pleasure,' he simpered.

That day, for the first time, Brienza asked us how we thought the work was progressing.

Every disparaging vignette starring Italian construction workers hunched over improvised card games staged on construction sites was made a lie by the crew at number 34. They worked as Titans. Dosing wine, singing, shouting, their dialects two dissimilar languages as they called to each other from distant parts of the space with instruction or encouragement. They worked from seven in the morning until seven in the evening, the stint interrupted by a proper lunch downstairs with Franco and two or three sprawls on whatever patches of unencumbered floor could be found for catnaps. One of Brienza's lackeys was always arriving with bottles of icy mineral water – which they mostly poured over their heads or spritzed down their shirts, their gullets being reserved for wine – or, from the shop downstairs, a gigantic tray, just out of the oven, of pizza topped with thin slices of potato and rosemary, or a sack of panini stuffed with mortadella. At the stroke of five, two barmen porting trays of pastries and thirteen cups of espresso mounted the stairs and served the crew royally, and at seven, like boys from school, they ran down the stairs to the rowdy freedoms of their evening. Brienza did take good care of his men.

We learned that he paid them handsomely, too, and that, in the Campanian and Sicilian villages and towns from whence the crew came, the chance to work up north for Il Brienza was considered golden. They told us that the *geometra* wouldn't accept just anyone who applied; he interviewed candidates, asked hard questions, offered each one a two-week trial at hunger wages, and only then, if all the hurdles were jumped to his standards, would a man be offered a job.

'Wouldn't it be simpler for him to hire local workers? Umbrians, Tuscans?' I ask them.

'But we're better craftsmen. Artists. And we're hungry. Most of us have been without work or our fathers have. We know what that feels like,' one of them says for the crew.

He rubs his stomach.

'And twelve hours a day, six or seven days a week? No one accepts those conditions anymore,' says another one.

'But we do,' many of them say almost as one.

There is no embarrassment in this admittance but, rather, a kind of awe at their good fortune.

ONE MORNING WHILE Fernando stays abed, I decide to surprise the crew with breakfast and so arrive at the ballroom at ten minutes before seven, carrying silver-paper-wrapped trays of warm croissants, sweet ricotta tarts, and almond cakes from Scarponi. I am greeted by a woman. Small and plump, she is stepping from the still unfinished but functional downstairs bathroom, an elastic between her lips, her hands busy with the gathering of her black curling hair. She is wearing jeans and a very prim white cotton brassiere.

'*Buongiorno, signora. Mi scusi ma* . . . Excuse me but . . .'

'*Buongiorno, sono Chou-Chou,*' I say, as though the job of identification rests with me.

'*Carmine,*' she shouts. '*Carmine, vieni qua. Subito, Carmine.*'

Who are you and what are you doing in my house gets lost
in my throat, but she's gone back into the bathroom and
slammed the door anyway. I'm about to ask her from the
other side of it, but my question is foiled by one of the crew,
who is rushing into the *salone* from the direction of the
kitchen.

'*Ah, signora, buongiorno.*' He takes the trays from me as though
I were the delivery person he'd been expecting and busies himself finding a place to set them down. I understand he's opted to
play it dumb. I have not learned all the names of the thirteen
men in the work crew.

'*Carmine,*' I venture. 'Your name is Carmine, yes?'

'*Si, si signora, e lei,*' he says, pointing at the bathroom door, '*è
mia moglie. Eleanora, voglio presentarti la signora de Blasi,*' he says
much too loudly.

No sound from Eleanora. Carmine repeats his desire to introduce us. Still no sound from Eleanora. Carmine knocks on the
door with the flat of his formidable hand, telling her something
in a Neapolitan dialect that I cannot understand but that I believe
warns her to come out or he'll break down the door. I wonder
if Eleanora might not be caught without a shirt, if that could be
her problem, and so I slip my sweater over my head, adjust my
thin silk camisole – my nakedness now only minimally less than

Eleanora's – go to the bathroom door and say, *'Eleanora, ti passo una maglia.'*

She opens the door a crack, takes the sweater, and, a moment later, exits flushed and weeping. She hugs me, and I think how easily women can be complicit.

We introduce ourselves again and she begins to tell me that she took the train yesterday from Salerno to Rome and then from Rome to Orvieto, that she missed her husband and wanted to surprise him, that she just didn't want to wait for his bimonthly Saturday-evening-until-Sunday visit.

I had already learned that the crew is lodged in a former monastery (another Brienza stroke of genius, I'd thought), where two or three lay brothers conduct a guesthouse activity. Eleanora explains that she appeared at Carmine's door, accompanied by the lay brother from the reception desk – and then only after he'd inspected her identity card and was convinced of her wifely status. It was just before eleven and Carmine and his three roommates were already sleeping.

'Signora.' Carmine takes up Eleanora's story. 'I couldn't invite my wife into that room. I hope you can understand that. And I didn't have the means to take her to a hotel. I knew that the back door here has a lock that, shall we say, presents small obstacle to entry, so I climbed up the exhaust pipe from the restaurant downstairs, jumped from it to the terrace, and opened the door. Went down the front way, where I'd told Eleanora to wait. We slept in the little room off the kitchen. Eleanora was getting ready to leave when—'

'I understand. Still, you were trespassing. You are trespassing. It's wrong. I have to tell my husband about this. We'll have to inform Brienza. The crew just can't use our home as a hotel.'

'You know that if you tell Brienza, I'll lose my job.'

'And I also know that if I don't tell Brienza, one or another of you is bound to repeat this episode. I'm sorry.'

I hear the other workers on the stairs. Eleanora weeps more plaintively and I want to hug her and help her find the rest of her clothes and invite her to Via Postierla for a proper bath and a good breakfast, but I know this would not be the best way to handle the events. I leave without a good-bye to the couple and greet the workers as they're entering, if a little less playfully than usual.

Even before I arrive in Via Postierla, my emotions cool, so that I present the story to Fernando in a reconciled way. He responds as if to a betrayal. Whereas the strongest emotion that the machinations of the Ubaldini and Samuele have thus far illicited from him has been frustration, this conjugal visit in our pantry causes him to feel violated. I envy Fernando his crystalline perspective, his sturdy barriers between criminal misuse and courtly bluestocking plots.

Our solution is a compromise. We tell Brienza that *someone* entered the apartment through the back door – via the restaurant's exhaust pipe, we think – that we found evidence of an overnight presence in the house. He is, of course, horrified, conducts an inventory, sets immediately to the task of installing a secure door on the back terrace as well as a security system that is linked directly to his phone and to the local *carabinieri* station. At his own expense, he assures us.

Several months later, Carmine would stay behind one evening after the rest of the crew had left. Out on the back terrace he was breaking down emptied cartons, generally tidying up the accummulation of debris. I'd gone out to check on his progress.

'Signora,' he'd asked, 'have you ever been to Napoli in April?'

'Yes, I have. And more than once. It's especially beautiful in the spring. But why do you ask?'

'Eleanora and I want to invite you and Signore Fernando to a baptism. In fact, we want to ask you to be godparents at a baptism.'

'Is it true?' I hold my splayed hands over my stomach.

'Yes, it's true.'

I point over my shoulder in the general direction of the little pantry.

'Yes. We're sure it happened on that night. Your house is blessed, signora. We'd begun to give up hope, you know. I mean, after four years of marriage and . . . Will you tell *il signore*?'

EVERY ONCE IN A WHILE, elegantly dressed men in twos and threes appear at the work site when we're present. Brienza always seems to be expecting them. He greets them nearly as slavishly as he did Edgardo but never introduces them to us. We are wallpaper waiting to be hung. The men observe quietly or ask a polite question of one of the crew. They run their hands over just-seamed walls, tap support beams, generally slink about. Perhaps they are State inspectors. Or potential clients of the *geometra* who've come to see how he works. One day I ask Brienza if this is the case, but all he says in answer is, '*Loro sono gente importante*. They are important people.'

I must ask Samuele when I see him, or Ciro or Concetta as soon as I can reach them. But Samuele is never around, the Ubaldini don't return my calls, and the brief periodic visits from the unknown men continue.

'Does their presence in our house strike you at all as an invasion?' I ask Fernando once as two of them pass slowly from room to room.

'Not really. They are unknown to us but not to Brienza, and while the work is in progress and he's in charge, I will trust him and his eccentric way of operating. When the work is finished and I have the only set of keys, I'll decide who comes and goes. I think that's how it is and how it will be.'

I say nothing, but once again I wonder about the Venetian's canny positioning of people and their deeds on his personal compliance sheets. The presence of unidentified men sniffing through our home at will — albeit in company with Brienza — is calmly placed in the category of *eccentric* behavior. Another quite acceptable piece of the courtly bluestocking plot.

THOUGH WE'VE ACCUMULATED some wonderful old furnishings, both during our days in San Casciano and during the wait for Palazzo Ubaldini, when we sketch out how we'll set up the new rooms, we are reminded of the far greater spaces to fill. Another sofa or two with some comfortable overstuffed chairs, a different dining room table since the one we have will be dwarfed in the depths of the ballroom. Chairs for it. Some good rugs. And for the kitchen, along with whatever else will or will not be in it, we'd like to trade in our falling-apart *madia* – a bread-rising dresser – for a sturdier one. We begin our search with the man next door.

Actually, it's a few meters down Via del Duomo to the *antichità*. But we find little there that interests us among the scant and mostly dainty inventory of gilt-trimmed settees and tea carts arranged under the crystal drips of Austrian chandeliers. The vulcanic-voiced patron, whom we've seen and passed by on the streets and stood next to in one bar or another for two years, sipping countless *espressi* and *aperitivi,* still doesn't recognize us or even greet us, save a thunderous *buongiorno* as we enter his precinct. We tell him, more or less, what we're looking for, tell him, too, that we'll soon be neighbors, as if he didn't already know that. Not even some slim gesture of welcome ripples his cemented posture as he broods in the far corner of the shop, wrestler's arms folded across his chest, feet splayed, eyes half closed. If he had the earth's most wonderful *madia* and priced it at twenty-five thousand lire – thirteen dollars – I would step around it and out the door.

'*Grazie, arrivederci,*' we say, already wincing in preparation for his salutation; but we needn't have bothered, since he says nothing at all.

Another *antichità* sits across the tiny piazza from number 34 and we head there. Comprised of the ground-floor rooms of a Filippeschi palazzo, it's strewn with seventeenth- and eighteenth-century museum pieces. The patron here, costumed like a golf pro in red plaid trousers and pink cashmere pull-over, seems kind, listens to our small litany of desires, says that though he has nothing right now, he will look about for us in his travels, and I think I've failed part one of his client require-ments by asking the price of a lamp that attracts me. Serious, elegant people don't talk about money. Why do I keep forget-ting that? The would-be golf pro tells us about a *magazzino,* a warehouse, situated just over the Lazio border. He says we might take a look there.

Later that same evening we dine at Miranda's, and just as we're finishing, Tilde arrives, sits with us. We ask her if she knows about the warehouse in Lazio and she says she does. Says she'll take us there and, in fact, she'll take us to several other places. She'll take us everywhere.

'Let me do the bargaining,' she warns and finds no quarrel from us.

The hunt is scheduled for the following Saturday, and we're surprised as we walk out from the garden in Via Postierla at the appointed hour to see both Tilde and Edgardo sitting in the back of the *marchese*'s dark green Range Rover. Piotor is at the wheel.

'Tilde wouldn't know a *madia* from a commode,' Edgardo tells us as we settle in.

'And he is simply envious of the fun he knew we'd have without him,' she says as though it's true.

Piotor brakes, as he is directed to do, in front of every barn and *magazzino* up and down the old Viterbo road to Rome. What Tilde doesn't know, Edgardo does, and between them we are admitted inside the rat-perfumed bellies of abandoned farmhouses and the fetid cellars of deconsecrated churches to probe dubious treasures. At last, Edgardo points Piotor in the direction of the village of Torre Alfina, where we stop inside the gates of a medieval hamlet. The *castelluccio* – small castle – the chapel, the farmers' lodgings, the barns and stables are all made of the same sullen gray stone, glossed now in a twilit rain. Its piazza is broad and deep and godforsaken, save for a small black dog howling more in welcome than menace. A tall, slouching figure stands in a doorway that has been cut into the massive portals of the *castelluccio*.

'*Buona sera, bello mio,*' he calls to Edgardo, who calls back, 'Is it the servants' night off?'

'Yes, I gave them all leave at once. Thirty-three years ago.'

The old men laugh and hug each other, look each other in the eye, hug again.

'*Madonnina Santissima,* most holy of little mothers, weren't you two together just last evening?' Tilde asks.

I have never seen this almost tender side of Edgardo, and it both baffles and pleases.

We are invited into a small space with plywood walls that has been outfitted with a folding table, a two-burner cooking plate set over a minuscule refrigerator, a sink where sour pots languish and a faucet drips. The black dog's bed is near the door. We learn that Edgardo's friend Fabio, also born a *marchese*, has constructed this little kitchen and a room beyond it as his living quarters. A space he can, if barely, afford to heat. Having long ago disbursed his liquid wealth, he has lived – since the end of the Second World War, when his farmers and their families left as a group to make new lives as factory workers in the relative luxury of Switzerland – by selling off the contents of the castle. Spoon by spoon, dish by dish. Furniture, silver, china, tapestries and rugs of immense dimensions, a medieval weapons collection. Jewels. A story not unlike that of Beatrice Ubaldini, late matriarch of the ballroom at number 34.

When Fabio goes to fetch some wine, Edgardo tells us, 'While there's still a shred to sell or trade, Fabio will stay right here. Truth is, he'll stay longer than that. The last soldier on the hill.'

'Does he have a family?'

'Two married sons. Both gone off a lifetime ago, just after their mother, Fabio's wife, passed away. There was nothing for them here.'

'Except their father.'

'I don't think they looked at things that way. When they realized that Fabio wasn't going to part with the land or the hamlet, divide the spoils, they went away. They visit, though, or at least Fabio tells me they do. What they don't know is that their father has willed every centimeter of his little realm to the *comune* of

Orvieto. One day this will be a school or a museum. Maybe a *casa di cura,* a home for old people who are alone. Something like that. Anyway, his will is iron-clad and uncontestable. The sons will get nothing. Exactly what they gave. Fabio is stronger than he looks.'

We are here because Edgardo thinks Fabio might have a dining room table for us. But Fabio can't remember the one to which Edgardo refers. Says he never had such a table. Edgardo describes it in greater detail, says it was draped in a fringed tapestry and covered all over with family photos in silver frames.

'Don't you remember that table?'

'Why must I remember it? Find it if you can and I'll sell it to you.'

Of course Edgardo knows the table's precise location and leads us up and up the spiraling stone steps directly to it, still draped in tapestry but without the silver-framed photos. Edgardo pulls back the cloth to reveal a beautiful dark wood table. It is long, somewhat narrow, and set upon great bulbous, curving legs on whose shanks pineapples are carved. *Pineapples were cleaved to the doors of sea captains' houses on Nantucket. Another ancient sign of welcome. The captain has returned from his voyage to the South Seas and, at last, he is at home. He awaits you.* Our ballroom is no longer mythical. We, too, will soon be at home. And here is our dining table, it no longer mythical either. Our harvest grows.

'If it's not too lurid a question, would you kindly ask *il marchese* the price of this table?' I say this to Edgardo while I am looking at Fernando, who looks back at me knowing I'm already composing menus, lighting candles. He nods his agreement. We both know our budget.

'I can tell you what it's worth and then I can tell you what it will cost, the difference between the two ciphers being bound to excite you. My old friend is not greedy. The greater his poverty grows, the less greedy he becomes. He has learned to live well with so little, you see,' Edgardo tells us.

The selling price Edgardo quotes seems unworthy of the table, much too low. Fernando and I conference, refereed by Tilde, and counter the offer with a sum half again as much. When Edgardo begins to protest, I tell him, 'We've also learned to live well with so little.'

Over the next weeks we make the short journey to Torre Alfina again and again and we buy more things from Fabio. Once, a set of six miniature silver spoons bedded in a green velvet box. Once a fourteenth-century *baule,* a bridal chest, rotted here and there but still intact enough. We buy a tall, narrow armoire, the interior and the shelves of which I'll upholster in apricot damask. Lit with an old gilt lamp and beset with crystal, it will be beautiful. Each time we leave him, wedged as he is among his faltering stones, his waning goods, we drive away saddened, always thinking of Barlozzo. *Most all of us abide in ruins, Chou. Our own, the ones we inherit.*

IT'S LATE OCTOBER and twilight flutters in by six. The crew lights the ballroom like a surgery and they work past seven most evenings. The end of their job is very near, and as though they've already gone away, they talk about another place while they work. Somewhere in Terni, I think, or close by it. In a week or so, they'll have forgotten the ballroom.

I come alone to the site in the afternoons now since Fernando has transformed a bedroom in Via Postierla into a workshop where he is restoring a dozen mismatched and wonderful old chairs, which will go around the table with the pineapple legs. In line after the chairs there are a pair of nineteenth-century country French dressers, whose oak surfaces he will reveal from under layer upon desecrating layer of white enamel. Leaving him among his oils and brushes, I arrive at the ballroom at five, when the barmen and the coffee and the pastries do, and then putter about, sketching, writing, sometimes following small commands for this and that. I wait for the crew to finish, see them out as though they were my guests.

'*Ciao, ragazzi. Grazie di tutto e buona serata. Presto a letto, eh? Ci vediamo domani.* Bye, kids. Thank you for everything and good evening. Get to bed early. We'll see you tomorrow.'

I like the quiet after their boyish noise. They've turned out most of the lights, left me in the shadows of a single bulb caged inside a metal grid, clipped to a painter's scaffold. I kill it, too. Outside, hung on the wall of the palazzo across Vicolo Signorelli, an iron lantern spills amber light on the cobbled street and yellow mists of it invade the ballroom. I open the terrace doors wide to the night, to the breezes, sometimes bold. I light a candle and carry it into the small vault-ceilinged room just off the *salone* that will be my office. Slowly and only partway, I open the shutters of its one window, then unhinge the window itself, hoping he'll be there. The man who lives in the apartment across the *vicolo*. His window looks directly into mine. A violinist who plays each evening; I find myself waiting for his music. Perhaps for him. Standing before his uncurtained, opened window in a nearly bare room, an old floor lamp with a faded green *abajour* behind him, he plays Brahms and Bach and Paganini. Splendidly he plays, magnificently sometimes, thick, lank hair falling over tightly closed eyes, a black crust of a beard about his broad pale face. Muffled in the dark of my little room, I am his unseen audience. He, his music, his bravura have become my end-of-the-day cure, a balm all the more consoling for its being private. *For most of us, it is exquisite to conceal. A lover; a bank account; a thought, recurring, flickering; a single after-noon sitting at a white wicker table, midst the languorous dancing of figs, pendulous as milky breasts. Another black skirt.* Brahms at eight o'clock from across the *vicolo*. Just for me.

Among his repertoire, how I wish there was a waltz. I wander back into the *salone* with my candle, settle myself among the debris. Pollyanna marooned, paint-scented tarps are my pillow. I close my eyes, too, all the better to see this room as it once might have been. Rose marble floors and blue-silk walls. And perhaps to introduce myself to the good Ubaldini ghosts. Surely one cannot inhabit a five-centuries-old space, go rum-maging about the allure of it, the taint of it, and not be humbled before it. Is that why I feel so small here? Another wispy ghost come to take her turn before she sleeps. An old house is a churchyard. I listen to the Brahms and I want to know, how was this place? And how was she?

Black hair massed, caught above the white shaft of her neck, which seems hardly made of flesh at all but some Venus fragment, retrieved, refastened to hard adolescent shoulders above a velvet gown the citrine color of a tiger's eyes. And he? What was he like? Breaking away from his mates in the far corner, he advances toward her. Draping the taut red stuff of his breeches, his sword chinks against its chain as he strides. They dance together in this room. Plotting small evils and expecting joy, they fall in love. Their magic lasts as long as a waltz. I think of Orfeo. *I preferred one waltz with a beauty to a lifetime with someone less rare.* Is love confined mostly to a waltz? Or a kiss? Miranda's kiss. *The first time he kissed me and I kissed him back, that was everything. That longing, that sense that you could curl up and die, smiling, coiled up inside him. You can tell love by a single kiss. I'm sure of that.* A waltz. A kiss. A life. Why do we ask for more? Why do we insist there *is* more? How I wish he'd play a waltz. The bells strike half eight and I spring to my feet. My consort is always on time. He's on the stairs, come to fetch me, to take me down to Franco's for supper, or maybe he's brought the car around so we'll go to Miranda's. His perfume precedes him. A Venetian man bent on a rendezvous.

'*Ciao, bello,*' I greet him.

His kiss is hard.

'Have you been crying?'

'Not very much. Mostly I've been waltzing.'

277

I don't tell him about Brahms at eight o'clock from across the *vicolo* just for me. Nor about her in the citrine-colored velvet nor him with the chinking sword. Nor about the good ghosts nor about how small I feel. I don't tell him. Not now. Not yet.

IT'S THE FIRST WEEK in November and the crew begins hauling away their ladders and buckets and makeshift tables. Generators, saws. Their work is done. Two years plus a few months later than projected, but it's done. *Time has a less perishable quality in Italy. Or a more perishable one.*

We shake hands and hug and thank each other and they're gone. Only Carmine lingers, tells us he'll keep in touch, call when the baby is born. He presents me with a small box of biscotti from Scaturchio, the pastry shop I'd once told him was my favorite in Napoli.

We set to the sweeping and scrubbing of what seem like acres of terra-cotta tiles and I consider Barlozzo's theory about the futility of washing floors. We dust the new white walls in preparation for the painters whose scaffolds and tarps had been delivered weeks ago, with the promise that they'd begin their work 'in a day or so.' We've collected sample tins of several shades of red from Angelo Bruzzi down on the *corso,* and Fernando brushes a meter-wide swath of each one on the longest wall. Once we've seen the colors in both morning and afternoon light, we'll choose.

When we return to the ballroom that next morning, Brienza is there in company with a duet of elegantly dressed strangers.

I think they are men who've been here before, but I truly can't recall. We enter, exchange good mornings. I sense an opportunity.

'I don't think we've officially met. I'm Marlena de Blasi, and this is my husband, Fernando.'

Brienza steps on me, 'There will be no red walls in an Ubaldini palazzo.'

He has moved to stand in front of the swaths of red paint, pointing to them, as a teacher to an equation on a blackboard. The gentlemen say nothing, look over our heads, away from the dread red.

'And what color would you prefer that I paint the walls of my apartment?' Fernando asks one of the men, stepping very close to him.

The man points his chin higher, mutters something to Brienza, who attempts his rescue from the looming Venetian.

'We are only guiding you away from abusive decisions that will corrupt the dignity of an historic palazzo,' Brienza defends.

'I neither need nor accept your guidance. In fact, I find this visit inappropriate, Signore Brienza. And as civil comportment dictates, I would include the names of your friends in my address, had I been introduced to them.' Fernando steps a centimeter closer to the man he's stalked and whose chin quivers now with the strain of its northern pitch. 'Since I have not been informed of the identity of these men, I can only term them trespassers. Interlopers whom I will ask to leave my home.'

'I am an Ubaldini and you will not ask me to leave my own palazzo,' the man howls, chin still pointed upward.

I wonder if this signifies a duel.

'The truth is, Signor Ubaldini, that I will, indeed, ask you to leave my home. The premises on which I have contracted to live. The same premises for which I have paid to restructure. And the same premises for which I will choose the color of the walls. Good day.' Fernando walks to the door, opens it wide.

I guess the duel is off.

PART THREE

In Via del Duomo

20

Where I Come From,
We Invite Our Neighbors
and Friends to Supper

*T*he red walls are beautiful. Red like the seeds of a ripe pome-
granate. Red like the underside of a tea rose. The other
rooms downstairs are painted in variations of it. Faded, paler.
Run through with cream. The walls in all the upstairs rooms
have been washed in a parched old ocher.

With Samuele's help, we've arranged to have our things
brought around from the *magazzino* on the last Saturday of
November. Meanwhile, the two French dressers, restored to
their original glory, sit on either side of the great granite hearth.
I've dressed the long terrace doors in layers of satin – apricot
and melon and peach – each drape a different length, bordered
and hemmed with silky fringes from Valmar in Florence. And
for days now, Signore Carlì and his son have been plumping and
stitching and tacking and stapling right here in the *salone*,

transforming sofas and armchairs, side chairs, a chaise longue with meters and meters of damask and moiré we'd found in a warehouse called Tessil Toscana, just off the *autostrada* near Val di Chiana. While the Carlì work, I do, too, upholstering the chairs that Fernando has refinished with the last of my treasured lengths of Venetian stuff from Rubelli and Bevilacqua. Just as the chairs themselves are all different, so are their cushions. Ferociously thrifty, the Carlì show me how to use every size and shape of scrap fabric to line drawers and the interiors of cabinets and armoires. I don't tell them I'd been saving a piece here and there to sew a skirt, a jacket. An undiscovered bolt of peach damask I hide from them in the bridal chest we bought from Fabio.

I run a soft cloth over the already cleaned and oiled table with the pineapple legs, place the chairs around it. Once again I take stock. The ballroom is no longer mythical, nor is the dining table nor are the chairs. All that remains to complete the journey of the myth to substance is to choose a date, invite our guests. And cook. I imagine who will sit where. I move Barlozzo farther from Miranda and closer to Orfeo, place Tilde next to Luca and sit Neddo on my right, Edgardo on Fernando's right. *You can't put people from here at the same table with people from town. You just can't. Not one of them would consent to such a thing.* There's time to get it right.

OUR BELONGINGS ARE transferred from the *magazzino* to Via del Duomo in the single journey of a not-so-large black truck, from whose bed and cab five men descend, unloading, shouldering, porting things up to the ballroom. Fernando guides them to the correct placement of the carefully marked boxes as well as the furniture. In less than an hour the five men are shaking my husband's hand, wishing us well, and the efficiency of the event is so extreme as to make it seem rude.

We are at home. Every stick and spoon in our life's inventory is in the same place. In the same place where we are, too. Without having decided, we go automatically up the dark, narrow stairs to our bedroom, begin our work there. Fernando bolts the yellow wooden bed together, hangs the heavy red-and-gold curtains from the wrought iron frame of the *baldacchino,* rolls the spring and mattress into place, and we heave ourselves onto it, limbs sprawled in triumph. *We're home.* I set about with the linens, and in my heart's eye I see Florí snapping these same burgundy sheets on our bed that first morning in San Casciano. I arrange the room, if in a temporary way, lay down carpets, fill the armoires with our clothes, set up lamps, and shove whatever remains in boxes against the wall. I need to set up the kitchen.

Miranda had offered to help and Tilde, too, but I'd refused, saying all I have is time. I know they'll be here anyway; at least I know that Miranda will, and I find myself listening for her on the stairs.

Brienza's non-upgraded kitchen includes quite wonderful appliances, all of which were delivered and installed a few days ago. Duly scrubbed and polished, they are lined up along one wall. But these were the extent of his offering. No cabinets, no work spaces, nothing else at all. He'd shown us his floor plan weeks ago – assuming we'd opt to complete the kitchen through him at our expense. According to Fernando. But all we said was, 'How lovely. That's just fine.' We then went about measuring the remaining spaces, remeasuring them, calling on a local carpenter who doesn't so much build furniture as dismantle old pieces and refashion them according to his clients' needs. He liked the dimensions of the kitchen, the soaring ceiling, even the murky light from the single small window cut high on the north wall. He showed us some richly grained cherry from a four-meter-long armoire he'd acquired from the sacristy of a deconsecrated church in Montepulciano and suggested two waist-high pantries and a broad, tall cupboard and we said yes. The carpenter took us to a *marmista* down by the train station who, once he heard our story, said it was *rosso di Verona,* the pink-red marble excavated in the hills near Verona, that we needed over the two pantries to form a work surface near the stove and sink, and another slab of it to place over a center table where I could make bread and pasta and pastries and where, when scrubbed and covered, we could dine sometimes. I liked the idea of kneading bread where we'd later sit to eat it. Both artisans gave clear estimates for the cost of materials and labor and reasonable dates of consignment, all of which were honored.

Meanwhile Fernando had constructed a simple frame with three crossbars from lengths of old wood, sunk butcher's hooks of varying sizes into it, and hung it above the sink – a magnificent pot and utensil rack. I unpack the copper, scrub and rinse and dry and arrange. I do the same with every whisk and spoon and sauté pan and the kitchen is wonderful. I go every now and then to peek into the dining room. To look at the table and the chairs.

'What doesn't get finished today might get finished tomorrow,' Fernando says, gray with fatigue.

We bathe and dress and walk the few meters up to Piazza del Duomo, step down into the tiny Cantina Foresi and call for a bottle of Sauvignon Blanc from Castello della Sala. We say we've no appetite for supper, that the bed sounds more inviting than the table this evening, that we'll go to Franco for a big, long lunch tomorrow. We share the Sauvignon with our postman, who's come in to choose a wine for his supper. And with a friend of his who stops by for an *aperitivo*. Buttoning our jackets against the wind, we walk back down the Via del Duomo, where Miranda is waiting at the door of number 34. A cardboard box covered with a white cloth sits on the step, and she's deep in conversation with Barlozzo.

'Where have you two been?' she asks like a mother superior.

'I thought you wouldn't come – I mean I knew you would – but it had gotten so late and . . .' I speak to Miranda while I'm hugging Barlozzo, and then I'm hugging her while I ask him, 'Why didn't you call so we'd have been here to greet you?'

I'm so happy to see these two people and suddenly I feel hungry rather than tired, starving, really, as Fernando picks up the white-cloth-covered box and carries it inside and up the stairs and Barlozzo slings a plastic shopping bag full of wine bottles over his shoulder and I think this means we're going to dine in this evening.

'Who's cooking at your place, tonight?' I ask Miranda.

'Everything's under control. Just made stew and soup, and the boys can handle *bruschette e insalata*. I wouldn't have missed this for the world,' she says as I open the door to the clutter of the ballroom.

Though I go through the motions of showing them about, take in their enthusiasm as best I can, my mind is occupied with the single thought that I could never have arranged for a house-warming lovelier than this one will be with the goddess and the duke.

Miranda begins unpacking the box she brought, pulling out small terra-cotta dishes of this and that, a pot of soup tied up in a dish towel, another one cradling a roasted rabbit stuffed with sausage and wild savory. She's bossing everyone, telling me to set the kitchen table with the silver and linens she's brought herself, sliding a corkscrew across the table to Fernando, pushing Barlozzo down into a chair as if she was trying to drown him in a pool. She apologizes and tut-tuts over what she fears are her meager offerings for the four of us as the buzzer sounds.

I open the door to Edgardo. And to two large palms planted in magnificent blue-and-white porcelain pots, behind which I can barely discern Piotor.

'We were here earlier and were going to leave these by the door, but I really did want to see how the table looks and . . .'

We're inside the *salone,* Piotor dragging the palms, Edgardo directing his path among the boxes and the sofas and chairs, Fernando coming to greet them, Barlozzo leaning against the frame of the kitchen door, hands in his pockets.

'Marchese d'Onofrio, voglio presentarvi a Gilberto Barlozzo,' I say, taking Barlozzo by the hand and extending my other one to Edgardo. I'd only just stopped myself from introducing Barlozzo by our nickname for him: the Duke, *il duca,* which is one grade higher on the title scale than *il marchese.* It could have been grand. I present Piotor to Barlozzo, and he seems to shake his hand with a bit more verve than he did Edgardo's. Seeing Barlozzo and Edgardo next to each other is breathtaking. They could be kinsmen. The truth is, they could be twins. Separated at birth, perhaps, and certainly having taken up with different tailors, yet their height and width are echoes, a pair of exotic long-stemmed, white-haired, black-eyed birds hung loosely in human costume. Even they, themselves notice.

Miranda comes out from the kitchen. Her audacious self checked, she nods her head toward Edgardo. *'Buona sera, marchese.'*

They merit no introduction, Miranda-of-the-Bosoms and *il marchese* d'Onofrio, she having cooked his supper and washed his noble underwear in one or another of their long-ago lives.

Edgardo, not extending his hand as he might have to her, wishes her a good evening in return. There is silence in the ballroom. I say I'll just set two more places around the kitchen table, but Edgardo is busy dismissing Piotor, telling him to wait downstairs, saying that he'll be along shortly.

Edgardo turns back to me. 'No, no but thank you, my dear, I'm expected to dine at home. I just wanted to take a look at things in situ, as it were, and to wish you both well. And be warned, I shall expect you to begin thinking about new draperies for my *salone*. You do have a good eye, flagrantly rococo.'

Miranda is back in the kitchen and – do I hear an irritated banging of pot covers? And a stage-whispering of '*flagrantly rococo*'? The buzzer sounds.

Tilde approaches, looking like an old, skinny, glittering child with filched diamond pendants in her ears, her mum's lynx swishing over the ancient stairs. I flash immediately to Katherine, the Englishwoman who'd disdained the Orvietana she'd once seen at the market. *Imagine a woman in lynx to her ankles asking for* qualcosa in omaggio, *something for free?* Of course the woman in lynx was Tilde. If only dear Katherine had had an inkling of Tilde's generosity with her neighbors. I pull her inside, hug the lynx and the velvet-sacked bottle she holds to her chest, my grasp never quite finding its way to either flesh or bone. I introduce her to Barlozzo, with whom she instantly strikes up a delicious flirt.

'It must be a hundred years that I've waited to meet you. Chou's right: you are the image of Gary Cooper. Come here and sit with me so I can look at you.'

Thus far ignored by Tilde, a stung Edgardo steps, blusteringly, between them to take the lynx. Tilde is on.

Without breaking stride, she has entered, sensed distress, disarmed it. She sashays into the kitchen and wraps her arms about Miranda while both the exotic birds watch from their perches in the *salone,* beaks wide open. Miranda, having missed not a beat of the scene, is laughing her church-bell laugh, which sets Tilde to laughing as she pulls the filter off a Gauloise, lights it from the gas burner, and they both set me to laughing and so the three men begin laughing, too.

'You are a hussy, Tilde,' says Miranda.

'I am that. Always have been.'

Surely Barlozzo has never seen or heard a woman quite like Tilde. Most of us haven't. In her wake, he is a half-ripe boy, a captive regressed to puerility, his long hands furtive about the buttons on his shirt, about his ears. Miranda's laugh has reached the teary stage, and she dabs at her eyes with a dish towel. The buzzer rings. Fernando opens the door to Neddo.

His distinctive shrill announces him to Miranda and Tilde and me, and all our laughing stops. He carries an armload of wood into the *salone*. Edgardo and Neddo have not been – knowingly, willfully – within a kilometer of each other in over sixty years. Since that morning in the peach orchard.

Miranda looks scoldingly at me, as if I've created this encounter, which I suppose I have by the very nature of my knowing both of these men, counting both of them my friends. Miranda is about to leap to Neddo's defense, to turn him

291

around, I think, and march him back down the stairs, safe away from his old foe, but it's still Tilde's night.

'*Neddo, amore mio,*' she says, hugging the unsuspecting little man about the neck, above his bundled wood, a man with whom, heretofore, she'd only shaken hands.

Neddo beams. Places the wood by the hearth. The exotic birds, each for his own reason, beam not at all.

'*Vieni, Neddo, vieni a vedere chi cé*. Come, come see who's here.'

Neddo has already seen. He allows Tilde to steer him toward Edgardo and Barlozzo. A Puckish imp he seems, looking up at the great, tall birds. The silence is long, and Barlozzo – privy to the history – knows it's not for him to break. It's Neddo who begins, falters. Recoups.

He says, 'If I have to look upon you one more time in my life, I say, Madonnina, thank you for letting it happen here. You've grown old, Signore Edgardo. You've grown very old. I guess when I thought of you during all these years, I always thought of you as the sixteen-year-old bastard you once were.'

Edgardo takes in a long breath.

'I suppose if I'd known you as you are, as you've become,' Neddo continues, 'I would have felt sorry for you. Fact is, though, I truly have felt sorry for you, if only once in a while between long stretches of despising you. You see, what I *did* know about you, even if I didn't know how decrepit you'd become, was that your heart would never change. Nor the state of your soul. No one changes, least of all a villain like you,

Signore Edgardo. That's why I feel sorry for you, having to live inside that black heart of yours.'

'This is neither the time nor the place for our reunion, Neddo. I might have someday died perfectly content never to have seen you again either, but since the Fates were to deny me that pleasure, there is a discourse I would choose to have with you. Privately, of course. Shall we go down to have a smoke, make a plan to meet?' Edgardo says all of this very quietly.

'How can I be sure you won't set fire to me, Signore Edgardo?'

It's become Neddo's night. Miranda is white with fear, motionless in the kitchen doorway, and Tilde, the hussy in her tamed, stands next to her. Barlozzo and Fernando fiddle with the firewood, as they're wont to do. I pace, get as far as the hearth and, reeling, back myself down into the safekeeping of a chair.

Puck and the *marchese* are heading for the door when Edgardo turns back, takes all the rest of us deliberately into his gaze. 'In honor of Chou and Fernando's much-anticipated move to this wonderful place and, now, in honor of my unexpected reconciliation with my old friend Neddo, I, with your kind and collective permission, intend to take a table for us downstairs, where we can celebrate these two events. I'm sure Piotor will join us.'

'Noblesse oblige.' Barlozzo says this very quietly as the door closes upon Neddo and Edgardo.

No one else speaks. Tilde, her diamond pendants swinging

hard, wraps the supper Miranda brought and places it in the refrigerator along with her gift of Piper-Heidsieck, unsheathed from its velvet sack. Miranda sits at the kitchen table, watches Tilde at work. She stands, then, in the doorway to the kitchen saying, 'Won't you go up to get ready, Chou?' As she speaks, she looks down at her hands as though she is just discovering them. Fernando and Barlozzo are on the terrace smoking, and I think she wants to speak to Tilde privately. I oblige. As I pass her, she reaches her arms out to me.

I climb the stairs to our bedroom, change my skirt, step into some pretty shoes. I take down my braids, brush my hair, head down. *It all worked out, didn't it?* I ask myself, as though I need my own defense. But against what? I didn't pluck a forbidden peach, nor did I burn down the peach orchard from which it came. Furthermore, I did not contrive to put those two men together here this evening and it's all beginning to seem biblical, or is it just Umbrian? Red lips tonight. Red like my walls. Opium.

'I'm on my way,' I call downstairs, but only Fernando has waited for me.

He's cracked the Piper-Heidsieck, pours it into two Bohemian crystal flutes, big as flower vases. So smug and unwieldy, the glasses want dexterous tipping into the maw lest the wine become a chest rub, so we use them only in moments distinguished by rapture or grievance. He's turned out the lights and we sit at a small tea table set before the terrace doors, the lantern in the alleyway throwing a yellow haze, making velvet creases on the polished stones of the floor, and I already understand what the big Bohemian flutes signify tonight.

'I just wanted us to have a few moments alone before we go down. There's no rush. By the time they get settled, look at the menu . . . Miranda and Tilde went for a walk, said they'd meet us all downstairs later. Barlozzo is staying close by the other two should the need arise for an intercessor.'

'Do I have something to be sorry for in all this?'

'No. No, of course not. It's only that they, all of them save Barlozzo of course, have been part of each other's life – up close or far away and in one guise or another – for a very long time. And I think what happened here, what, perchance, happened here this evening was a *private* thing. A thing that would have happened far more justly without the presence of strangers. Without you and me and Barlozzo looking on. I don't know whether their meeting will turn out to be prodigious or not. Barlozzo was right about noblesse oblige. Edgardo, quite valiantly, tried to and is still trying to save the evening and maybe much more than that, but still I doubt any of them are comfortable. Oh, perhaps Tilde is. Her character can bear more drama than most others. But even she is clearly distressed for her friends. I guess what I wanted to say to you, what I wanted to ask you before we go down, is to please – not tonight, not ever, perhaps – raise the question of this dinner of yours. This dinner party you'd like to have here with all of them along with who knows what others. Miranda told me you want to invite Orfeo and Luca as well as Beniamina and Magda, is it? The two

grande-dame terrors of Via Malabranca. Darling, help me understand why you are choosing to claim ignorance of what you know
are ancient, sacred cultural and social boundaries. Could you
really expect those jeweled, cane-wielding, hundred-year-old
patricians to sit down to dinner with a shepherd? Or, for that
matter, for a shepherd to sit down with them? I'm tempted
to ask, *How dare you, Chou?* Miranda has told you in her own
undeniably direct way that you are being presumptuous. Out of
line. Impertinent. Disrespectful of how people do things here. I
have to agree.'

'Is there any defect of mine either one of you might have
missed?'

'Vanity, perhaps. No, let me call it immodesty. Your very
selfish desires are at work here. Your needs and wants. Oh, your
generosity is part of it all, too, but you could implement generosity in many ways apart from suggesting, insisting that, along
with a couple of shepherds just for spice, an estranged group of
people, related by history and pain and not very much joy, come
to sit around your table together to be, I don't know, is it *healed*?
Is that the right term? You seem to be suffering from some com-
pulsive, vainglorious *Babette's Feast* dream. You are not Babette
and our friends are not little mean-spirited Swedes whom you
can bring to tears and harmony over a pot of turtle soup.'

'They were Norwegians. And I have *insisted* upon nothing.
I've yet to make a single invitation. And if I do, no one must, per-
force, be obedient to it. Anyone who wishes to refuse can do so.
Will do so. It's supper I'm talking about, Fernando, not a royal

edict to attend a hanging. I don't *see* the cultural boundaries that horrify you and Miranda. They are not my cultural barriers. That's one of the benefits of being an outlander. A fresh, unchained outlander. An outlander who carried her own cultural and social attitudes from across the sea. Even if she's had precious little chance to practice them in half a decade. Where I come from, we invite our neighbors and friends to supper. And inviting my neighbors and friends to supper is all I had in mind.'

'Will you forget the idea of the dinner, Chou?'

If I did not understand before, I know now that I am a social adolescent plowing through the lavish rage and the epic silences of these Latins. A New World pup, unlicked and gnawing at the heels of the ancients. My husband knows that my silence is surrender. I resist when he tries to take me in his arms. Put my fists up to my chest. He kisses me, but I don't kiss him back.

21

Black Ties and Pretty Dresses

*L*ife in the Via del Duomo is hardly new to us, what with our having both frolicked and stumped up and down the narrow parish of it for more than two years. And, having witnessed – day by day, nail by nail, and stud by stud – the rebirth of the formerly abandoned ballroom in Palazzo Ubaldini, neither is *it* unfamiliar. Yet having been here and *being* here are hardly the same.

Where we once drifted in and out, always on our way to somewhere else, now we wake up to it, a former lover we finally married. Taking in the imperishable rhythms of the neighborhood, we watch for, wait for each small juncture in a day and an evening, perhaps fit ourselves into one or another of them, or take pleasure in them from an ever shorter and shorter distance. Like trying to step in with a marching band, we – more

I – use the wrong foot before using the right foot but, soon enough, we find our place.

The grocer downstairs, Giovanni, is the first person we greet of a morning. We open the doors onto the *via* just after eight and find him unloading newborn bread from a wooden box attached to his *moto*. Unwrapped and piled haphazardly like stones, he's fetched the bread from the baker in Piazza Scalza. He holds out a hand to us, palm up, and when we take it, say good morning, the rough hard flesh of it is warm from his handling of the bread and I think this must be the most splendid way to begin a day.

In perpetual sartorial splendor, a linen-wrapped Franco sweeps his steps, drenches the cobbles in sudsy water, directs the arrivals and departures of delivery wagons and small trucks with the verve of a London bobby, each one come with some treasure for him or Giovanni or Emilio, whose shop down the *via* is stacked to its rafters with handmade wild boar sausages and artisinal cheeses and jugs and tins of Umbria's most prized extra virgin oil, pressed from the fruit of his own ancestral trees. Raffaello, the tobacconist, sweeps his cobbles, too, and when we stop to greet him he pulls out from his sweater pocket Fernando's package of cigarettes, mumbles that the Venetian should pay him some other time, turns then to help Giovanni unload milk and butter. The goldsmith, whose minuscule laboratory-cum-*bottega* is set between the tobacconist's and Franco's, always saunters onto the scene at this point. He is Alessandro, with curly brown hair caught in a ponytail, a woolen cap pulled low over smiling eyes, and he, like Giovanni, shakes hands with each of us, wishes us a good day, turns back to unlatch the door to his bejeweled kingdom. All the players are now assembled. By half eight, a busload of Germans or Spaniards or Americans is haunting the ceramics shops, and children, their pale blue aprons flapping out from under their jackets, scream their way to the school. And even though it's December, a tribe of local elders collects, shake hands and kiss and hug each other, seat themselves, faces to the sun, on the benches placed for their particular comfort along the thirteenth-century walls of the chapel across the way. Like a Sunday-morning minister, Giovanni walks the line of bundled, booted old children, shaking each one's hand, wishing them a good morning.

'*Ringraziamo Dio per un altro giorno, ragazzi,*' he shouts, looking up at the sky. Let's thank God for another day, kids.

The truth is that Franco, Giovanni, Emilio, and Raffaello, each of whom has his place of business within fifteen meters of one another in Via del Duomo, were all born in the same year and raised within these same intimate environs. The four have gone through school together, shared childhood, coming-of-age, courting, marriage, the births of their children, the deaths of their parents, and now, at sixty, they coexist in a brotherhood of prickliness and affection, of temperate chivalry, which seems not to preclude periodic machinations and vendettas.

An hour later, after a stroll and a cappuccino, we are back

upstairs to tend to our own work. We light a fire in the *salone,* open the terrace doors to the commotion of the nine o'clock bells and to the sopranos who, up in the practice rooms of the Palazzo di Sette, fling their young voices to high E. Like sun piercing the fog.

Though we'd never admit to it, both of us fuss about with some contrived job that keeps us near the terrace doors. What we're really doing is waiting for the spectacle of the baskets.

To persons living on the upper floors of the palazzi of the Via del Duomo, the squeeze of bicycle horns announces the delivery of the post or of shoes — newly soled and shined and wrapped in brown paper tied with a string – or of chops or cheese or an ounce of crushed fennel flowers, forgotten yesterday afternoon at Gli Svizzeri and necessary for this morning's veal stew. There is the shuffling of feet then, old or young, the unfastening of shutters, the letting down of baskets on ropes to hold the goods. *Ecco fatto,* there, I've done it, they say. Pulleys screech as the baskets ascend and the postman or the shoemaker's boy – standing back, eyes upward, cheering on the voyage of the goods until they reach safe hands – returns to his bicycle, quietly awed, I always think, as though he'd *seen* that cow jump over the moon. '*Buongiorno, buona giornata, grazie mille.* Good day, a good day to you, and a thousand thanks,' all of them say like a te Deum.

Only days of this new residential life in Via del Duomo pass before I begin to fear for it. I like it so well that I want it to last. I want it to stay the same. Joy – like beauty, like love, like a flower — is partly made of dread, changing, dying even as it blooms. And so, early on I begin to wonder if, when I look out onto the Vicolo Signorelli the next morning, it will be gone. How can I be sure that Franco and Giovanni and Emilio and Raffaello and Alessandro will be going about their work? Will Giovanni's hands be warm from unloading the new bread? Could it be that the squeaking of the pulley baskets and the shouting of all the players were figments, lustrous, vanishing? Chroniclers, charmed by a place, will muse over one or another of its inexorable passages, caused by nature or made by man. And they are right to do so. *That* was then, and so *this* cannot be. Somewhere about 40 B.C., Horace wrote, grievingly, about the sour taste of the wild leeks — once sweet as hyacinth bulbs — that grew on the steeps of his Lucanian village. And he liked neither the way in which Marcellus's tomb was being cared for nor the strange tilt of the headdresses that the younger village women had taken to. He'd been gone a year.

WE WORK LONG and hard over the next days, affectionately disregarding what might not have been our first choices in the refurbishing of the ballroom. Hollow doors, scanty woodwork, factory-made floor tiles — about all these and more we throw up our hands, position another good lamp beside a plump chair, or pull a set of delicate Nippon plates farther forward on the second shelf of the lighted armoire. Just as we said it would be, the ballroom is lovely enough. And to calm the atavistic hungers of gypsies newly encamped, one or the other of us performs swift forays for midmorning *cappuccini,* a pastry, maybe two. Two, maybe three cuts of white pizza wrapped in thick gray paper. Galumphing slowly up the stairs when there's a lull in his own traffic, Giovanni carries lunch to us. Ruffles of mortadella or *salame* showing out from thick trenchers of bread, a bottle of Rubesco, uncorked, two paper cups upside down over it since we are, in a real way and by choice, only taking shelter up in the ballroom. Or auditioning for the parts of house patrons. We nap on the rugs as though we have no beds and tell ourselves that if we yield to boudoir afternoons and to shopping and cooking and sitting down at table, all else will fall beyond the pale. We stay more than a week in that interlude between having moved into but not yet having begun to *live* in the ballroom. So good have we become at waiting.

WHEN I THINK about the events of our first evening in the ballroom – the grand convergence between Neddo and Edgardo; Neddo's lunge; Edgardo's knightly move – I feel chastened, an oaf desiring to atone, and yet, for what sins? I neither caused their plight nor schemed their encounter. Fernando and I never talk about that evening nor does Edgardo when he stops by around twilight, pulling tins of Russian tea from the deep pockets of his voluminous coat or handmade chocolates he's ordered from Gilli in Florence. I whip eggs and cream and brandy with black sugar, carry glass cups of it for us to sip by the fire, and he says he loves it and I know he also means that he is as content to be quiet with us as we are to be with him.

Nor does Barlozzo talk about the first night's events when he arrives at eight or so, insinuating himself between us and our rags and polishes and goading us to get to work cleaning our unkempt selves, to get ready for supper, damn you. He himself is fairly luminous these evenings, hair parted in the middle and smelling like a barber shop, clean, ironed shirt tucked into thick blue-black wool trousers I'd not seen before. The new ritual is that he drives us to Miranda's and that Tilde is already there waiting for us and that we four dine together. Miranda joins us as soon as she can. When Orfeo and Luca are about, they pull up chairs, unwrap their cheese, and we all drink more wine than we would without each other.

Lynx-wrapped and spirited, the temptress in Tilde does not, however, hold forth. Aware that she has enchanted the old duke, she lures him not closer but gently away. *Hey, you're a very nice man but all that was just a scherzo.* Of course Barlozzo knew her game even as she played it, but still he clings to the spell of her, asking nothing from her save a passing presence, and nothing from the enchantment itself but *to feel* it. Pleasuring in his own capacity to be pleasured, Barlozzo is smitten with Tilde and he is better for it.

WHEN I DO GET around to thinking about shopping and cooking, it's a simple supper I long for. I go early to the winter marketplace, dark and misty like a cellar where grapes were just pressed. Wrapped in shawls and scarves, the farmers are wraiths emerging and disappearing among the fogs, arms full of cabbages or gloved fingers setting matches to coals or twigs piled in pots under metal birdcages, more often in old buckets, rubbing their hands, slapping at their shoulders. I find tables lush with stalks of ivory cardoons and pumpkins and squash slashed to bare their orange flesh, and turnips and parsnips and the roots of celery built up into pyramids, teetering. But Tomassina has peppers. A basket of gorgeous yellow peppers and a smaller one of the long, twisting green ones sometimes called witches' noses. Dear Tomassina fills my canvas sack with them, alternating yellow with green, composing a still life and all the while telling me how wonderful the peppers would be roasted together with wild fennel and chunks of some good potatoes if I can find them. I find them.

I walk in the still-sleeping *vicoli,* the wheels of shopping carts rattling over the cobbles, a softly spoken *buongiorno,* here and there, the only smudges on the silence. A fir tree, its swooping branches like the wings of a great black bird, has been set up in the *piazzetta* behind the bank. A different sort of Christmas tree, it is hung with scrawled notes. There are perhaps a hundred of them, skewered on branches or tied to them with yarn or ribbon or butcher's twine. I stop to read them.

Lisabetta, do you still love me? Please forgive me, Federico

You know that I can't live without you, so come home, come home now, Giovannino, please come home. Yours forever, Nicoletta

Gioachino, bring soap or I can't wash your shirts. And bread, two hundred grams of cooked ham, half a liter of milk, and something sweet. I love you, Rosanna

Ciao Romeo, on your way home, please look at the green sweater in the window at Anna's. It doesn't cost very much. Would you get it for me for Christmas? With hope, Sara

Back home I spread Emilio's oil over my old, beloved, oval terra-cotta gratin dish, recently rescued from two years' imprisonment in Samuele's *magazzino*. I toss the seeded, rough-cut peppers with the potatoes and more oil, crushed fennel flowers. Coarse sea salt. I put the dish in a quick oven, wait half an hour, toss the mass and adjust the heat to very slow, so the peppers and the potatoes will soften, fairly melt into each other, both of them taking in the sweet breath of the fennel. I set corn bread from Biarritz to rise. Roasted peppers and corn bread. A rough red.

We go about our day, the oven perfumes beguiling us every once in a while. Beguiling us for the goodness of the scents themselves and for the goodness of having an oven of our own. In a kitchen of our own, in a house of our own. Our own along with the Ubaldini, of course. Seven or eight hours pass and I take the dish from the oven, set it to slowly cool on a table near the terrace doors. I bake the bread, set the two rounds of it on an iron plate rack next to the peppers.

It's after seven and we run down for *aperitivi* and to take a good heft of Castelmagno – a cheese made from the milk of cows and goats and ewes that feed on the wild herbs and flowers of the mountain pastures of the Piemonte. It's Emilio who procured the cheese, from a person who knew a person up north. 'I thought you might be nostaglic, every once in a while in this land of *pecorino,* for a cheese from closer to "home,"' he'd told the Venetian. We buy some each day until the high, narrow wheel of it is gone. We choose a Sangiovese from Giovanni.

'*Sangue di Giove,* blood of Jove,' he whispers as he expertly wraps the bottle in brown tissue, handing it, horizontally, over the counter, slapping it into my hand. 'To be drunk exclusively in bed.'

'It's a good idea,' Fernando says, piling napkins and silverware into a basket along with a tea cloth, plates, glasses. He goes up to arrange the yellow wooden bed for our supper and I follow with the peppers and the bread. The cheese. Huffing from the climb under the weight of my offerings, I find the candles lit, the bed set for two. The Venetian is pouring out the blood of Jove and finally we are *living* in Via del Duomo 34.

IT'S THE TENTH day of December, and as the town prepares for Christmas, we ready ourselves for a week-long tour with six Americans from Miami Beach. We'd resisted the idea of hosting a tour so close upon the holidays when it was presented, nearly a year earlier, by one of the three couples. But these were people who'd traveled well and enthusiastically with us twice before. After some consideration we'd finally agreed to plan a preholiday jaunt for them through several Umbrian and Tuscan hill towns and to instruct them in the cooking and baking of the genuine dishes of an Umbrian Christmas. When the tour was reserved, we'd had not an inkling that we'd already be living in the ballroom and so had made plans for most of the cooking demonstrations to be staged in the kitchens at La Badia, a twelfth-century convent hotel that sits just outside Orvieto and where our guests would also be lodging. And even though we are now in residence here in the Via del Duomo and could conduct the cooking demonstrations in our own kitchen, the arrangement at La Badia still feels like the right thing to do. Also, one of the more casual of the demonstrations would be presented in Miranda's kitchen. For Miranda herself to perform. For all the world, I would not tamper with this, for as the date draws near, she grows nearly bridal in her excitement.

She has colored her gray-brown hair a dark chestnut. New clogs from the Saturday market – handsome leather ones with pale wooden platforms – and a pinafore splashed with huge poinsettias compose her trousseau. Miranda-of-the-Bosoms is going big-time. A diligent star, she has been practicing her welcome to 'da pipples of-ah Mee-am'-mee Bich'-e' along with her recipe for gratinéed cardoons, holding up bowls and pots as she's seen television cooks do, tilting her head dulcetly. Since I will be her translator, she repeats and repeats her instructions to me until I am loath to even be in the same room with a cardoon and not much happier to be near her.

As we prefer to do with our guests, we'd talked back and

forth at length, listening to the particular needs and wants of this group, and then carved out an itinerary to reflect them. All in their late sixties and 'fit but lazy,' as they put it, these food and wine enthusiasts said they wanted to walk in countryside and village settings and to dine and drink divinely, if more rustically than formally. Except for the last evening. 'On the last evening, surprise us. As long as the surprise includes black ties and pretty dresses,' Will had said. 'And no museums this time, Chou' was his final plea.

They wanted to know something more about olive oil and cheese-making. And they wanted to learn enough about Umbrian Christmas food so they might return to Florida prepared to re-create a genuine festival for family and friends. Hence, I'd scheduled morning or early-evening cooking demonstrations and left sufficient time for the walking and 'dining and drinking divinely' parts of the tour and to visit the undusted splendors of village churches and broken castles along our way. One day we'll visit Sant'Antimo, an eighth-century abbey built by Charlemagne, where we'll hear the monks of Santo Norbert sing Gregorian chants – a prelude to lunch in the nearby wine village of Montalcino, which will be followed by an eight-year vertical tasting of Brunello. On another day, we'll drive to Pienza to lunch on wild mushrooms and suckling pig roasted over grapevine cuttings in the ponderous medieval dining hall of a mycologist/vintner, after which debauch we'll heave ourselves onto a truck-drawn hay wagon. Fortified with quilts and grappa and a flautist's serenade, we'll submit to being pulled over back roads and sheep paths under the leaving sun for nine kilometers to a *caseificio,* a furtively operated cheese-making hut where unlicensed artisans turn out some of the best pecorino in Tuscany. Bootleg cheese much like the one called 'ignorant' that is made in Umbria. A Homeric fire will be burning outside the hut, around which a good simple supper will be served under the winter stars. Such 'off the path' events as those that we offer our guests have not, as yet, been presented in guidebooks or on Internet sites, and when they are, if they are, Fernando and I – knowing that the very nature of their unusualness must, perforce, be changed by greater traffic – already have a pact sealed for our exit from this work.

We'll taste Emilio's newly pressed oil one afternoon around the fire in an old stone mill. His wife will roast thick slices of her fine bread over the cinders, drizzle it with the good, impossibly green oil, still turbulent and tasting both sharp and delicate and something like raw baby artichokes and roasted hazelnuts on the tongue. Along with the *bruschette,* she'll serve platters of wild boar prosciutto, handmade *salame* perfumed with wild fennel, and jugs of red – a little post-lunch, preprandial *spuntino,* Umbrian style. We'll hunt truffles in Norcia with Barlozzo and his friend Virgilio, and on another morning suffer a ten o'clock tasting of the prestigious whites of Antinori at Castello della Sala. Now, as I review the plans, already approved and arranged for, the single change I'd like to make regards the 'black ties and pretty dresses' desire. The surprise.

We'd hired a good local chef – one of the bevy who'd shunned my request to rent his kitchen for my recipe testing years before – to cater a dinner to be served in the rather royal dining room of a sixteenth-century castle that guards a hamlet on a hill just off the road to Todi. And that is sometimes rented to travelers. As grand as I know such a dinner would be and as much as I suspect it would fulfill our guests' wishes, I begin to think it would be somehow lovelier, maybe grander yet, for us to dine at home. To dine in the ballroom. Along with our Miami Beach six, we could invite Miranda and Barlozzo. Including Fernando and I, we'd be a party of ten, enough to inaugurate the table with the pineapple legs and the chairs of many colors. I could prepare parts of some dishes in advance of the tour and work on others into the wee hours after we've bid our guests good night. I'd have the entire afternoon of the last day to finish things since post-lunch until *aperitivi* has been scheduled as free time for our guests, allowing for a shopping tour through Orvieto, some time to pack. I can do it.

'I can do it. And-since-we've-known-Mary Grace-and-Will-since-Venice,-I-mean-they've-always-wanted-to,-you-know,-sort-of-follow-our-comings-and-goings-and-I-think-the-ballroom-*merits*-a-good,-rousing-kind-of-party-don't-you? And I think it will be a lovely way to thank Miranda for her help and Barlozzo and—' I'm breathless from trying to put forth both my wishes and their justifications before Fernando can strangle the whole of them, but I needn't have rushed. I needn't have doubted him. Serene is the Venetian before my plan.

'I think Mary Grace and Will would especially love this. Shall we call them, just to let them know?' is all he asks.

That Will is a retired U.S. senator, that Mary Grace is an heiress to the still estimable fortunes of a now threadbare, former Fortune 500 company and a woman whose great-grandmother was a lady-in-waiting to the last court of the czars does not enter into the Venetian's calculations about how they will *especially love this,* even though they might well be seated at table with a dead-ringer-for-Gary-Cooper forager and a brown and bosomy maid-of-all-work. Fernando trusts that Will and Mary Grace will love this, in part, simply because they are Americans.

Thank God for Will and Mary Grace and for America and the Americans, even those Americans who talk too loudly and through their noses and wear white sneakers or pointy boots and Stetsons and lean against the walls of a twelfth-century church to read the Red Sox news from the *Herald Tribune,* instead of going in to light a candle or gaze at a Filippo Lippi madonna, while telling me, 'Chou, my darlin', I've already seen the insides and the outsides of too many churches in my life.' And God bless the Americans who assure me that 'Atkins would never have lived in Italy, I can tell you that. There's just too many carbohydrates. Oh, no, no, no, I don't eat bread or pasta or rice or sugar or, for that matter, I don't eat anything that's white. And, yuck, I don't eat bunnies or lambs or wild pigs either. I'll want a steak and salad twice a day, two hard-boiled eggs at breakfast, and half a cup of All-Bran, dry, before bed. Can you arrange that for me, Chou?' God bless the Americans who long to travel in Italy and yet have not a whit of longing to *be* here and who will mistake a host or a teacher for a therapist or a servant. Yes, God bless America and the Americans, and while you're at it, please bless these old, maybe dying, maybe already dead friends of mine here in this land called Umbria.

Umbria. Umbra. The very roots of the word conjure shade, darkness. Hence, is the Umbrian temperament nothing more and nothing less than a birthright? Are they only being themselves, wailing separatists whose blood still throbs with the spleen of feudal lords in a land where grudges are collected like Sèvres teacups? Where an umbrage is hoarded like gold? Could it be that everywhere about Italy itself – despite all the razzle about *la dolce vita* – there endures a fierce and incorruptible expression of the human tendency toward bitterness? Nevertheless, I am an American woman who can love and feed and, yes, embrace a shepherd and a *marchese* and a maid-of-all work and sit down with them to dip good bread into good wine at my table or any other one to which I have been made welcome. I can do that. And, in my aging bread baker's hand, I can hold tight to the small evergreen hope that these ancients in this ancient world might, now and then, live a night of their lives past their pain.

THERE WILL STILL be two empty chairs at the table with the pineapple legs. Four, if I finagle. I don't let myself think further. Not now. Not yet.

Would the Lady Be Pleased
by a Waltz?

*O*nly a few days remain until the tour begins, and knowing
how much racing about the countryside and how much
waiting for the post or the delivery truck are involved in finding and collecting the elements of a fine supper – not
counting the time for the cooking and baking of it – I sit by
the fire in the *salone* with a glass of Vin Santo, doubting the
wisdom of my plan for the grand gala, *black-ties-and-pretty-
dresses* last evening of the tour. I riffle the pages of my book of
numbers and addresses – intimate guide to the forever wily
paths of my cherished suppliers. No simple directory this:
each entry is a sonnet, a complex series of instructions
including, for instance, the number and address of the
Calabrese cheese maker's mother or those of the ex-wife of
the sausage man in Foligno or of the cousin of the former

lover of the saffron lady in Navelli or those of the men- or women-next-store should the artisan himself, herself have moved on or should the ring of the telephone be less than inspiring on a day when I call one or another of these children of nature. Or if the telephone itself lies inert and unpaid for, as has more than once been the case. I learned long ago to secure auxiliary routes to their lairs. Battered is this red leather book, tied around with a length of wide black grosgrain, its pages long ago loosed and stained and scribbled on, crossed out and over and between which are pressed blossoms and leaves and weeds and herbs, a wine label here and there and recipes saved in bleeding black ink on paper napkins, all of them clutched in the refuge of the old book so I will remember what I could never forget. I began keeping it during my earliest journeys up and down the peninsula and long before I came to live here, and so by now it is more map than address book. No matter where I might be in Italy, I could call one or two or more of these numbers and find a friend and, more than likely, a place at his table. Too, no matter where I might be in Italy with the desire to cook, I would not do it without gathering in what I needed of their good honest stuffs. And so, with the book nearby, I write the menu.

Each *portata,* course, will have a significance. The antipasto will reflect a lushly interpreted version of one of the first suppers for which man himself *prepared* a part. For which he *cooked* something. Stone Age shepherds were already cheese makers of a sort, cooking a portion of a day's milk over a twig fire, leaving it apart, adding cooked milk each day until the vessel at hand was full, the milky pap set enough to be turned out onto asphodel or fig leaves or a bed of pine needles. Covering it with same and burying it in a cave or mounting stones about it like a safe, the shepherd left the cheese to age, a promise of future suppers, something fine to eat on some later day and with a shard of broken, dripping honeycomb or a purloined pear. Foiling the salt in the cheese against the sweetness of honey or the fruit, the shepherd, unwittingly, craved both flavors, one to exalt the other. And by composing this relatively sophisticated supper, he soothed his hunger more roundly than he might have with only the cheese. Or only the honey or the pear. In a very real way, early shepherds were gourmands, foraging, gathering as they walked, always intent on supper.

For the first course I will roll out the rough, thick ropes of pasta which are nearly sacred to an Umbrian supper and sauce them with a glossy rich paste of fat, fleshy olives. Once built from the overripened olives which fell from the trees before the harvest began, it was the children's job to collect the bruised, still precious black fruit, to fill their pockets and sacks with it, dispatch it as treasure to the kitchen door. Smashing the olives with a wooden mallet to relieve them of their stones, the cooks would tumble them then into a mortar, pounding them into a savory paste with a handful of wild herbs.

The main course will be a dish Florí loved and which, when

I first served it to her, she called *una tenerezza di maiale,* a tenderness of pork. Two stalwart nutriments of both the Umbrian and the Tuscan cuisines compose it: grapes and the courtyard pig. A tour de force of sorts and therefore welcome after the shepherd's supper and the humble pasta, it wants two days for a dry-spice massage to penetrate the lean white flesh of the pig. Then a long languishing in a slow oven, a while to rest from all the ministrations, and finally, the ceremonious carrying of the grand haunch into the dining room, trailing the primal mists of supper, of a welcome home to the fire after a day at war or in the fields or any place at all from which a body needs to restore his peace.

An intemperate sweet at the last, in three-part harmony and about which there is neither gastronomic nor historical significance save that I love to eat them. To eat all three of them together. Brown sugar gelato churned to silk with extra-virgin olive oil and set down with wedges of caramelized blood orange. I'll go about the table then with a tray of just-fried *frittelle alla sambuca* — small, crusty, sugar-dusted fritters of wild black elderberries. *Sambuca* berries, in Italian. Having already gorged on them alone in the kitchen, I will sit there at table, demure, sipping at the Moscato Fernando will have just poured. *Oh, no, thank you. You go ahead. I never do have appetite when I cook. You know how that is.*

Antipasto

Pan-Sautéed Winter Pears with Pecorino and Walnut Focaccia

Primo

Umbrichelli con Olivada

Secondo

Leg of Spiced Pork Slow-Braised in Red Wine with Prunes

Roasted Chestnut Polenta

Dolci

Brown Sugar Ice Cream with Caramelized Blood Oranges

Warm *Sambuca* Fritters

Rustic, refined. Invention, tradition. Not so many courses. I scratch out a copy and take it to Miranda, invite her to join us.

Anticipating the same joy she's exhibited over her participation in the cooking demonstrations, I am quietly stunned when she refuses.

'I couldn't sit through a dinner with all those strangers. I can't speak to them and they can't speak to me. Why, I'd be so nervous, Chou. I just couldn't.'

'Language is the least effective way to communicate sometimes. Besides, at least two of the guests do speak a bit of Italian, and as for the rest, we'll be there to translate.'

'I'd need a store-bought dress.'

'I could go shopping with you.'

'I'll think on it.'

'I'm going to invite Barlozzo. Will his presence help your comfort?'

'Not a bit. He'll just sit there behind a wine bottle muttering ugly things about Miami Beach and either he'll make me laugh or make me mad.'

'WHY IN HELL would I want to sit through all those fancy dishes of yours, never mind in the company of some old people from Miami Beach?'

'They're all younger than you are.'

'I'm doing my part by tramping through the woods with them, a promise that I made in a weakened, overfed state and that I regret only less than I would the promise of a walk with the devil himself. If Virgilio's bitch doesn't like them, she won't hunt anything but the flesh of their haunches.'

'You could wear your Florentine leather trousers.'

ONCE THE GOODS are in house or on their way to us by dint of express couriers, dairy trucks, or, in the case of the blood oranges, by train from Catania, I begin thinking about the ballroom itself. I'd called on Neddo to beg branches of olive leaves, only just harvested of their fruit. And would he take Fernando and me into the woods beyond La Svolta to gather pine boughs? I ask Barlozzo, too, if he'll wander about his own territories to collect the same, and next evening he arrives with both olive and pine branches enough to decorate the Duomo. I call Neddo to tell him we're set, but he's already been out collecting, too. 'I'm on my way, Chou,' he says, like a succoring angel with an ambulance. And after he and Fernando and I relieve his truck of magnificent boughs of fir and pine and even more olive branches than the duke had brought, we sit sipping grappa by the fire. Too reticent to inquire the why or what for of the branches, he seems content only to have provided them.

'We're hosting some American guests next week, and on the last evening of their visit, we'll all dine here. I wanted to make a sort of Umbrian Christmas setting in the ballroom, and so all you brought will be put to fine use.'

'Well, if you need more . . .'

'No, there is more than enough. But I do thank you, Neddo.'

'Listen, how about wood? Are you fixed for wood?'

'Plenty of wood.'

'If you'd like, I could help to serve or wash up. I've done plenty of that in my time. Mostly when I was younger and the Orvietani used to have wonderful parties with orchestras and midnight suppers. It's been a while, but I'm sure I could make myself useful.'

'Well, if you're free that evening, why don't you join us at dinner?'

I hear myself saying the words if more with my heart than my head, but still, I've just invited Neddo to the gala. Loud and clear and without discussing it with the Venetian. It seemed a natural thing to do. As natural as inviting the duke or Miranda.

'Yes, Neddo, please do come to the dinner.' Fernando seconds the invitation, and not just to be gracious. He's smiling broadly, beginning to tell Neddo about the menu and how we've known Will and Mary Grace for a long time. Neddo seems to levitate slightly from his chair.

'Will you be wearing a *tight?*' he asks Fernando.

In Italian, a *tight* is, oddly enough, a tuxedo.

'Yes, I'll be wearing a *tight,* but it's hardly necessary—'

'I want to wear a *tight*. My eldest son wore a *tight* at his wedding – when was that? – nineteen years ago, and the thing is still hanging in the winter armoire. I look at it every once in a while and think about trying it on myself, but then I never do. It belonged to his bride's uncle, killed in the war. The suit is very old, but as I recall, very handsome and if I can get Sibilla – do you know the *sarta* who lives right in the next palazzo here? Well, she'll fix it so it will look as if it were made for me. Yup, Sibilla will fit that *tight* to me so I'll be like those Russian cavalrymen who would put their doeskin breeches on, jump into tubs of cold water, and then let the pants dry, tense as drums, to their hides. That's how the *tight* will fit me. But tell me this: can I wear brown shoes with a *tight?*'

'Surely you can. I've always loved brown and black together,' I tell Neddo.

Neddo's face, at this moment more Puckish than ever, takes over all the other reasons for my wanting to have this dinner. And because there's nothing else to say, he laughs and laughs and so I do. Fernando does.

I calculate numbers as I close the door on him. Our six American guests, Neddo, Fernando, and me. Nine for sure. Maybe Miranda. Maybe Barlozzo. Maybe eleven. One chair left. One chair plus two finagled chairs. Should the need arise.

We pile the bounty of branches on the terrace and in the cold room behind the kitchen. Not always cold, I think, as Carmine and Eleanora come to mind.

IN THE CERAMICS *bottega* across from the Duomo, I ask the *padrona,* with whom we are only barely acquainted but who clearly sees us as potential clients, if she might be willing to rent us six of her largest *anfore,* explaining that I'll fill them with olive branches and place them about the ballroom for a dinner party. She is agreeable, and so her husband and son and Fernando each hoist a beauty – all of them painted in a different, bold design – down the Via del Duomo to number 34. Cheered on by the merchants along the way, they make a second trip. The street buzzes.

I buy every white candle in every shape and size in every shop where any can be found, and the buzz swarms. It reaches Tilde.

'You're causing great speculation these days, what with all the candles and the loaned vases and the deliveries in the dark of a whole forest of green things. It was the box of oranges from Catania, though, that got my attention. The conductor in whose hands it was placed for guarding is the brother of Luigina from the *pulisecco,* the dry cleaner. He told Luigina they were addressed to "that American woman in Via del Duomo" and that there was another, smaller box filled with orange blossoms and marked "Chou-Chou." She said her brother was crazy with curiosity, couldn't stop asking why a person wouldn't just go to the normal *fruttivendolo* and buy normal oranges. Of course Luigina thought I'd be the one to bring some light to the question, and so I did. Told her it was quite obviously a lover's gift, what with the blossoms and all. From a Sicilian who wears black Armani shirts and has orchards.'

'That should help my reputation. Anyway, I thought Miranda would have told you about the dinner. I invited her to join us, but she refused.'

'Invite me, too, and she's sure to come.'

'Consider yourself expected. Maybe now Barlozzo will say yes, too.'

That makes ten for sure. Ten and counting. I think again about the table.

For efficiency, I will set the table even before the tour begins – one thing less to do later. From the fabric trunk I pull a length of saffron silk velvet with a rolled hem, bordered in silk roping of the same color. I cover the table with the pineapple legs, and the velvet drips, puddles about the stones of the floor. Over it, I position two handmade single-bed patchwork quilts – early-nineteenth-century American heirloom pieces, family legacies of a friend in St. Louis, which she'd sent to me after visiting with us in Venice. I'd forgotten how gorgeous they were and, smoothing them out, their width is flush with the edges of the table. I love how the rough, bright fabrics of them seem right against the luxury of the velvet. There is a fine resonance, too, between the quilts and the chairs of many colors, and the ballroom seems more beautiful to me. I lay luscious branches of hard red berries along the center of the table. And among the tendrils and the thorns of them I nest thirty silver cups, a prized collection meant for sherry but lovely stuck with candles. I unpack the Deruta plates, reproductions of ancient Umbrian designs, thrown and baked and glazed and painted by a master ceramicist in the little town so rich with artists. We'd given them to each other last year for Christmas, undespairing symbols of trust at a time when we had neither table nor house. We'd thought to keep the dishes packed until we could find an armoire especially to hold them, but I know these plates belong on this table and so I wash and dry them, line their red-and-gold beauty along the old quilts, set down my mishmash of good silver collected piece by piece over the years of my long life. Large as kitchen towels, I knot the napkins on one end, leave the fine red damask of them to lie as it will beside each plate. We will be drinking only red wines at table but of two very diverse styles and vintages and so, accordingly, I choose two sets of crystal, tying a small sprig of olive branch to each stem with a length of jute ribbon. When I stand back to look at the table, its effect is, I think, happy. A meeting of eighteenth-century Budapest and nineteenth-century New England here in medieval Umbria, where, somehow, a waltz would not be out of place. Splendid, opulent to be sure but, far more, it seems favorable to joy. Awaiting the lighting of the candles, the pouring of the wine, lavishingly and from some great height, to splash into the deep, round bowls of the glasses. We need music.

When I call the local conservatory to ask after a violinist, I am, quite naturally, thinking of my own who plays in the small, bare room across the *vicolo*. And when I know him, if I am meant to know him, perhaps it will be he, *thick, lank hair falling over tightly closed eyes, a black crust of a beard about his broad pale face,* who will play Brahms in the ballroom. But for now:

'Yes, Signora de Blasi, if I'm not mistaken you are fond of Brahms, yes?'

The question perplexes.

'We have two young men who perform as soloists for such occasions as yours. Both are senior students and experienced concertists. Shall I send them to meet with you?'

'Actually, I would prefer that you choose between them. May I expect him then at seven on that evening? Yes, in Via del Duomo 34. Yes, thank you very much.'

Certain desires are easily accomplished in small hill towns in Umbria.

'What do you think?' I ask the Venetian about the table.

'Well, if only you had trimmed the quilts with the tails of Russian sables and maybe added one more layer of fabric, it might be perfect. This will do, though.'

'I HOPE I'M NOT disturbing you,' a throaty morning voice says through the *citofono*. It's seven-thirty on the first day of the tour and Fernando has gone with our driver in the van to Fiumicino to fetch the Miami six. I am to go at nine to La Badia to await the group and to bring fruit and flowers and chocolates to their suites. To see that all is set for the welcome lunch. I am dressing when the outside buzzer rings.

'I just wanted to catch you before you left, Chou. May I come up?' It's Edgardo.

'I'll ring you in, but please give me a moment.'

I pull on boots, button my jacket, and run down the stairs to find Edgardo standing by the front door, looking somehow sheepish for a *marchese*.

'Sit down, make yourself comfortable.'

'No, no, I won't stay. I know this is a big day, but I just wanted to leave this note for you. It will explain everything.'

'Well, now that you're here, won't you tell me about it? Shall I read it?'

'I'll read it to you, but I should explain . . . I hear from Tilde that you're having a dinner here, that you have guests from America this week, and I just wanted you to know that it would be an honor for me if you and they would dine with me one evening. At Palazzo d'Onofrio, I mean. Here, the note is an invitation.' He breaks the seal on a small sheet of folded paper so thick it looks like cloth. 'It reads, "*Il marchese* Edgardo d'Onofrio requests the pleasure of your company and of your guests on – I left the date blank – for cocktails and dinner à la Russe."'

I find this strange. The early-morning visit, a formal invitation sealed in green wax. His face almost twitching with tension. 'I don't know what to say except that each and every moment of the next seven days has been scheduled, programmed. Fixed. You know what I mean. We're expected somewhere each evening, and I would hate to disappoint the people who've been preparing for us, counting on us. Your generosity is very touching, Edgardo, but there just isn't time.'

'I understand, of course I understand. It's just that I thought it might be exciting for your guests to sit down to a real Moldavian dinner. Piotor would be cooking, you know.'

'The truth is that our guests have traveled here to Umbria because they are looking forward to a perhaps more *local* sort of experience. But who knows – someday we might be able to arrange a Russian dinner with one of our groups. Not this time, though.'

'Will I get the chance to meet them?'

The light comes. Even I, after a few stuttering moments, can now recognize an Umbrian ruse. Edgardo never expected me to accept his invitation. What he came here for, what he anticipated is that I would return the favor. He waits for me to invite *him*.

I bite. 'But I have an idea. Why don't you join us here?'

He looks admiringly at the table.

'Do you have room for me, Chou? I mean, I wouldn't want to impose.'

'Neddo will be here, Edgardo.'

'I know. Actually it wasn't Tilde who told me about the dinner. It was him. It was Neddo. Now that he no longer considers my place the twelfth circle of hell, he came down to look at some equipment my manager wants to sell. And when I saw him from the window, I asked him inside for a grappa. You know, to warm himself by the fire. Don't get all weepy, because neither Neddo nor I are going to live long enough to become friends. No, not friends. Too many untraversable spaces between us for that. And I say this without reference to class or caste or birthright. I say it only because that's the way it is. But I do find myself thinking about him since that *episode* here a few weeks ago. He's a worthy fellow who's living a good life. Much of mine seems empty by comparison. But anyway, as we were sitting there watching the fire, out of nowhere he asked me if I thought it would be proper to wear brown shoes with a *tight*. He had to ask me the question twice before I understood he wasn't asking about a generality but about his own wearing of brown shoes with his own *tight*. "Where in hell are you going in a *tight* and brown shoes, if I may ask?" I said. And then he realized his own trap, knew that if he told me, I might feel left out. So he softened the story, said he'd invited himself and that you were just too kind to refuse him.

'Anyway, I guess I came here to ask for an invitation, too. First time in my life. And now that you have invited me, I can tell you that Neddo's presence will only add to the joy of being here myself. We all want that second chance, don't we, Chou? Don't you think we do? The second time around. I don't mean with a lover. A second chance with ourselves. A second chance at goodness. To get right what we did wrong. And I'm not talking about regret. Anyone at all can strike and hold that pose. I think this is something harder than regret. Trying to see our young selves, as we were, as we thought we were, trying to rebirth ourselves into more noble beings. Yes, a second chance at goodness. I feel Neddo might be able to help me with that. Shall I bring caviar?'

'No. No caviar. Just be sure to wear brown shoes so Neddo will feel spiffy.'

Eleven and counting. That's without Miranda. Without Barlozzo. Thirteen if they come. I will not have thirteen at table. I rearrange the place settings for fourteen. Gather up my things and head for La Badia.

IT'S WONDERFUL TO see Will and Mary Grace, and their chums are lovely. No one warns me about lactose intolerance or even asks me how in the world I can walk around in 'those heels.' They are bright, beautiful people who are prepared to be delighted. Rapt during the cooking sessions, thrilled with the dining and drinking divinely, eager for the sunset climbing through forgotten stone villages flung out like lost chords among the hills, they are of a chivalric tribe who leave a fine trail of well-wishers along our routes.

And though we tell them little enough about the plans for the dinner in Via del Duomo, we do tell them about the other guests who will be joining us. This prospect seems to excite them inordinately and they say how grand it will be to meet and dine with local people, to get to know a few Orvietani up close.

By way of pre-introduction, we tell them some small symbolic story about each one of our friends, and they listen like children to a fairy tale. They are especially interested to meet Neddo, they say.

But when we bid our guests good evening, it's always after midnight and the last part of our workday is still to come.

It feels like being at Miranda's back in those early days as we light candles and set to plumping figs and stirring polenta – always clockwise – marinating the haunch of a pig, plunging the scarlet flesh of Sicilian oranges into a pot of roiling black sugar. Fernando chops and sings and we talk about the day. As the evening of the dinner approaches, there is always more and more we can accomplish in these post-midnight hours, until we find ourselves barely climbing the stairs to the yellow wooden bed at all. Enthusiasm keeps us upright. The night arrives.

SWEET NEDDO, THE evening's self-appointed firekeeper, arrives long before the other guests are due and he bends into the work of stoking and bellowing and the arranging of the burning logs with deference to his fine clothes, patting his trousers and his jacket sleeves between operations. Pressing a blue checked handkerchief to his brow. He is George Raft in the thirties – wide, wide lapels and a wasp-waisted double-breasted jacket, his hair slicked back. His brown shoes are polished. We talk back and forth from the *salone* to kitchen, where I am sitting in front of the oven, watching the bread. I buckle black satin sandals over bare feet, toenails painted the same good red as my lips are painted. It's too warm in the kitchen for the cook to wear stockings. My dress is not a cook's dress anyway. Black velvet, strapless. From a draped, bias-cut bodice, it goes down straight to the midcalf, where it meets with a flaring fishtail ruffle. After all, Will did say 'pretty dresses.'

Miranda had continued to reinforce her refusal to join us until Tilde accepted for her, bought her a dress — navy chiffon with a shawl — and promised to lend her jewels. Tilde is holding the dress and the jewels hostage at her place, just to make certain that Miranda won't get all ready and then decide to pan-fry a few lamb chops before she comes to town. She's to be at Tilde's at six-thirty. Meanwhile, she's here.

Fresh from her ascendency over the cardoons and the Miami six, Miranda has been haunting me and walking the ballroom. Inspecting things and sniffing about and adjusting flames under pots, she's finally offered to do something useful. To braid my hair. Four thick shiny plaits she makes of my hair, which is still the color of hot copper wires, and I clasp the braids together, low on my neck, with a wide Chanel bow.

'Isn't it time for you to go now, Miranda? Tilde will be waiting.'

'Cut me another piece of cheese, will you, Chou? For the walk.'

Miranda had brought a gift, an apron she'd made for me from the same white Montefalco linen she uses to make sheets and kitchen towels. So wide it goes twice around me and covers every centimeter of my dress, and now I twirl in it, show it off to Neddo, who keeps repeating that I'm sure to burn my décolleté when it's time to fry those *sambuca* fritters. What's keeping Fernando up there beyond the narrow dark stairs?

He is wonderful. And wearing his wedding clothes. Except for the brown shoes. I hug him and I'm back right there outside the little red-brick-faced church on the Lido, thinking, *This is the way the world should end,* and that makes me blush. Makes me feel shy, and so I go to look at the bread again.

The Venetian begins to light the candles, nearly fifty of them stuffed into every candlestick and candelabra of our lives. He uncorks eight bottles of '85 Sagrantino from Arnaldo Caprai. Then eight of the '90 Brunello from Altesino, which he will later decant. He lines the bottles up like soldiers on a sideboard near his place at table.

The borrowed *anfore* are filled with immense bouquets of olive branches and set about the perimeter of the room, and the pine and fir branches and boughs we've laid along the edges of the stone floor, creating a sort of carpet of them, and then stood the rest of them in fat sheaves in the corners. There is everywhere the scent of Christmas in the ballroom.

Miranda insisted that two of her nephew troupe help with serving, and they, too, arrive early, having put their thumbs out and taken passage into town from Buon Respiro with a trucker. Their shirts are made from the same linen as my apron, and we make a fine trio in the kitchen. I have drawn sketches of how each course should look, how it should be plated, and they study the pages, converse, study them again.

'*Fatto*,' they say in unison. 'It's done.'

As I finish the elements of each course, they will plate them. Carry them to table. They are better trained than Culinary Institute students in their thirty-seventh week of instruction, these boys from Buon Respiro.

As each batch of bread is finished, I carry the loaves to the terrace, set them on the balustrade, on racks covered with branches of wild rosemary. Hot and wet is the new bread's perfume, the thick crusts of it coaxing the oils from the herbs, and I think everything is ready. The others will be here in a moment and I'm already missing Barlozzo, even if I understand his desire to stay away tonight. Part shyness, part misanthropy. Part missing Florí. Not even Tilde can distract the old duke from Florí. Not truly. Florí is his love, his timber in the boiling sea, and he clings to her.

There is one small task left to do. I should seek Fernando's aid, since surely he would make a better job of it. Or Neddo's; he would be thrilled by the pure exoticism of the act. But I want to do it myself. I take the beautiful pineapple that I'd left a few days ago on the *madia* to ripen, whack it more or less in two with a cleaver, carry the larger piece in a bowl to the front door. I skewer the fruit with my oldest, best French knife and, with due force, plunge the knife into the old brown door. It sticks. It stays, and the pineapple is angled to show both its flesh and its skin, and the long, dark fronds of it lie nicely against the pine boughs and berries and the lush bunches of black grapes that I'd hung there earlier. Signore e Signora de Blasi are at home.

I stay outdoors fussing with the last batch of bread, resting my arms on the balustrade between the cooling loaves and the pots of basil and the branches of a lemon tree, my legs pressing against the velvet of my dress into the wisteria, into the jasmine. It's warm on this evening in December, and I lift my face to every sublime trembling of a breeze. I arrange and rearrange the bread, a carnival lady with her walnut shells. I've always liked to bring bread or cakes or whatever I've just pulled from the oven to cool outdoors. Pies on a windowsill in Saratoga. But I'm not in Saratoga anymore. Nor in Cold Spring nor Sacramento nor St. Louis. Not in Venice, not in San Casciano, but here on a great stone island in an ancient palazzo on a terrace in the sky and I stand here watching the moon. Half a moon: tenuous, pale, barely glistening up out of the white fogs the clouds make. Who knows why, but a scene comes to mind, powerful in its way and which I'd witnessed not so long before on a train to Rome. Now, of all moments, it plays itself over and over again.

In a second-class car, I sit behind an American couple. 'You're over the top, Susan. This whole trip is over the top. Did you really have to have that hat? That ridiculous hat. And that wine you just had to drink at lunch cost thirty-five dollars. And now you sit here in ecstasy over cornfields and cows and a few decrepit villages. Hell, if you wanted to see cornfields I could have taken you to Iowa. Could have saved myself a whole lot of trouble. We travel seven thousand miles to look at cows.'

'I'm not just looking at cows, Jeffrey. I'm looking at Italy. That's the part you don't understand. And I love my hat. And I'll

tell you another thing, Jeffrey. I *am* over the top. Almost everything and everyone in this world is over the top, over your top.
And I'll tell you why. Your cup is too small. Your cup is mean
and small and nothing fits in it except whatever drips and drib-
bles you pour into it yourself. There isn't room for another
thing. But let me tell you, Jeffrey, there's more to life than what
you can fit into your cup. Get a bigger cup. For God's sake,
Jeffrey, get a bigger cup.'

As I passed them on my way to exit the train, the two sat
there separated by a large black felt hat stuck with a full-blown
pink rose, she, still looking out the window, he, staring straight
ahead or deep inside or maybe even into the bottom of his cup.
And on this evening, especially on this evening, I am wishing
that Jeffrey has found a bigger cup.

The door to the palazzo across the way opens, shuts. It's he of
the *thick, lank hair falling over tightly closed eyes*. Carrying his
violin.

He looks up at me. '*Buona sera, signora. Arrivo.* Good evening,
my lady. I'm coming.'

It was him, him of the crusty black beard, with whom I'd
spoken. It's he who is the conservatory director. And when I'd
told him my address, perhaps before I'd told him my address,
he'd decided to choose himself as our violinist.

Fernando opens the door to him.

'*Giacomo Serafini, molto lieto.*' He introduces himself all around.
Wants nothing at all to drink. *No, grazie.* Steps over to the terrace doors, unpacks his violin, begins to play.

'Did you know that this floor of the palazzo was once a ballroom, signora?' he asks as he tightens his strings, strokes and plucks at them.

'Yes. Yes, I did know that.'

'*La signora gradirebbe un valzer?* Would the lady be pleased by a waltz?'

Let life shape itself.

Fernando is leaning against the far wall, smoking. He flicks the cigarette into the flames of Neddo's leaping fire, beckons me with his eyes, a quarter nod of his head – an Italian boy summoning his girl – and I go to him. Let myself be held. Hold him tighter than he holds me and take in the Italian boy smell of him all mixed up with coffee and red wine and wood smoke. And now with Opium.

'Will you dance with me?' he wants to know.

We walk to the center of the room and, as in the films, we bow to each other extravagantly. I still have my apron on. Serafini interrupts Brahms in a gentle, diminishing refrain. The Venetian and I take our positions; Serafini takes his. He plays Il valtzer dell'Imperatore and we dance. We dance as though we know how to dance, we dance better than we've danced ever before and perhaps better than we ever will again, and I think perhaps Serafini plays better, too, for our dancing so well and I hope the Ubaldini ghosts are all watching. Neddo is watching and striding about in front of the fireplace just as he strides his meadow. *A warrior, swinging his scythe, high, wide, in rhythm with the wind.* The nephews are watching, too. Watching us and looking out from the terrace for the others.

'They're coming up the *vicolo*.'

We all go out to the terrace save Serafini, who continues with the waltz.

That they have all arrived in Piazza Scalza at the same moment is a small kismet. There is Tilde, lynx-wrapped against the sultry night, diamonds swinging in her ears. Fanning herself with her shawl, Miranda-of-the-Bosoms is a goddess in midnight blue. And the American women wear very pretty dresses. Tilde and Miranda weave themselves among the other three and, arm in arm, they strut the *vicolo* like a runway, laughing, splendid, clearly prepared to be delighted. Edgardo waits for the men to reach him at the turn onto the Via del Duomo. Far less ebullient than the women, all the men wear brown shoes. Connection enough.

None of them seems to notice the two men who round the corner from Piazza Scalza a few moments after them. One clutches a cape about him; the other one wears leather breeches and a velvet vest and I can only hope they've not brought cheese.

I can hear them all shuffling into the courtyard now and, from the *salone,* I shout, *'Benvenuti, benvenuti, belli miei.'*

It's not what's on the table but who's on the chairs. Fourteen places set round the table with the pineapple legs, fourteen chairs of many colors where good people will sit down to supper. Will be at home with us. *At home.* Such a long road it's been to get here.

Ten red tickets.

A thousand days.

Il telefono è per lei, signora.

Stringing time like pearls. Enough pearls to make a life.

A tiny silver shovel.

Tell me who I was when we were fifteen. Do you remember me then?

Dolce e salata, *sweet and salty. Because that's how life tastes to me.*

Ubaldini ghosts.

The night train to Paris.

The 7:16, Cold Spring to Grand Central.

Why shouldn't I go and live on the fringes of an Adriatic lagoon with a blueberry-eyed stranger?

Mom, can we get a puppy?

The band is practicing here tonight, Mom.

Mom, can we get a puppy tomorrow?

Mom, please don't wear that white cape to my basketball game ever again.

I love you, Mom.

I love you, baby.

Mom, I've decided for sure. Certain sure. I'm really going to be Superman for Halloween.

My hair is not purple, Mom. It's aubergine.

Mrs. Knox, you have a baby girl.

Spiced figs.

Caramel oranges.

New bread.

Old wine.

A sunlit peach.

Brown shoes.

Pretty dresses.

I wanted death to find me dancing.

For God's sake, Jeffrey, get a bigger cup.

A kiss.

A waltz.

La signora gradirebbe un valzer?

Yes, la signora would be pleased by a waltz.

Serafini has taken up Brahms once again and I go out to the landing, peer down over the stairwell. I look for you even though I know you're not there.

The Feast

*B*ut even though you weren't there, all the rest of them filed in, flooding the ballroom with the *allegria* I'd been longing for.

Serafini played and played and Tilde waltzed with Will and I did with the nephews while Mary Grace and Neddo managed something like a minuet. Giovanni-the-downstairs-grocer-of-the-bread-warmed-hands pressed the buzzer importantly every quarter hour or so to ask how we were doing for *aperitivi*.

'*Volete un altra oppure due?* Would you like another or maybe two?' he'd inquire, laughing softly at the fun even he was having just being a supplier. Fernando or I would run down to take two more iced bottles of the local sparkler from the crooks of his arms, an arrangement he'd offered us after assessing the size of our refrigerator. He rang once again just as we were sitting down at table and we fibbed then about our need for yet more; said we were in the middle of cooking and would he mind awfully coming up.

'*Solo per mezzo minuto.* Only for a half minute,' he'd shouted into the *citofono*. Grinning and puffing from the climb, he presented himself at the door and I pulled the aproned, smocked bulk of him inside, introduced him all around, insisted him into a chair. Handed him a glass of the first-course wine. He sat there for his half minute and nearly four hours more. The final chair was offered to Serafini, who balked and bleated until all were seated except me. He came to the kitchen and, his fingers gingerly cupping my elbow, he escorted me to the table, pulled out my chair, settled me into it. Only then did Serafini, too, take his place at the table with the pineapple legs. Tuxedos, velvet breeches. An apron. Pretty dresses and brown shoes. There we were – all sixteen of us – and there we stayed. There we supped and quaffed and groaned our way through two changes of candles and a pyramid of olive wood. Piling up memories. The feast that night in Palazzo Ubaldini has, over the years, become a kind of legend here in our tiny parish on the rock. The truth of it retold. Shined up and passed about – a talisman – among our neighbors. We laugh when we hear about some who tell the story of it in one place or another, claiming they were here. Saw it all. Tasted it all. Danced with an American princess. No matter how many suppers we host, no matter who will sit in those chairs, at that table, I think there was, there must have been something of quintessence about that night. Of course I know it was they who made it so. That singular collection of good souls. And the knowing that you, too, would have been here if you could.

Hence if it's the now-famous feast one might think to recreate, please remember that the recipes for it matter less than those who'll be there to partake of it. Much less.

Recipes

Pan-Sautéed Winter Pears with Pecorino and Walnut Focaccia

*T*he combination of pears and pecorino is traditional in Umbria, the sweetness of the fruit soothing the saltiness of the cheese. The delicious compatibility of the two is less the result of invention than of the timeless availability of the two components.

'We had sheep and so there was cheese. And in one season or another, there was almost always some sort of pear ready to eat either from a wild bush or an orchard tree. So that's what we ate, and that's what we still eat. And the undisputed best way to go about this little meal is to first steal the pear,' says the incorrigible Neddo. 'Then find a hillside facing the afternoon sun. Once settled, pull a pocket knife from your sack, peel and slice the pear a sliver at a time, eating it from the knife between crumbles of pecorino, also pulled from your sack. Red wine and good bread would not be out of place.'

Though surely a dandified reading of the original, this following one is also quite good.

Pan-Sautéed Winter Pears with Pecorino

To serve 6

6 ripe but still firm winter pears, preferably Bosc
55g/2oz unsalted butter
1 tablespoon olive oil
About 55g/2oz (½ cup) very fine yellow or white cornmeal or
  maizemeal
sea salt
a pepper grinder
225ml/8fl oz (1 cup) Orvieto Classico
About 280g/10oz medium-aged pecorino
150ml/¼pint (¾ cup) chestnut or buckwheat honey, warmed to a
  liquid

'Stripe' the pears with a vegetable peeler, cut them into halves, leaving the stem intact – either on one half of the pear or split between the two halves – and core and seed the fruit. In a large sauté pan, heat 40g/1½oz of the butter with the olive oil over a medium flame until the butter just begins to foam. Pour the cornmeal or maizemeal out into a shallow plate and press each pear half into it, lightly coating the cut sides only. Place each pear half, cut side down, into the hot fat. Sprinkle the pears with sea salt and generous grindings of pepper. Sauté only as many pears at a time as will fit comfortably in the pan without touching. Leave the pears undisturbed for 5 to 6 minutes to form a good, golden crust and then turn them carefully with a spatula to cook the other side, salting them and grinding on pepper as before. Once again, leave the fruit undisturbed for 5 minutes. Remove the sautéed fruit to warmed plates. Use large or even oversize dinner plates for this presentation, allowing people to smudge bits of the focaccia in the honey and the pear without sending it sailing off the edge of some delicate little dessert plate. Raise the flame and rinse the pan with the Orvieto Classico, stirring to dissolve the pan residue. Allow the wine to reduce for 2 to 3 minutes. Off the flame, gloss the sauce with the final 15g/½oz of butter, swirling the pan to melt it. Place four or five roughly-cut slivers of the pecorino next to the pears on each plate, drizzle with the sauce and threads of the warmed honey. Send around the table a just-baked focaccia for people to tear and pass. Pour the same Orvieto Classico used in the sauce, chilled rather than cold.

Walnut Focaccia

A roundish, flat cake made of water and grain and cooked quickly over the red-hot ash of a fire or a hot stone was perhaps the earliest form of bread. Focaccia is its most direct ancestor. Even the name is derived from *focus,* fire in Latin. The French *fougasse* – a ladder-shaped bread often made with walnut oil – is of the same clan. But as it is with so many foods which travel far from their roots, what is passed off as focaccia in many parts of the world can be a cottony, oily, flavorless travesty. Make your own.

To make three 23–25cm/9–10in breads

About 500ml/18fl oz (2¼ cups) tepid water
3 teaspoons dried active yeast (or a small piece of fresh yeast,
  about 20g/¾oz)
6 tablespoons extra-virgin olive oil, plus extra to drizzle
1½ tablespoons fine sea salt
750g/1lb 10oz strong plain white flour
85g/3oz (⅔ cup) stone-ground wholemeal flour
140g/5oz (1 cup) finely stone-ground white or yellow cornmeal or
  maizemeal
additional tepid water, if necessasry
200g/7oz (2 cups) walnuts, lightly toasted and lightly crushed
sea salt

Place 75ml/2½fl oz (⅓ cup) of the tepid water into a large mixing bowl and sprinkle or crumble in the yeast. Stir to dissolve and let stand for five minutes. Meanwhile mix together 6 tablespoons of olive oil, the remaining 425ml/¾ pint (2 cups) of tepid water, and the fine sea salt. Add the liquids to the yeast, add the three flours, all at once, and stir to form a rough mass. Turn the mass out onto a lightly floured work surface and begin to knead. If the mass seems dry, sprinkle over a few drops of additional water at a time until the mass is workable. Continue to knead the mass until a soft, satiny, and elastic dough is achieved; flatten the dough into a rough rectangle and sprinkle over the walnuts. Work the nuts into the dough and reshape it into a rough ball. Set the dough into a lightly oiled bowl, cover tightly with clingfilm, and set it to rise in a warm, draft-free place. Allow to rise until the mass is doubled. This might take as long as two hours. Deflate the dough and cut it into three pieces, shaping each one into a flat round each about 23–25cm/9–10in diameter. Place the rounds onto oiled baking sheets which have been lightly sprinkled with cornmeal or maizemeal; cover with tea towels and allow to rise for half an hour. Press your knuckles into the dough, creating lovely little pockets which will eventually hold oil and salt. Cover the rounds once again and let them sit for the last rise, about an hour. Preheat the oven to 200°C/400°F/gas mark 6. Now sprinkle or grind sea salt over the breads. Do this generously. Drizzle them with olive oil, hitting the pockets when you can, and bake the breads for 20 to 25 minutes, until they are puffed and nicely golden. Transfer immediately to racks to cool slightly before serving. These can be successfully reheated in a hot oven for a very few minutes.

Umbrichelli with Olivada

Umbrichelli are rough, hand-rolled and hand-cut ropes of pasta made from only flour, water, and salt. If making fresh *umbrichelli* seems daunting (which I can assure you it is not; see below), don't be tempted to substitute fresh pasta made with eggs, which is so widely available now. Its silky texture and richer flavor is not the best foil for the frank rusticity of the olive paste. Better to approximate the *umbrichelli* with a thick, dried spaghetti such as *bucatini*.

Kin to the Provençal tapenade, Umbrian *olivada* is made with great, fleshy black or purple olives whose briny quality is chastened with a dose of black rum rather than intensified with anchovies as it is in the south of France. Less salty, less aggressive, a pot of the Umbrian paste in the cupboard is gold. Apart from dressing pasta with it, smear it on roasted bread to serve as an antipasto, spoon it over grilled fish or alongside a roast chicken, or stuff it into the hollows of August tomatoes, raw or grilled. In summer, I tend to spoon it into small white cups and set it down as an antipasto with little silver spoons and a tangle of battered and just-fried sage leaves. Except for cold white wine, nothing else seems necessary.

Umbrichelli

To serve 12

450g / 1lb plain flour
2 teaspoons sea salt
water, to mix

On a large pastry board or in a large mixing bowl, pour out the flour, add the sea salt, and mix well. Urge the mixture into a mound, make a crater in its center with your thumbs, and into it, begin pouring water in a thin stream while you work it into the flour with your free hand. The desire here is to achieve a thick, consistent, if rough mass of dough. Once that's accomplished, begin kneading the mass on a lightly floured surface until it begins to smooth out and take on some elasticity. About 8 minutes. Here the fun begins. If you've ever worked with egg-based pasta dough, you'll be familiar with the feverish rolling and rolling and expanding and turning and rolling again and again until the stuff is thin as yellow silk. A magnificent feat and well worth its trouble to be sure. However, traditional Umbrian pasta-making is a much less precise art. What that means is that once you've made this dough, there are several ways to proceed in the shaping of the *umbrichelli*. One can begin by cutting the dough into thirds and, on a lightly floured surface, rolling out each third into a sheet about 5mm/¼ in in thickness. A little bump, a little tear – nothing can hurt the final result here. At this point one can roll the pasta sheet swiss-roll fashion and cut it into thinnish strips, approximately 5mm/¼in wide, dust the strips very lightly with flour and leave them to dry in a flat basket or on a tray lined with a tea towel. Repeat the process with the other two-thirds of the dough.

Alternatively, one just pulls off pieces of the dough and rolls them into long thin ropes, drags the rope gently through a dish of flour, and heaves the thing onto the same sort of cloth-lined tray. This is an especially good method for those wishing to either engage or distract any householders beyond the age of four. It's fine child's play, which means it's also fine adult's play. The *umbrichelli* can be left to dry for half a day or overnight covered loosely in a cool place. Do not refrigerate them. When ready to cook them, bring a large pan of sea-salted water to the rapid boil and tumble the pasta into it. Stir, reduce the heat to keep a quieter boil, and cook the pasta until it rises to the surface. Meanwhile, pour the *olivada* into a large serving bowl. As the pasta rises to the top, catch it with a skimmer or pasta spoon (or slotted spoon) and place it in the bowl. Repeat until all the pasta is cooked. Toss the *umbrichelli* with the *olivada* and serve.

This is absolutely not a pasta which is enhanced by the addition of Parmigiano.

Olivada

Makes approximately 450ml/16fl oz (2 cups)

675g/1½lb large black or purple Italian or Greek olives, pounded
*   lightly with a mallet and relieved of their stones*
3 fat, firm cloves of garlic with no trace of green sprout, peeled
*   and crushed*
3 tablespoons grappa or cognac
3 tablespoons dark rum
2 teaspoons red wine vinegar
2 tablespoons raisins, plumped in warm red wine and drained, the
*   wine reserved*
Approximately 50ml/2fl oz (¼ cup) extra-virgin olive oil

By hand:

Place the stoned olives and the garlic in a large wooden or marble mortar and begin crushing them with a pestle, grinding them against the sides of the mortar until a rough paste is achieved. This takes only a minute or two. Combine the grappa or cognac, the dark rum, and the vinegar and add the mixture, a teaspoon or so at a time, all the while continuing to smooth out the paste by using a grinding motion with the pestle. Add the raisins and their soaking liquid and continue to smooth the paste. Lastly, a drop or two at a time, beat in the olive oil – using the pestle now as a whisk – until a smooth, light, and glossy paste is achieved. All of the olive oil may not be needed. Never refrigerate the paste. If not using it immediately or within several hours, transfer it to a glass or ceramic vessel, cover the top with a very thin layer of extra-virgin olive oil, cover the vessel tightly, and store in a cool place. The *olivada* will keep for several weeks if stored properly.

With a food processor:
In the bowl of a food processor fitted with a steel blade, process the olives with the garlic, grappa or cognac, rum, vinegar, and the raisins with their soaking liquid to a coarse paste. Scrape the bowl.

With the machine running, add drops of the olive oil through the feed tube, thinning the paste, glossing and emulsifying it. See above for storing suggestions.

Leg of Spiced Pork
Slow-Braised in Red Wine
with Prunes

This is an ancient celebration dish in both Umbria and Tuscany, historically cooked in December during the harvesting of the olives and the pig-sticking. Stories abound among the farmers about how they'd build olive-wood fires in their outdoor ovens and cook two haunches at a time to feed the troupe of harvesters who hand-picked the olives, feasted, rested, and then moved on to the next estate to repeat the events a few days later. Though recipes and general narrative change from one storyteller to the next, all of them agree about the epic hungers raised up by the clove and cinnamon smoke which curled from the ovens and hung maddeningly, promisingly in the cold blue air of a winter's day.

Even without the glory of an olive-wood-fired oven, the scent of the charring spiced flesh seeps into every millimeter of the house, bringing otherwise well-behaved people to loiter fussily about the kitchen. And if I stand on my terrace for a moment, putting out bread to cool or to greet my neighbor across the alleyway, or if Fernando and I sit, swaddled in winter coats and sipping at warm spiced wine, to watch the sun set, I have seen people stop short on the little street below, look up, inhale. Swoon.

Since I must stay in or near the kitchen for all those hours of its braising, I use the time to lay the table and put together the rest of the supper. Set the bread to rise, stir up the polenta, make a sweet.

Surely on the night of the feast, this was the dish which sparked the most nostaglia. Strangely, even our American guests likened the tenderness and sweetness of the flesh to that of the 'baked fresh ham' of their childhoods. When this sentiment was translated to the Umbrians, there was a great shaking of heads and the darting of pitying glances at the New Worlders who would pretend such a dish could be had anywhere but here.

One caveat: no matter how many prunes I cook along with the pork, I never have enough. The supply is always less than the demand. Even people who wouldn't eat a dried prune on a bet start digging about in the sauce for another one. And another one.

To serve 12

2 tablespoons fine sea salt
2 teaspoons just-cracked pepper

1 tablespoon ground cinnamon

1 tablespoon ground allspice

2 teaspoons ground cloves

1 5.4–6.3kg / 12–14lb leg of fresh pork, its bone intact, its fat
*   well trimmed*

6 tablespoons extra-virgin olive oil

2 medium onions, peeled and minced

3 fat cloves of garlic, peeled, crushed, and minced

2 bay leaves

1 10cm / 4in stick of cinnamon

Up to 1.4 litres / 2½ pints young red wine

675g / 1½lb prunes, stoned

Combine the sea salt, the pepper, and the dry spices together and massage the potion into all the surfaces of the pig's haunch. Place the perfumed leg in a non-metallic vessel, covering it tightly with clingfilm, and allow it to rest in the refrigerator for 2 days.

Preheat the oven to 220°C/425°F/gas mark 7. In a large terra-cotta or ceramic casserole or a roasting tin, warm 2 table-spoons of olive oil and sauté the onion and garlic to translucence. Massage the haunch with the remaining 4 table-spoons of olive oil, place it over the sautéed aromatics, and roast it for 20 minutes, gilding it and sealing in its juices. Reduce the heat to 170°C/325°F/gas mark 3 and add the bay leaves, the cinnamon stick, and 450ml/16fl oz (2 cups) of the red wine. Braise the pork, uncovered, basting it at 15-minute intervals with its juices and judicious doses of red wine to compensate for evaporation. Known here as it is in many parts of the world as the *angels' portion*.

Meanwhile, plump the prunes in more of the red wine over a low flame.

After 3½ hours have passed, add the plumped prunes to the roasting tin and continue to baste and braise the haunch for another ½ hour to 1 hour, or until its internal temperature reads 65°C/150°F. Remove the haunch from the oven and allow it to rest in its juices for 30 minutes.

Remove the pork from its tin, carve it into thin slices, and present it with its braising juice – cinnamon stick removed, corrected for salt – studded with the prunes.

Roasted Chestnut Polenta

To serve 12

450ml/16fl oz (2 cups) whole or full-fat milk
1125ml/39fl oz (5 cups) water
225ml/8fl oz (1 cup) Orvieto Classico or additional water or milk
1 tablespoon fine sea salt
1 teaspoon light soft brown sugar
3 tablespoons extra-virgin olive oil
40g/1½oz butter
250g/9oz (1½ cups) coarse, stone-ground yellow cornmeal or
    maizemeal
55g/2oz (½ cup) chestnut flour (available in specialty food shops
    and Italian groceries) or use extra cornmeal or maizemeal
freshly ground nutmeg

In a large heavy-based saucepan set over a high flame, combine the milk, water, wine (or additional water or milk), salt, sugar, oil, and 15g/½oz of the butter and bring the mass to a boil. Stir the cornmeal or maizemeal with the chestnut flour (or additional cornmeal or maizemeal) and pour the mixture into a pitcher or measuring jug with a lip. With a large wooden spoon in your stirring hand and the pitcher in the other, begin stirring and, very slowly, begin pouring out the mixture in a thin, constant stream. Stirring all the while. And always in the same direction, if you recall the story about Saint Anthony's feast. Lower the flame and continue to stir until the mixture becomes very thick and bubbles and puffs steam, which should be the case somewhere about twenty minutes into the process. Building a fine, smooth polenta wants a bit of coordination and a willing arm. Off the flame, grate a good quarter of a nutmeg into the polenta and add the final 25g/1oz of unsalted butter. Give it all a good stir and pour it out into an oiled tin – or two of them if that's easier – to a depth of about 5cm/2in. Allow the polenta to cool. Cut it into squares or rectangles or even cut it out with a large biscuit cutter and lay the pieces on an oiled baking sheet. Under a preheated grill, grill the polenta until the edges are crisped and the little cakes are thoroughly heated. Transfer to a heated platter and pass it along with the pork and its braising juices.

Brown Sugar Ice Cream with
Caramelized Blood Oranges

*E*xtra-virgin olive oil employed as a component in dessert making is as natural here as are butter or cream. Again, oil is at hand and so it's used to every possible advantage. Stirred into simple cakes, it imparts a tender, luscious crumb. In crusts for sweet and savory tarts, in anise-scented cookies, in the batters for pancakes or fritters, olive oil exalts flavor and lightens texture. Its use in ice cream is, however, not at all typical.

It was during the ninth-century Saracen reign on Sicily when, along with a rich patrimony of pastry cooking, the art of ice-cream making was introduced in Italy. Since then every conceivable fruit and herb and seed and essence and perfume has been dedicated to the embellishment of the smooth, satiny stuff, which may very well be the earth's preferred sweet. But the addition of olive oil is a relatively recent conceit. And just as it does in other sweet cooking, the use of extra-virgin olive oil in ice-cream making lightens the texture of the finished cream and exalts the flavors of the other components. Either finely crushed cinnamon bark, lightly crushed espresso beans, the scraped seeds from the heart of a fresh, plump vanilla bean, Grand Marnier, Cognac, Cointreau, or crystallized ginger might be substituted for the cloves in this recipe. I confess to the occasional debauchery of making the ice cream with all of these perfumes and spirits at the same time, dosing the base with the instinctive, restrained hand of an alchemist. The olive oil suspends each layer of flavor so that, on the tongue, rather than tasting their amalgam, one is treated to a series of soft explosions and dissolutions. An extended fireworks display. Should you opt to make the ice cream this way, do forget the oranges and the fritters. Forget the dinner.

Brown Sugar Ice Cream

To serve 12

10 large egg yolks
175g / 6oz (¾ cup) dark soft brown sugar
8 whole cloves, lightly bruised
450ml / 16fl oz (2 cups) double cream
450ml / 16fl oz (2 cups) whole or full-fat milk
115g / 4oz extra-virgin olive oil

Whisk the yolks and sugar together in a large bowl.

Combine the bruised cloves, cream, and milk in a heavy-based saucepan and, over a medium flame, bring almost to the boil. Strain the mixture. Then, whisking constantly, drizzle the hot cream mixture into the yolk mixture. Return the combined mixtures to the saucepan and, over a low flame, stir the mass with a wooden spoon until the custard thickens enough to coat the back of a metal spoon, about 8 minutes. Transfer the custard to a clean bowl and allow to cool for several hours. Stir the custard and then whisk in the olive oil, incorporating it thoroughly. Either freeze the custard in an ice-cream maker according to the manufacturer's directions or pour the custard into ice-cube trays and place them in the freezer. At 15-minute intervals, remove the trays and stir the mass thoroughly before returning the trays to the freezer. The freezing and stirring process permits a slow and thorough chilling of the mass and helps to avoid the formation of ice crystals and uneven freezing. After three or four 15-minute intervals, the custard will be lightly set. If you prefer a firmer texture, repeat the process once or twice again.

Caramelized Blood Oranges

8–10 seedless oranges or 10–12 blood oranges
55g / 2oz unsalted butter
100g / 3½oz caster or granulated sugar

With a small, sharp knife, peel the oranges, relieving them of both their colored peel and white pith. Horizontally, cut the oranges in thirds or fourths, depending upon their size. Since the fruit will be enduring the perils of hot caramel, it must be cut into sturdy pieces so as not to break apart.

In a heavy-based sauté pan, large enough to accommodate the oranges, melt the butter over a low flame. Add the sugar and stir constantly with a metal spoon until the sugar turns a very dark brown. Carefully add the oranges to the caramel, turning them about to coat them in the sauce. Be patient if the coolness of the fruit causes the caramel to seize, since it will melt again once the oranges are heated through. Just keep tossing things about. Transfer the caramelized orange slices to a nonstick or lightly buttered baking sheet and cover lightly with clingfilm. Set aside in a cool place but not in the refrigerator. The oranges can be completed to this stage up to 24 hours before serving.

Preheat the grill. Ten minutes before serving, place the baking sheet with the caramelized oranges 10cm/4in below the grill heat and grill the fruit until the edges begin to take on color and the caramel begins to melt. No need to turn them. Have at the ready warmed, shallow soup plates. Spoon some of the oranges and their sauce into the warmed plates, top immediately with the ice cream, and serve with large soup spoons. The idea is to get the dishes to the table and to convince your guests to begin eating while the oranges are still very, very warm and the ice cream is still very, very cold. A sensation worth pursuing. The only thing to sip here is an iced Moscato.

Warm Sambuca Fritters

S *ambuca* berries grow wild along nearly every country road in
our part of Umbria. Small, shiny blackish berries in fan-
shaped clusters atop tall, sturdy stalks, they are called
elderberries in English. The clusters of berries – still clinging to
their thin, threadlike stems – are removed from the stalks,
rinsed, and dried, then dragged through a beer batter, fried in
olive or peanut oil, and rolled about in baker's sugar. Served
pan-to-hand-to-mouth, these, like warm evanescent kisses, signify the feast's end. In some Umbrian homes, additional to the
fritters served at table, one is gifted a paper sack of them to eat
on the way home. Or in bed.

Lacking access to wild elderberries, wild or cultivated
blueberries can be used with success, as can blackberries,
raspberries, or redcurrants – all of these, of course, wanting

sugaring 'to taste.' Halves of ripe black plums or apricots first soaked in Cointreau are also good.

First prepare the batter. Precise proportions are nearly impossible to recommend since, depending upon the fruit to be used, you will require more or less of the batter. The dose here is generous and, if not entirely needed, make thin, post-feast pancakes the next day and serve them with butter and a squeeze of lemon.

115g/4oz (1 cup) plain flour
140g/5oz (1 cup) very fine stone-ground white or yellow
 cornmeal or maizemeal
2 good pinches of sea salt
55g/2oz (¼ cup) caster or granulated sugar
beer, to mix

Combine all the dry ingredients in a mixing bowl and slowly whisk in the beer until the batter achieves the consistency of thick double cream. Cover the batter lightly and let it stand for at least an hour. Whisk again. The batter will have thickened slightly to the consistency of a loose custard as the flour and cornmeal or maizemeal swell.

Use a large skillet, about 7.5cm/3in deep, filled two-thirds full with peanut oil or extra-virgin olive oil. Even here in the land of extra-virgin, some consider it an extravagance to use it in frying. These find peanut oil an acceptable substitute. Over a medium flame to avoid cool spots, heat the oil to

185–188°C/365–370°F or – avoiding the fussiness of a thermometer – once the oil begins to sway, test the temperature by dropping a half teaspoon of the batter into it. If the batter colors deeply and bobs about within a few seconds, the oil is ready.

Stir the batter. If using other than *sambuca* berries, add the fruit directly to the batter and stir. With a tablespoon, remove some of the batter and fruit and drop it into the hot oil. Repeat until the pan is full but the fritters are not at all crowded. If using *sambuca* berries, drag a cluster through the batter and place it into the hot oil. When the fritters take on a dark golden color and float to the surface, turn them gently with a skimmer or slotted spoon. As each fritter becomes thoroughly golden and crisp, remove it with the skimmer or slotted spoon to kitchen paper to drain. A sugaring assistant is helpful at this point, one willing to roll the hot things about very lightly in caster or sifted icing sugar and pile them onto a serving plate. Guests should be lined up at the stove. There's nothing more deflating after all this battering and frying and skimming and sugaring if everyone else is engrossed at table, missing out on the spectacle.

Acknowledgments

For the loves of my life: Lisa Elaine Knox and Erich Brandon Knox.

For her quiet, constant brilliance: Annette Barlow.

For a splendid tribe of idols, heroes, cavaliers, and muses: Miranda Lopane, Matilde Zatti, Neddo Terrosi, Gilberto Barlozzo, Franca Magi, Rosanna Giombini, Mario de Simone, Maria Rosaria Leonori, Federica Spaccini, Simona Rocchi, Anna Romagnoli, Sharona Gury, and Mimi Baram.

A THOUSAND DAYS IN VENICE

Marlena de Blasi

When Fernando spots her in a Venice café and knows immediately that she is The One, Marlena de Blasi is caught off guard. A divorced American woman travelling through Italy, she thought she was satisfied with her life. Yet within a few months, she quits her job as a chef, sells her house, kisses her two grown-up kids goodbye, and moves to Venice. Once there, she finds herself sitting in sugar-scented pasticcerie, strolling through sixteenth-century palazzi, renovating an apartment overlooking the seductive Adriatic Sea, and preparing to wed a virtual stranger in an ancient stone church.

As this transplanted American learns the hard way about the peculiarities of Venetian culture, we are treated to an honest, often comic view of how two middle-aged people, both set it their ways but also set on being together, build a life. *A Thousand Days in Venice* is filled with the foods and flavours of Italy and peppered with recipes and culinary observations. But the main course here is about a woman who falls in love with both a man and a city, and finally finds the home she didn't know she was missing.

A THOUSAND DAYS IN TUSCANY

Marlena de Blasi

Continuing from A Thousand Days in Venice, this is the story of Marlena and her Venetian husband, Fernando, as they make a life for themselves in rural Tuscany. Amongst the many people they befriend is Barluzzo, an old sage who takes the couple under his wing and initiates them in the age-old traditions of Tuscan life: since their house lacks electricity, he helps them build a traditional brick oven in the garden; in autumn he wakes them at dawn to gather chestnuts and porcini mushrooms, and at the onset of winter he takes them to pull grapes from the vines and beat olives from the trees. Beautifully written and richly seasoned with mouth-watering recipes of the region, this book is filled with the carpe diem attitude that so captivated readers of *A Thousand Days in Venice*.

www.virago.co.uk

virago

To find out more about Marlena de Blasi and
other Virago authors, visit:
www.virago.co.uk

Visit the Virago website for:

- Exclusive features and interviews with authors,
  including Margaret Atwood, Maya Angelou,
  Sarah Waters and Nina Bawden

- News of author events and forthcoming titles

- Competitions

- Exclusive signed copies

- Discounts on new publications

- Book-group guides

- Free extracts from a wide range of titles

PLUS: subscribe to our free monthly newsletter